TIARA GLASS

by Dr. Angela M Bowey

Published by OAR Publishing with KDP.

CONTENTS

Tiara Glass History

Author: Angela M. Bowey

"Tiara Exclusives" of Dunkirk, Indiana, USA, was set up in 1970 as a subsidiary of Indiana Glass within the Lancaster Colony Corporation, to exploit the "home parties" concept of selling to housewives. Tiara Exclusives marketing focussed on the housewife as homemaker/home entertainer. Their products, collectible glassware, were projected as enhancing the home decor and especially the home entertainer's dining table. They sold matching sets of table glassware and accessories in reproduction antique designs, some hand-made and some machine-made and mostly to a high standard. They recruited thousands of agents, called "Hostesses", who sold Tiara Exclusives glassware at their own home parties, between 1970 and 1998.

Tiara Exclusives did not make glass, they commissioned it from other glass manufacturers. They used molds which had formerly belonged to other glass companies, many of them genuine antique molds. They often enhanced these sets of antique molds with new items based on the same designs. And for nearly thirty years they were highly successful. Although they closed in 1998, all the molds which belonged to Tiara still belonged to the Lancaster Colony Corporation which still made glass and occasionally produced patterns from the Tiara Exclusives range marketed through their Home Interiors division. In 1999, for example, the Tiara Sandwich Glass dinnerware was offered in Plum color. The Sandwich Glass wall clock has quite often (since 1998) been advertised in periodicals, available in Spruce and Peach.

Who Made Tiara Glass?

The offices of Tiara Exclusives were adjacent to the Indiana Glass Company, and both companies belonged to the Lancaster Colony Corporation. So initially Tiara commissioned glass from Indiana Glass and most of their early designs were made at Indiana Glass. When sales demands exceeded capacity other companies were commissioned and as time went by Tiara added products to their range which exploited the specialities of other glass manufacturers. Both before and after the closure of the Indiana Glass hand shop (about 1989), Tiara Exclusives commissioned glass from Fenton Art Glass, L.E.Smith, Fostoria, Pilgrim, Dalzell-Viking, Durand (in France) and Anna Hutte (in Germany).

Tiara by Fostoria in 24% lead crystal, first appeared in the Fall 1984 Tiara catalogue in the following designs:

- the Suzanne vase
- Coronation vase
- Exclusively Yours goblets and glasses
- Venetian candleholders
- Brilliant tidbit tray
- Leonardo Wedding bowl and cover
- Radiance dinner bell
- Leonardo footed urn and cover (hostess gift)

In the Spring 1985 Tiara catalogue these same pieces were shown, plus the folowing additions:

- Egg and cover
- LOVE paperweight

And in the Fall 1985 Tiara catalogue all the above items plus the following:

- Inspirational paperweight
- Suzanne candy box and cover
- Suzanne salt and pepper set

In 1991 Lancaster stopped marketing lead crystal and transferred the molds to Indiana glass who produced some of the above designs in "crystal without the lead".

More information on the products made by the various companies for Tiara can be found in the 1995 document "Tiara Exclusives Product Information Manual" which is contained on this e-Book.

Where Did the Designs Come From?

Tiara Sandwich glass was the original mainstay of the company, introduced in their first catalog in 1970. Ruby was the first color in 1970, followed very shortly by "golden amber". The sandwich glass pattern goes all the way back to Deming Jarvis in 1825, and was one of the first designs ever made in pressed glass in the USA. It was a popular pattern when Jarvis introduced it, and very similar designs were made by many later glasshouses, including Indiana Glass. In the 1920s a set of molds for this pattern were made and used by Indiana Glass. Some of these were the same molds rehabilitated by Tiara in the 1970s, specifically the tumbler, goblet, vegetable bowl, snack set, dinner plates, salad plates, cups and saucers.

In the late 1970s Tiara designed new pieces in Sandwich glass patterns, including the Sandwich Glass basket, ashtray, salt and pepper, dinner bell, candle holders and pitcher; and in the 1980s they added more items. In 1995 the Sandwich Glass spoon holder was made for Tiara by Fenton Art Glass from molds which formerly belonged and were used by Imperial Glass. Duncan & Miller also produced a similar Sandwich pattern during the Depression Era, and some of their molds were also rehabilitated and used by Tiara Exclusives.

Tiara sold *Sandwich Glass* in several colors (see catalog pages). In their 1978 Tiara catalog, the company wrote "To the best of our knowledge, Sandwich Glass dinnerware has never before been made in the Golden Amber color". However, Indiana Glass did produce their Sandwich pattern in amber during the Depression Era, albeit a lighter shade of amber than some of the Tiara pieces.

The **Lord's Supper Tray** was a very popular design introduced by Tiara in 1972 and produced in several colors. The design goes all the way back to the Model Flint Glassworks (Albany, Indiana) in the 1880s. About 1902, after that company closed, the molds were purchased by Indiana Glass who made versions with gold or platinum decoration around the edges or on the back.

Ponderosa Pine was another very popular Tiara design made by Indiana Glass. It was introduced in 1981 and was designed by Art Harshman specially for Tiara, so it is not an antique design.

Avocado or Sweet Pear was an Indiana Glass Company design from 1929 which was adapted and introduced by Tiara in 1982 and discontinued in 1988. There was a very attractive water set offered in a wide range of colors, as well as serving dishes, sugar and cream, sherbert and pickle dishes and other items.

Crown Dinnerware was introduced by Tiara in 1986 in Imperial Blue. The original antique molds came from different sources including Indiana Glass and the US Glass Tiffin factory. They were called by names such as Kings Crown and Thumbprint. Indiana Glass re-introduced Kings Crown in the early 1950s and it was a very popular design. There were new items designed by Tiara (Crown Pillar Candle) and by Fostoria for Tiara (Suzanne Salt and Pepper). The Veronique Egg Tray and Wall Clock and other patterns were original Indiana Glass Molds in this pattern.

Tiara's **Cape Cod** pattern was made from original 1940s molds from Imperial Glass. The Tiara color "Vintage Blue" was said to distinguish these Tiara Cape Cod pieces from the originals because Imperial did not use blue for the particular shapes offered by Tiara (Basket, bud vase, 2-part relish). This pattern was made for Tiara by L.E.Smith from 1993 to 1995.

The **Venetian** range of candle lamps was designed and made for Tiara by Fostoria Glass in 1984 and continued to be made into the 1990s.

You will find more information about more patterns in the various documents included in this e-Book. It is clear that Tiara Exclusives rescued old molds from many US sources and reproduced some beautiful glass using those molds and other complementary designs that they commissioned. Apart from paper labels, their glass was not normally marked "Tiara", except for a few Indiana glass items made for Tiara which were marked with the name Tiara in the mold. This lack of permanent marking has produced some confusion, but on the whole Tiara tried to keep away from the colors that had been originally used for patterns they reproduced.

Tiara Glass is collected with enthusiasm by many people. It was, after all, designed to be desirable and not just useful. No doubt our grand-children will put a very high value on it just as we value Depression Glass today!

-

Tiara 1974 Catalog Contents

Exclusive Gifts By Tiara

THE HISTORY OF GLASS

Over 4,000 years ago, perhaps on the Sands of Egypt, Syria, or Babylonia, the manufacturing of glass began. Since then mankind has added, little by little, to the glassmaker's art. The skill of the glassmaker has been a source of beauty treasured by all people. Making glassware by hand is the oldest industry in the Jamestown Colony in 1608.

In the manufacture of Tiara Exclusives many of the techniques and tools of the early days are used. It is natural that you, a Tiara Customer, should want to know something about the way the line is created. Much of it is hand made, either pressed or blown, and in molds dating back many, many years. Each item is exclusive with Tiara, and will not be found in any other line.

Glass is made of Silica, Soda Ash, Lime, and Feldspar. Small amounts of various other chemicals such as Copper, Selenium, Manganese, Cadmium, etc. are added to make a "batch." After careful mixing of the selected ingredients, a quantity of broken glass—called cullet—is often added to the "batch" mixture to speed up the melting process. Glass is truly the product of earth and fire! The tank into which the glassworker shovels the "batch" has been pre-fired to an intense heat of about 2700°F. In about 18 hours the glass is ready to be gathered and blown. It takes a shop of 6 to 10 skilled workers to make one item.

A blowpipe is a hollow tube of steel with a special "head" which the gatherer dips into the tank of molten glass. Turning it in the glass, he gathers just the right "gob" on the end of the pipe. He hands it to the blower after first shaping it on a marveling plate. The blower then shapes the "ball" with apple wood tools and paddles, and with carefully controlled puffs, forms a hollow bulb. His tools are varied and adapted for each item, and include the Pucellas, often called just the "tool." Like a huge pair of tweezers, the "tool" becomes a set of additional fingers for the skilled craftsman.

Now the piece is ready to be removed from the blowpipe and turned over to the stick-up boy, who picks it up and takes it to the "glory-hole", a reheating furnace kept at about 2500°F. Here the glass is reheated and taken to the finisher for further shaping. He, with the skilled touch of practiced hands, forms the decanter, bowl, pitcher, etc. When the item is to have a handle, or requires additional work, it is handed to a second finisher.

As this finisher completes the piece, a carry-in boy appears with a special fork, snaps the piece from the punty and carries it to an annealing oven or "lehr." Here it travels on a slowly moving, endless chain through several hours of diminishing heat, emerging at the end ready to be inspected. It is then labeled with the Tiara Exclusive sticker, boxed, and put in stock.

Since many Tiara Exclusives are blown and shaped by hand, variations in size, shape, and color lend real individuality to each item.

The original Sandwich Glass was named after Sandwich, Massachusetts, on Cape Cod. It is one of the most famous of all Early American glass styles. Glass Collectors treasure it. Museums display any pieces they can get. It was first made in 1825 by Deming Jarves, who developed the ability to press glass by hand. The beautiful patterns were cut in iron molds by hand!

The star and scroll design was described by the early writers as "sparkling like dew-moistened leaves." In spite of its lacy quality it has tremendous sturdiness and durability and can be machine washed.

Every conceivable item for the table is available to Tiara customers now, or will be in the near future. To the best of our knowledge, Sandwich Glass dinnerware has never before been made in the Golden Amber color. On a gold tablecloth the rich color speaks quality, and marks the owner of it as a discriminating homemaker! The Golden Amber recaptures the glamour and authentic coloration of Early American glass.

The use of this exclusive line for shower gifts, wedding gifts, birthday and anniversary gifts, and for Christmas affords the giver a continuity unmatched in beautiful glass! Every piece is hand pressed in our own plant, and is exclusively yours through Tiara!

5

These pieces are all reproduced in the ORIGINAL molds, and therefore, are valuable collector's items. No color is so flattering to the wood tones of the dining room, and no color is as scintillating in a sunny window as Golden Amber. The many faceted surfaces of the Sandwich pattern are at their best in Golden Amber.

(A) 10231 Sandwich Gold Bridge Set—4 pcs.—These trays make a conversation piece for your card parties! Used with the dinnerware, they provide the final touch of elegance.

(B) 10215 Sandwich Gold Wine Set—9 pcs.—Perhaps one of the most priceless gifts in Sandwich is this truly breathtaking Wine Set! Six minature Wine Goblets surround this handblown bottle on the hand pressed tray. One would expect this creation in glass to cost upwards of a hundred dollars, yet Tiara makes it available at a remarkable price! Filled with one's favorite wine, the hand ground stopper prevents evaporation. A wedding gift of unmatched beauty and usefullness, this Wine Set will forever remind the user of the thoughful and discriminating giver!

SANDWICH REPRODUCTIONS

(A) 10208 **Sandwich Gold Goblet Set**—4 pcs.—Certainly add prestige to any dining table! These footed goblets are hand pressed jewels that speak quality table service. The continuity of this line provides the gift giver with many chances to add to a loved one's collection over a period of time! Birthdays, Christmas, Valentine's Day, Easter, Anniversaries, etc., each offer an opportunity to add to the collection! (5¼" high).

(B) 10212 **Sandwich Gold Sugar / Cream Set**—Matches your dinnerware, affords you a chance to set a distinctive table, whether formal or informal.

(C) 10233 **Sandwich Gold Ftd. Sherbert Set**—4 pcs.—Ice cream and puddings take on an elegance you'll appreciate, when served in these footed sherberts.

(D) 10209 **Sandwich Gold Place Setting**—4 pcs.—10210 **Sandwich Gold Starter Set**— 4 place settings—The Sandwich Starter Set of dinnerware is unmatched in beauty and durability. The large 10" dinner plate, the 8" salad or bread plate, and the 6½ oz. cup and 6" saucer form a place setting that will enhance your table! Sandwich Glass dates back to the early 19th century, and we are proud to be the sole user of this heavenly pattern.

(E) 10227 **Sandwich Gold Salt and Pepper Set**—The only Sandwich salt and pepper still in existence, as far as we can ascertain! These twin beauties, 4¾" high, will mark the user as a discriminating hostess.

SANDWICH COLLECTION

(A) **10226 Sandwich 8 pc. Snack Set**—This authentic Early American Snack Set is the rage of all who see it! The oval plate, petite in size, 8½″ x 6¾″ dia., marks it as the most unusual set to be found in America. What an outstanding gift!

(B) **10216 Sandwich Gold Candlestick**—Pair.

(C) **10217 Sandwich Gold Console Bowl**—Decorates your dining room table in glorious fashion! Filled with fruit or flowers the bowl sets the atmosphere for your dining enjoyment.

(D) **10230 Sandwich Gold Tiered Ensemble**—For the living room, dining room, hall, or bedroom, this 3 tiered ensemble can be utilized for mints, or nuts, jewelry, or spices.

(E) **10229 Sandwich Gold Puff Box and Cover**—A relic of Early America! This delightful gem provides us with a most unusual gift.

SANDWICH COLLECTION

(A) 10220 Sandwich Gold Butter Dish and Cover — At the turn of the century butter was churned on the farms of America, and formed into round balls. This fascinating covered dish reminds us all of our great heritage. Many use these lovely dishes for Eggs Benedict and Squab under glass! You'll be proud to entertain with this most unusual product of early America. (6'' high).

(B) 10221 Sandwich Gold Handled Basket—The Console Bowl is hand paddled into this attractive basket, and then a handle is affixed to it. As a centerpiece, or an accent piece on an end table or mantle, it is unsurpassed. (10'' high).

(C) 10213 Sandwich Gold Pitcher — Will be a treasured gift! Patterned on the bottom as well, it adds its full measure to the formal table setting. Filled with flowers or a plant it is a most unusual vase! The star and scroll pattern shine brilliantly in this useful gift! (8'' high).

(D) 10219 Sandwich Gold Serving Platter — This 13'' Platter is excellent for sandwiches or for your favorite cake! It is also handy for small roasts and fried chicken! You'll find it handy for serving at almost every meal.

(E) 10228 Sandwich Gold Berry Set — 5 pcs. — The 8'' Berry Bowl can serve as just that, or it can be utilized as a server for potatoes or vegetables. When serving ice cream for dessert remember this bowl will easily hold a full quart! These small 4'' Nappies are just right for an individual serving of berries, vegeatbles, or dessert! You can't have too many of this handy size!

SANDWICH COLLECTION

(A) **10029 Crystal Iris Wine Set**—9 pcs.—The supreme gift for the discriminating homeowner! This radiant Iris Wine Set is produced in the original molds dating back many years! Regardless of color combination this set fits in perfectly, and is truly an elegant addition to the Tiara line!

(B) **10406 Crystal Mardi Gras Punch Set**—Consisting of 1 bowl, 1 ladle, and 12 cups—this radiant Mardi Gras Punch Set of 14 pieces is handmade from molds purchased from the old United States Glass Company many years ago. This very beautiful set is the epitome of good taste, and affords one the opportunity to give an unusual wedding gift that will become an heirloom. (8 qt. cap.).

(C) **10407 Crystal Mardi Gras Plate**—Was once a punch bowl, but has been paddled flat to make a base for the Punch Set, and to be used separately as a serving platter. (21" dia.).

(B-C) **10408 Crystal Mardi Gras Punch Set**—Complete as a 15 piece Punch Set the above two items make their mark as the Top Of The Line in Tiara! A gift of incomparable beauty, it is just the thing to give to that person "who has everything."

FESTIVE ACCESSORIES

(A) 10028 Sunset Jar and Cover — Is a vivid reminder of bygone days! The brilliance of this piece makes it an ideal accent piece in any room, and for those who wish utility for this captivating item, it makes an unusual cookie jar! (9'' high).

(B) 10001 Sunset Classique Urn —A revival of the classically traditional urn shape for flower arrangements or to grace the mantel. (8¾'' high).

(C) 10027 Sunset Lord's Bread Tray — Listed in many antique books, and we have now produced this outstanding item in sunset color in the original mold. An ideal gift to men of the cloth, it is also available to churches to raise needed funds! Makes an unusual wedding gift, and one that will be long remembered. (7'' x 11'' dia.).

(D) 10034 Sunset Colonial Vase — This brilliant colonial vase has all the fire of a summer sunset! The crimped top affords individuality, as all are done by hand. (8'' high).

(E) 10003 Sunset Leaf Bowl — Encircled by a wreath of ruby leaves, this bowl takes full advantage of the subtle gradation of sunset colors. (5½'' high-8'' dia.).

(F) 10002 Sunset Leaf Footed Compote —This aristocratic piece stands tall and proud on its solidly kneaded stem. An outstanding piece from its golden foot to the fiery ruby wreath. Useful for small plants, candies or a decorative piece.

(G) 10030 Sunset Handled Basket — The square facets of this unusual piece are repeated in its overall shape graced with a deeply scalloped edge and applied handle.

SUNSET COLLECTION

(A) 10005 **Blue Handled Basket**—This gorgeous hand crafted basket is in a class by itself! Filled with fruit or flowers it creates a conversation piece for all occasions. Pressed first into a bowl, the sides are paddled in its molten form into its present shape, and then the handle is attached. The time spent by the craftsmen in this most unusual accent piece, makes it an outstanding value, and an unusual gift. (10" high).

(B) 10020 **Blue Colonial Water Bottle**—In Colonial days the water bottle was always on the table, filled with ice water. The convenience in pouring is unmatched. Modern American beverages of all kinds can be dispensed attractively with this creation. No home bar is complete without this bottle. Handblown in a turn of the century mold, it exemplifies your good taste in gifts, as well as the glassblower's art! (8" high).

(C) 10009 **Blue Strawberry Jar and Cover**—Strawberry preserves have been made by housewives for centuries, and this Early American jar is a reminder of the talents of these pioneer women! A collector's item now, we have a limited number available. What a treasured gift for the bride-to-be! This beautiful blue jar and cover is hand-pressed, and will appreciate in value in the years to come. (9½" high).

(D) 10031 **Blue Sugar and Cream Set**—This unusual set was designed over 50 years ago and sold for a very short period. The unique double lip and square handles are a distinct novelty found in no other set.

HORIZON COLLECTION

In 1925 the International Exposition of Decorative Arts opened in Paris and introduced to the world a bold new design style. The sleek geometric style that was borrowed from the Cubists came to be known as Art Deco.

Tiara has dusted off the old moulds, dating from World War I, and given them new life with its black patent-leather glass. The crisp wet-look is as modern as tomorrow, yet coordinates beautifully with your crystal or colored ware—gold, carnival or horizon blue.

The original glass, made from these same moulds over fifty years ago, is widely sought by collectors and listed in their catalogues as the "Pyramid" pattern. This is truly the glass for tomorrow's collectors, for it is, as far as we have been able to discover, the only black glass being made in America today.

(A) 10325 **Art Deco Salad Service**—5 pcs.—Salads obviously—but use it for desserts too!

(B) 10323 **Art Deco Center Bowl**—Float a gardenia or carnation in this— or some sugared grapes!

(C) 10324 **Art Deco Dessert Set**—2 pcs.—The simplest dessert with a cloud of whipped cream assumes real importance here!

(D) 10319 **Art Deco Handled Relish**—An intricately moulded triumph of the art of glass making—fondue sauces zing in this!

(E) 10320 **Art Deco Sugar, Cream and Tray Set**—This dashingly tall set takes formal command of any table setting.

(F) 10321 **Art Deco 8 oz. Tumbler Set**—4 pcs.—See how they set off your place settings!

(G) 10322 **Art Deco 12 oz. Tumbler Set**—4 pcs.—Smart elegance for tall drinks.

ART DECO COLLECTION

These masculine gifts can be used in the den, rumpus room, bar or patio and will delight the user.

(A) 10008 Tankards — set of 4 — These 12 oz. Tankards have been used in America for almost 400 years, and are a symbol of good times. Excellent for beer, they are equally handy and desirable for soft drinks. The satin finish befits the quality of these tankards, and the man in your life would love to have 4, 8, or 12 of them (5⅝" high).

(B) 10006 Mugs — set of 6 — A real treat for children in drinking their morning juice, milk, etc. Makes unusual conversation for adults for the service of any cold drinks. (3½ oz.).

(C) 10025 Crystal Etched Smoker Set—A most unusual gift, this 6 piece set (lighter, cigarette urn, and 4 ash trays) will make its mark in thousands of homes. The satin finish in the crystal is heaven to hold, and gorgeous to behold! Blending with any decor, it is the perfect answer for a wedding gift, and is priced far below what one would expect.

(D) 10021 Lime Eagle Ash Tray—The American Eagle has always been a symbol of early Americana, and the exceptional art work on this massive tray makes it a very outstanding gift! The gold tray is popular as a gift for a man's desk, while the crystal etched tray will blend with any color in any room! (10½" dia.).

(E) 10023 Crystal Eagle Ash Tray.

(F) 10022 Gold Eagle Ash Tray.

FOR THE MAN OF THE HOUSE

(A) 10101 **Lime Mountaineer Decanter**—Jolly Mountaineer Decanters trace their origin to the turn of the century. We present them to Tiara customers EXCLUSIVELY as an unusual gift! Used on a home bar they create much conversation. The hat is easily removed and used as a "shot glass." These treasured collector's items make a most unusual bottle for the family mouthwash, too! (10¼" high).

(B) 10100 **Blue Mountaineer Decanter, Etched.**

(C) 10045 **Gold Demijohn**—These handblown creations will add to your decor in a vast variety of ways. Used as a terrarium, vase, umbrella stand, or accent piece.

(D) 10044 **Blue Demijohn**

(E) 10013 **Gold Honey Dish and Cover**—Another bit of Americana is the famous Tiara Honey Jar and Cover! Hand pressed into the mold, it holds a full honey comb, and recalls the delicious taste of fresh honey! One of the most nutritious foods available, it is rarely found in the American home today, as few people are fortunate enough to have a dish that will hold the whole comb. This collector's item will increase in value over the years. The golden color is beautiful. (6" high).

(F) 10409 **Smoke Collector Bottle 1 Satchmo**—Released late last year in a limited edition of only 3,000 pieces, we have a limited number left of this first in the series, so it's first come, first served. Each bottle is numbered on the bottom.

(G) 10411 **Rose-Pink Collector Bottle 11 Miller**—The release of the 2nd of the series honoring men of music. Created by Tiara, this work of art is also produced in a limited edition of 3,000 numbered pieces.

COLLECTOR'S ITEMS

(A) 10104 Gold Accent Group—6 pcs.—2 Antique toothpick holders (for cigarettes or hors d'oeuvre picks) and 4 salt minatures—that double for individual ash trays or nutmeats.

(B) 10102 Lime Rose Vase—Going back to the early twenties, we have selected this 15'' vase for your decorating ideas for the fireplace, hall, or other location. It holds a myraid of flowers.

(C) 10105 Amethyst Rose Vase.

(D) 10103 Gold Salt Dip—1 pair—The classic Grecian crater shape in minature. A revival from the 1800's for salt or nutmeats.

ACCENT GROUP

(A) 10518 Zodiac, Goblet Vase, Collection

10506	Aquarius, Blue	Jan. 21-Feb. 19
10507	Pisces, Lime	Feb.20-Mar. 20
10508	Aries, Red	Mar. 21-April 20
10509	Taurus, Pink	April 21-May 22
10510	Gemini, Yellow	May 23-June 21
10511	Cancer, Violet	June 22-July 22
10512	Leo, Orange	July 23-Aug. 22
10513	Virgo, Gold	Aug. 23-Sept. 22
10514	Libra, Rose	Sept. 23-Oct. 22
10515	Scorpio, White	Oct. 23-Nov. 21
10516	Sagittarius, Turquoise	Nov. 22-Dec. 22
10517	Capricorn, Green	Dec. 23-Jan. 20

27

(B) 10039 Black Weiss Candy Box and Cover—This massive weiss goblet, 32 oz., with cover allows you to use your imagination! A candy box—a decorative accent—a covered glass for your favorite beverage—it could be any one or all of them!

(C) 10040 Black Baluster Zombie Mug — Pr. — This unique design was created exclusively for Tiara! For the tall Polynesian drinks, it is perfect! For a Harvey Wallbanger, it is unequaled! For iced tea and all soft drinks it affords beauty and comfort. Handmade, and priced reasonably for the man in your life!

UNUSUAL GIFT COLLECTION

(A) 10041 Rose—Pink Sweet Pear Pitcher—A real collector's item that marks the giver of this gift as most discriminating. Recalls the days of yesteryear adding charm to any setting.

10042 Rose—Pink Sweet Pear Tumbler Set—4 pcs.
10043 Rose—Pink Sweet Pear Beverage Set

(B) 10026 Crystal Magna-Weight — Set of 3 — Down through the years paper-weights have been made in all sizes and shapes, with many decorations. Selling from two dollars up to several hundreds of dollars, most of them have lacked the usefulness of our Magna-Weight! A domed lens of crystal, it magnifies whatever is placed under it, and thus it becomes a useful showcase for valuable stamps, coins, pictures, etc.! The plastic backing snaps off for easy access to the placement of a picture, coin, or stamp. The thoughtful gift for all occasions, the box of three is priced for multiple purchases. (3¼'' dia.).

(C) 10032 Blue Egg and Cover — From the Art Department of Tiara comes a modern miracle in glass! This magnificent covered egg is the envy of all who see it! Notice the three feet, instead of four, which assures there will be no rockers! From the inside these feet appear as beautiful rosettes. This most unusual addition to the Tiara line has received much acclaim! (7½'' high).

(D) 10046 Lime Egg and Cover

OLD AND NEW

WHAT IS A FLAW IN GLASSWARE?

Is a small bubble in a fine piece of stemware a flaw? How about a cord, or a mold mark? The answer is definitely no, but it's sometimes difficult to convince a customer of this.

Most dinnerware and glassware departments and specialty shops have had trouble at one time or another with customers who seek flawless perfection in the tableware merchandise they buy.

Such perfection can be achieved only in assembly-line products, of course. It is not possible or even desirable in quality ware whose manufacture depends so much on the skill and artistry of individual craftsmen.

Slight variations and tiny imperfections in glassware pieces are actually a confirmation of craftsmanship and individual artistry. Most customers who appreciate good glassware understand this.

For those who don't, here is a series of questions and answers that a salesperson can use to promote better understanding of the product.

Does a "seed" or bubble in glassware constitute a flaw?

No. One of these tiny "seeds" or bubbles the size of a pinpoint may sometimes be observed in a piece of glassware when it is examined closely against a strong light. The bubble is formed by gases when chemicals are united in the fusing or melting of the raw ingredients. It does not affect the quality of the beauty of the glass.

Should all pieces in a set be exactly alike?

No. There are almost always slight variations in diameter, height, and other dimensions in any group of tumblers, goblets, plates, or other articles of glass. These variations are usually so slight that they can be detected only with a micrometer, rarely by the naked eye. This is the hallmark of fine hand craftsmanship.

What is a cord?

A cord is an almost invisible difference in density in the glass which occurs during the fusing of the molten glass. It is visible only by reason of the fact that it reflects light. When a goblet with a cord in it is filled with water, no light is reflected and the cord becomes invisible.

Is a mold mark a sign of imperfection?

No. A mold mark is merely a ridge on a molded glassware piece that indicates the point at which the mold that formed the item was separated for removal of the finished ware. If it is overly prominent, however, it may be an indication of careless workmanship.

What is a shear mark?

A shear mark is a slight puckering of the glass caused when the artisan snips off excess molten glass when shaping the piece, as for example the end of the handle of a pitcher. It is a normal characteristic of glass and should not be considered a flaw.

Is hand-made glassware really made by hand, or merely hand-finished?

The production of hand-made glassware is indeed a hand process. The skilled hands and eyes of many men, working in teams, go into the making of every piece. The amazing thing is that such a high degree of excellence can be attained; that piece after piece coming from any individual or group of glass blowers or pressers is so nearly and accurately a duplicate of every other piece.

Why can't small irregularities be entirely eliminated from hand-made glass?

For the very reason that the glass is hand-made. No matter how deft the touch of the sensitive hands of glass craftsmen, it is impossible to eliminate completely small variations. These should not, therefore, be considered flaws. Glass is one of the trickiest materials to work with. Even machine-made glassware cannot be made absolutely perfect. But consider this: even the finest diamond, examined under a jeweler's loupe, rarely reveals absolute perfection.

How can the salesperson and the customer judge the quality of glassware?

There are certain simple tests and guides. Look for clarity and luster by holding the piece against a pure white background. Good glassware is quite clear, while inferior grades show a cloudy bluish or greenish tinge.

Quality glassware is also marked by a permanent polish or luster that results from fire-polishing.

Look for smooth edges. Glassware edges should be even, never rough and scratchy. In hand-cut ware, the design should be sharp and accurate. In etched ware, each tiny detail should be distinct and clearly defined.

Fine handblown glass frequently contains lead, which improves its clarity and adds to its weight. If a piece of stemware rings with a clear musical tone when struck lightly, this indicates lead content. Lime glass, on the other hand, does not have this resonance, but this does not make it any less desirable. The lime in such glass adds to its toughness and strength.

Reprinted from
CHINA GLASS & TABLEWARES

NO.	DESCRIPTION	COST	NO.	DESCRIPTION	COST
10001	Sunset Classique Urn	$ 8.50	10212	Sandwich Gold Sugar/Cream Set	$ 8.50
10002	Sunset Leaf Compote	6.50	10213	Sandwich Gold Pitcher	9.90
10003	Sunset Leaf 8" Bowl	8.90	10215	Sandwich Gold Wine Set—9 pcs.	33.90
10005	Blue Handled Basket	12.50	10216	Sandwich Gold Candlestick 1 pr.	7.50
10006	Crystal Frosted 3½ oz. Mugs—6 pcs.	5.90	10217	Sandwich Gold Console Bowl	7.50
10008	Crystal Frosted Tankards—4 pcs.	8.50	10219	Sandwich Gold Serving Platter, 13" dia	7.50
10009	Blue Strawberry Jar & Cover	8.90	10220	Sandwich Gold Butter Dish & Cover	8.50
10013	Gold Honey Dish & Cover	9.90	10221	Sandwich Gold Handled Basket	12.50
10020	Blue Colonial Water Bottle	5.90	10226	Sandwich 8 pc. Snack Set	8.90
10021	Lime Eagle Ash Tray	8.50	10227	Sandwich Salt and Pepper	8.90
10022	Gold Eagle Ash Tray	8.50	10228	Sandwich Berry Set—5 pcs.	8.50
10023	Crystal Eagle Ash Tray	8.50	10229	Sandwich Puff Box & Cover	4.90
10025	Crystal Etched Smoker Set—6 pcs.	8.90	10230	Sandwich Tiered Ensemble	8.90
10026	Crystal Magna Weight Set—3 pcs.	6.50	10231	Sandwich Bridge Set—4 pcs.	3.50
10027	Sunset Lord's Supper Plate	9.90	10233	Sandwich Ftd. Sherbet—4 pcs.	6.50
10028	Sunset Jar & Cover	12.90	10319	Art Deco Blk. Hld. Relish	8.90
10029	Crystal Wine Set—9 pcs.	39.90	10320	Art Deco Blk. Sugar/Cream/Tray	12.90
10030	Sunset Handled Basket	11.90	10321	Art Deco Blk. 8 oz. Tumbler—4 pcs.	14.90
10031	Blue Sugar & Cream Set	8.50	10322	Art Deco Blk. 12 oz. Tumbler—4 pcs.	15.90
10032	Blue Egg & Cover	12.50	10323	Art Deco Blk. 8½" Center Bowl	6.50
10034	Sunset Colonial Vase	6.90	10324	Art Deco Blk. 4¾" Dessert Bowl 1 pr.	5.50
10039	Black Weiss Candy Box/Cover	10.90	10325	Art Deco Blk. 5 pc. Salad Service	15.50
10040	Black Baluster Zombie Mug pr.	8.90	10406	Crystal 14 pc. Punch Set	39.90
10041	Sweet Pear Pitcher	10.90	10407	Crystal Plate	14.90
10042	Sweet Pear Tumblers—4 pcs.	13.50	10408	Crystal 15 pc. Punch Set	49.90
10043	Sweet Pear Beverage Set	19.90	10409	Collector Bottle—Satchmo	18.50
10044	Blue Demijohn	29.50	10411	Collector Bottle—Miller	18.50
10045	Gold Demijohn	29.50	10506	Aquarius Goblet Vase	4.50
10046	Lime Egg & Cover	12.50	10507	Pisces Goblet Vase	4.50
10047	Flowered Multicolor Paper Weight	9.90	10508	Aries Goblet Vase	4.50
10048	Crimped Multicolor Paper Weight	9.90	10509	Taurus Goblet Vase	4.50
10100	Blue Mountaineer Decanter, Etched	9.90	10510	Gemini Goblet Vase	4.50
10101	Lime Mountaineer Decanter	9.90	10511	Cancer Goblet Vase	4.50
10102	Lime, Rose Vase	9.90	10512	Leo Goblet Vase	4.50
10103	Gold Salt Dip 1 pr.	4.90	10513	Virgo Goblet Vase	4.50
10104	Gold Hostess Accent Group—6 pcs.	9.90	10514	Libra Goblet Vase	4.50
10105	Amethyst Rose Vase	9.90	10515	Scorpio Goblet Vase	4.50
10208	Sandwich Gold Goblets—4 pcs.	10.50	10516	Sagittarius Goblet Vase	4.50
10209	Sandwich Gold Place Setting—4 pcs.	11.50	10517	Capricorn Goblet Vase	4.50
10210	Sandwich Gold Starter Set	29.90	10518	Zodiac Goblet Set—12 pcs.	34.90

Tiara 1975 Catalog Contents

INDEX

EXCUTIVE OFFICES

Tiara Exclusives

DUNKIRK, INDIANA 47336 PHONE: 317-768-6789

ROGER W. JEWETT
NATIONAL SALES
MANAGER

RONALD A. KRATZ
NATIONAL SALES
COORDINATOR

RALPH WADDELL
ADMINISTRATIVE
DIRECTOR

SECTIONAL SALES LEADERS:

Barbara Ackmann
366 N. Spring St.
Elgin, Ill. 60120
Phone: 312-741-3608

Lynn Baird
Rt.# 13 Emory Rd.
Knoxville, Tenn. 37918
Phone: 615-922-7879

Robert Hnath
754 Tucker Rd.
Stone Mountain, Ga. 30083
Phone: 404-921-6357

Bette Hug
1860 Parker Rd.
Florissant, Mo. 63033
Phone: 314-837-7521

Sandra W. Zant
1001 N. Natchez Rd.
Chattanooga, Tenn. 37405
Phone: 615-265-0694

Wilma Jackson
5307 Carrolton Way
Speedway, Ind. 46224
Phone: 317-244-5965

Judy Longmore
2570 Sand St.
Portage, Ind. 46368
Phone: 219-762-8201

Jerrald Maynard
13981 13 Mile Rd.
Warren, Mich. 48093
Phone: 313-296-0998

Arthur McMahon
2100 Norfolk Dr.
Arlington, Tex. 76015
Phone: 817-469-7618

Judith A. Fiala
4336 N. Judd Ave.
Schiller Park, Ill. 60176
Phone: 312-678-8351

Beverly Roraus
1060 Nantucket Dr.
Cicero, Ind. 46034
Phone: 317-984-3494

L & H Shawbell
6020 N.W. 58th Terrace
Okla. City, Okla. 73122
Phone: 405-721-0657

Mark Tomich
1027 Fountain Ave. N.E.
Grand Rapids, Mich. 49503
Phone: 616-458-4058

Edward Weakley
293 Gary Dr.
Nashville, Tenn. 37211
Phone: 615-832-1893

YOUR COUNSELOR

The History Of Glass

Over 4,000 years ago, perhaps on the Sands of Egypt, Syria, or Babylonia, the manufacturing of glass began. Since then mankind has added, little by little, to the glassmaker's art. The skill of the glassmaker has be a source of beauty treasured by all people.

Making glassware by hand is the oldest industry in America, it started in the Jamestown Colony in 1608.

In the manufacture of Tiara Exclusives many of the techniques and tools of the early days are used. It is natural that you, a Tiara Customer, should want to know something about the way the line is created. Much of it is hand made, either pressed or blown, and in molds dating back many, many years. Each item is exclusive with Tiara, and will not be found in any other line.

Glass is made of Silica, Soda Ash, Lime, and Feldspar. Small amounts of various other chemicals such as Copper, Selenium, Manganese, Cadmium, etc. are added to make a "batch." After careful mixing of the selected ingredients, a quantity of broken glass – called cullet – is often added to the "batch" mixture to speed up the melting process. Glass is truly the product of earth and fire! The tank into which the glassworker shovels the "batch" has been pre-fired to an intense heat of about 2700°F. In about 18 hours the glass is ready to be gathered and blown. It takes a shop of 6 to 18 skilled workers to make one item.

A blowpipe is a hollow tube of steel with a special "head" which the gatherer dips into the tank of molten glass. Turning it in the glass, he gathers just the right "gob" on the end of the pipe. He hands it to the blower after first shaping it on a marveling plate. The blower then shapes the "ball" with apple wood tools and paddles, and with carefully controlled puffs, forms a hollow bulb. His tools are varied and adapted for each item, and include the Pucellas, often called just the "tool." Like a huge pair of tweezers, the "tool" becomes a set of additional fingers for the skilled craftsman.

Now the piece is ready to be removed from the blowpipe and turned over to the stick-up boy, who picks it up and takes it to the "glory-hole", a reheating furnace kept at about 2500°F. Here the glass is reheated and taken to the finisher for further shaping. He, with the skilled touch of practiced hands, forms the decanter, bowl, pitcher, etc. When the item is to have a handle, or requires additional work, it is handed to a second finisher.

As this finisher completes the piece, a carry-in boy appears with a special fork, snaps the piece from the punty and carries it to an annealing oven or "lehr." Here it travels on a slowly moving, endless chain through several hours of diminishing heat, emerging at the end ready to be inspected. It is then labeled with the Tiara Exclusive sticker, boxed, and put in stock.

Since many Tiara Exclusives are blown and shaped by hand, variations in size, shape, and color lend real individuality to each item.

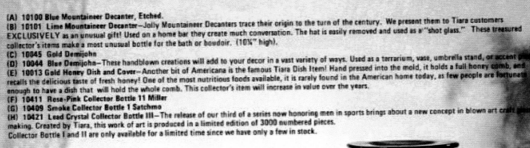

(A) **10100 Blue Mountaineer Decanter, Etched.**
(B) **10101 Lime Mountaineer Decanter**—Jolly Mountaineer Decanters trace their origin to the turn of the century. We present them to Tiara customers EXCLUSIVELY as an unusual gift! Used on a home bar they create much conversation. The hat is easily removed and used as a "shot glass." These treasured collector's items make a most unusual bottle for the bath or boudoir. (10¾" high).
(C) **10045 Gold Demijohn**
(D) **10044 Blue Demijohn**—These handblown creations will add to your decor in a vast variety of ways. Used as a terrarium, vase, umbrella stand, or accent piece.
(E) **10013 Gold Honey Dish and Cover**—Another bit of Americana is the famous Tiara Dish Item! Hand pressed into the mold, it holds a full honey comb, and recalls the delicious taste of fresh honey! One of the most nutritious foods available, it is rarely found in the American home today, as few people are fortunate enough to have a dish that will hold the whole comb. This collector's item will increase in value over the years.
(F) **10411 Rose-Pink Collector Bottle 11 Miller**
(G) **10409 Smoke Collector Bottle 1 Satchmo**
(H) **10421 Lead Crystal Collector Bottle III**—The release of our third of a series now honoring men in sports brings about a new concept in blown art craft glass making. Created by Tiara, this work of art is produced in a limited edition of 3000 numbered pieces.
Collector Bottle I and II are only available for a limited time since we have only a few in stock.

Collector's Items

(A) 10419 Monarch 8½" Bowl
(B) 10420 Monarch Sugar and Creamer
(C) 10423 Monarch Butter and Cover
(D) 10422 Monarch Large Pitcher—The Monarch Line is a true work of art, a fully deep cut pattern painstakingly designed to reflect light simular to a precious Gem. A treasure to grace any table top in formal or informal dinning.

(A)

Monarch Collection

(B)

(C)

(D)

(A) 10012 **Sunset Leaf Sherbets**—4 pcs.—Vanilla ice cream looks unusually delicious in these red sherbets, they add that right touch to your table setting.
(B) 10002 **Sunset Leaf Footed Compote**—This aristocratic piece stands tall and proud on its solidly kneaded stem. An outstanding piece from its golden foot to the fiery ruby wreath. Useful for small plants, candies or a decorative piece.
(C) 10001 **Sunset Classique Urn**—A revival of the classically traditional urn shape for flower arrangements or to grace the mantel. (8¾" high).
(D) 10011 **Sunset Leaf Candleholders**—1 pr.—The fire color of these twins will add the right flash to your table setting! Feel free to use them with your Gold Dinnerware for accent, with tall taper candles.
(E) 10034 **Sunset Colonial Vase**—This brilliant colonial vase has all the fire of a summer sunset! The crimped top affords individuality, as all are done by hand. (8" high).
(F) 10027 **Sunset Lord's Bread Tray**—Listed in many antique books, and we have now produced this outstanding item in sunset color in the original mold. An ideal gift to men of the cloth, it is also available to churches to raise needed funds! (7" x 11").
(G) 10028 **Sunset Jar and Cover**—In a vivid reminder of bygone days! The brilliance of this piece makes it an ideal accent piece in any room, and for those who wish utility for this captivating item, it makes an unusual cookie jar! (9" high).
(H) 10003 **Sunset Leaf Bowl**—Encircled by a wreath of ruby leaves, this bowl takes full advantage of the subtle gradation of sunset colors. (5½" high·8" dia.)
(I) 10030 **Sunset Handled Basket**—The square facets of this unusual piece are repeated in its overall shape graced with a deeply scalloped edge and applied handle.

Sunset Collection

(A) **10031 Blue Sugar and Cream Set**—This unusual set was designed over 50 years ago and sold for a very short period. This unique double lip and square handles are a distinct novelty found in no other set.

(B) **10020 Blue Colonial Water Bottle**—In Colonial days the water bottle was always on the table, filled with ice water. The convenience in pouring is unmatched. Modern American beverages of all kinds can be dispensed attractively with this creation. No home bar is complete without this bottle. Handblown in a turn of the century mold, it exemplifies your good taste in gifts, as well as the glassblower's art! (8" high).

(C) **10005 Blue Handled Basket**—This gorgeous hand crafted basket is in a class by itself! Filled with fruit or flowers it creates a conversation piece for all occasions. Pressed first into a bowl, the sides are paddled in its molten form into its present shape, and then the handle is attached. The time spent by the craftsmen in this most unusual accent piece, makes it an outstanding value, and an unusual gift. (10" high).

Horizon Collection

(A)

(B)

(C)

(A) 10102 Lime Rose Vase
(B) 10105 Amethyst Rose Vase—Going back to the early twenties, we have selected this 15" vase for your decorating ideas for the fireplace, hall, or other location.
It holds a myraid of flowers.
(C) 10046 Lime Egg and Cover
(D) 10032 Blue Egg and Cover—From the Art Department of Tiara comes a modern miracle in glass! This magnificent covered egg is the envy of all who see it!
Notice the three feet, instead of four, which assures there will be no rockers! From the inside these feet appear as beautiful rosettes. (7½" high).

(B)

(A)

(D)

Accent Group

(C)

Sandwich Reproductions

The original Sandwich Glass was named after Sandwich, Massachusetts, on Cape Cod. It is one of the most famous of all Early American glass styles. Glass Collectors treasure it. Museums display any pieces they can get. It was first made in 1825 by Deming Jarves, who developed the ability to press glass by hand. The beautiful patterns were cut in iron molds by hand!

The star and scroll design was described by the early writers as "sparkling like dew-moistened leaves." In spite of its lacy quality it has tremendous sturdiness and durability and can be machine washed.

Every conceivable item for the table is available to Tiara customers now, or will be in the near furture. To the best of our knowledge, Sandwich Glass dinnerware has never before been made in the Golden Amber color. On a gold tablecloth the rich color speaks quality, and marks the owner of it as a discriminating homemaker! The Golden Amber recaptures the glamour and authentic coloration of Early American Glass.

The use of this exclusive line of shower gifts, wedding gifts, birthday and anniversary gifts, and for Christmas affords the giver a continuity unmatched in beautiful glass! Every piece is produced in our own plant, and is exclusively yours through Tiara!

Most of these are all reproduced in the ORIGINAL molds, and therefore, are valuable collector's items. No color is so flattering to the wood tones of the dining room, and no color is as scintillating in a sunny window as Golden Amber. The many faceted surfaces of the Sandwich pattern are at their best in Golden Amber.

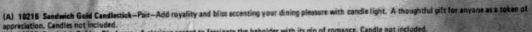

(A) 10216 Sandwich Gold Candlestick—Pair—Add royality and bliss accenting your dining pleasure with candle light. A thoughtful gift for anyone as a token of appreciation. Candles not included.
(B) 10237 Sandwich Golden Glo Lamp—A glorious accent to fascinate the beholder with its glo of romance. Candle not included.
(C) 10217 Sandwich Gold Console Bowl—Decorates your dining room table in glorious fashion! Filled with fruit or flowers the bowl sets the atmosphere for your dining enjoyment.
(D) 10204 Sandwich Gold Wine Goblet—4 pcs.
(E) 10203 Sandwich Gold Wine Set—11 pcs.—Now one of the most priceless gifts in Sandwich, consisting of 8 Wine Goblets, that surround this Handblown Decanter, on the hand pressed serving tray. An exquisite set that will be noteworthy of compliments by all who see it.

Sandwich Collection

(A)

(B)

(C)

(D)

(E)

A 10209 Sandwich Gold Place Setting—4 pcs.

B 10210 Sandwich Gold Starter Set—4 place settings—The Sandwich Starter Set of dinnerware is unmatched in beauty and durability. The 10" dinner plate 8"
salad plate, 6½ oz. cup and 6" saucer form a place setting that will enhance your table!

C 10201 Sandwich Gold 3 oz. Juice 4 pcs.—Another accessory of elegance to fulfill your formal dining service. We suggest their use for cocktails.

D 10208 Sandwich Gold Goblet Set—4 pcs.—Certainly add prestige to any dining table! The continuity of this line provides the gift giver with many chances
to add to a loved one's collection, Birthdays, Christmas, etc. offer an opportunity to add to the collection! (5¼" high)

E 10200 Sandwich Gold 12 oz. Tumblers—4 pcs.—This stunning Tumbler adds special elegance to your table top. Excellent for iced tea, sodas and cold beverages.

F 10227 Sandwich Gold Salt and Pepper Set—These twin beauties, 4¾" high, will mark the user as a discriminating hostess.

G 10239 Sandwich 7" Bread and Butter Plate—4 pcs.—A new release for the irreverent connoisseur of formal table settings. An ideal gift for a bride.

H 10212 Sandwich Gold Sugar/Cream Set—Matches your dinnerware, affords you a chance to set a distinctive table, whether formal or informal.

I 10233 Sandwich Gold Ftd. Sherbet Set—4 pcs.—Ice Cream and puddings take on an elegance you'll appreciate, when served in these footed sherbets.

(A) 10228 Sandwich Gold Berry Set—5 pcs.—The 8" Berry Bowl can serve as just that, or it can be utilized as a server for potatoes or vegetables. When serving ice cream for dessert remember this bowl will easily hold a full quart! These practical size 4" Nappies are just right for an individual serving of berries, vegetables, or dessert! You can't have too many of this handy size!

(B) 10220 Sandwich Gold Butter Dish and Cover—At the turn of the century butter was churned on the farms of America, and formed into round balls. This fascinating covered dish reminds us all of our great heritage. Many use these lovely dishes for Eggs Benedict and Squab under glass! You'll be proud to entertain with this most unusual product of early America. (6" high).

(C) 10202 Sandwich 6" Deep Nappy—2 pcs. An item in great demand, we have taken the cobwebs off this original mold, and proudly present the Sandwich everything bowl; soup, salad, or vegetable bowl! It's a winner! !

(D) 10221 Sandwich Gold Handled Basket—The Console Bowl is hand paddled into this attractive basket, and then a handle is affixed to it. As a centerpiece, or an accent piece on an end table or mantle, it is unsurpassed. (10" high).

(E) 10219 Sandwich Gold Serving Platter—This 13" Platter is excellent for sandwiches or for your favorite cake! It is also handy for small roasts and fried chicken! You'll find it handy for serving at almost every meal.

(F) 10213 Sandwich Gold Pitcher—Will be a treasured gift! Patterned on the bottom as well, it adds its full measure to the formal table setting. Filled with flowers or a plant it is a most unusual vase! The star and scroll pattern shine brilliantly in this useful gift! (8" high).

(G) 10238 Sandwich Celery Tray—This tray affords a pratical addition to your collection that can be used for a multitude of relishes.

(A) **10226 Sandwich 8 pc. Snack Set**—This authentic Early American Snack Set is the rage of all who see it! The oval plate, petite in size, 8½" x 6¾" dia., marks it as the most unusual set to be found in America. What an outstanding gift!

(B) **10230 Sandwich Gold Tiered Ensemble**—For the living room, dining room, hall, or bedroom, this 3 tiered ensemble can be utilized for mints, or nuts, jewelry, or spices.

(C) **10229 Sandwich Gold Puff Box and Cover**—A relic of Early America! This delightful gem provides us with a most unusual gift.

(D) **10231 Sandwich Gold Bridge Set—4 pcs.**—These trays make a conversation piece for your card parties! Used with the dinnerware, they provide the final touch of elegance.

(E) **10235 Sandwich 16" Platter**—Can not be exceeded in it's variety of use. This Platter will complement each discriminating Hostess. A gift truly functional in every household.

(A)

(B)

(C)

(D)

(E)

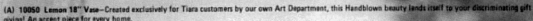

(A) **10050 Lemon 18" Vase**—Created exclusively for Tiara customers by our own Art Department, this Handblown beauty lends itself to your discriminating gift giving! An accent piece for every home.
(B) **10049 Sunset 18" Vase**—Like its lemon twin, this lemon vase will pick up the colors in your home, and add that "something extra" to the decor.
(C) **10014 Black South Seas Soap Dish**—A treasure to behold that will embrace your favorite scented bath or hand soap. 4 3/8" X 4". The design in deep relief allows it to be an ideal gift that has multiple usage in your home; such as a wall plaque or as an ash tray, for instance.
(D) **10052 Sweet Pear Tumbler Set in Lemon**—4 pcs.
(E) **10051 Sweet Pear Pitcher in Lemon**
(F) **10053 Sweet Pear Beverage Set in Lemon**—5 pcs.—Truly an all season gift of distinction. A reminder of years gone by, adding a delicate charm to any setting, and admired by collectors.

Old and New

(F)

(D)

(E)

(A)

(C)

(B)

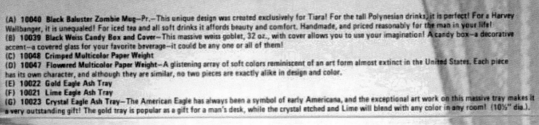

(A) 10040 Black Baluster Zombie Mug—Pr.—This unique design was created exclusively for Tiara! For the tall Polynesian drinks, it is perfect! For a Harvey Wallbanger, it is unequaled! For iced tea and all soft drinks it affords beauty and comfort. Handmade, and priced reasonably for the man in your life!

(B) 10039 Black Weiss Candy Box and Cover—This massive weiss goblet, 32 oz., with cover allows you to use your imagination! A candy box—a decorative accent—a covered glass for your favorite beverage—it could be any one or all of them!

(C) 10048 Crimped Multicolor Paper Weight

(D) 10047 Flowered Multicolor Paper Weight—A glistening array of soft colors reminiscent of an art form almost extinct in the United States. Each piece has its own character, and although they are similar, no two pieces are exactly alike in design and color.

(E) 10022 Gold Eagle Ash Tray

(F) 10021 Lime Eagle Ash Tray

(G) 10023 Crystal Eagle Ash Tray—The American Eagle has always been a symbol of early Americana, and the exceptional art work on this massive tray makes it a very outstanding gift! The gold tray is popular as a gift for a man's desk, while the crystal etched and Lime will blend with any color in any room! (10½" dia.).

Unusual Gift Collection

Art Deco Collection

In 1925 the International Exposition of Decorative Arts opened in Paris and introduced to the world a bold new design style. The sleek geometric style that was borrowed from the Cubists came to be known as Art Deco.

Tiara has dusted off the old moulds, dating from World War I, and given them new life with its black patent-leather glass. The crisp wet-look is as modern as tomorrow, yet coordinates beautifully with your crystal or colored ware.

The orginal glass, made from these same moulds over fifty years ago, is widely sought by collectors and listed in their catalogues as the "Pyramid" pattern.

(A) 10319 **Art Deco Handled Relish**—An intricately moulded triumph of the art of glass making—fondue sauces zing in this!
(B) 10322 **Art Deco 12 oz. Tumbler Set**—4 pcs.—Smart elegance for tall drinks.
(C) 10324 **Art Deco Dessert Set**—2 pcs.—The simplest dessert with a cloud of whipped cream assumes real importance here!
(D) 10325 **Art Deco Salad Service**—5 pcs.—Salads obviously—but use it for desserts too!
(E) 10323 **Art Deco Center Bowl**—Float a gardenia or carnation in this—or some sugared grapes!

Zodiac Collection

Tiara's new Zodiac Collection lends itself to your gift giving. The multiple uses for these goblets are limitless! ! The ideal gift for the newborn baby, your favorite man for his favorite beverage, the "his and hers" wedding gift, the girls in your card club, etc.!

10524	Aquarius,	Blue
10525	Pisces,	Lime
10526	Aries	Red
10527	Taurus,	Cream
10528	Gemini,	Yellow
10529	Cancer,	Cherry

10530	Leo,	Orange
10531	Virgo,	Gold
10532	Libra,	Pink
10533	Scorpio,	White
10534	Sagittarius,	Turquoise
10535	Capricorn,	Green

10534   10527   10525   10528

10526   10531   10533   10524

10532   10535   10529   10530

These masculine gifts can be used in the den, rumpus room, bar or patio and will delight the user.

(A) **10006 Mugs**—set of 6—A real treat for children in drinking their morning juice, milk, etc. Makes unusual conversation for adults for the service of any cold drinks. (3½ oz.).

(B) **10025 Crystal Etched Smoker Set**—A most unusual gift, this 6 piece set (lighter, cigarette urn, and 4 ash trays) will make its mark in thousands of homes. The satin finish in the crystal is heaven to hold, and gorgeous to behold! Blending with any decor, it is the perfect answer for a wedding gift, and is priced far below what one would expect.

(C) **10036 Etched Patio Beverage Set**—5 pcs.—These crystal etched beauties mark the user a knowledgeable host or hostess! This cool, refreshing set was an instant success.

(D) **10008 Tankards**—set of 4—These 12 oz. Tankards have been used in America for almost 400 years, and are a symbol of good times. Excellent for beer, they are equally handy and desirable for soft drinks. The satin finish befits the quality of these tankards, and the man in your life would love to have 4,8, or 12 of them (5 5/8" high).

(E) **10035 Etched Pitcher 64 oz.**

(A)

For The Man Of The House

(B)

(C)

(D)   (E)

What Is A Flaw In Glassware?

Is a small bubble in a fine piece of stemware a flaw? How about a cord, or a mold mark? The answer is definitely no, but it's sometimes difficult to convince a customer of this.

Most dinnerware and glassware departments and specialty shops have had trouble at one time or another with customers who seek flawless perfection in the tableware merchandise they buy.

Such perfection can be achieved only in assembly-line products, of course. It is not possible or even desirable in quality ware whose manufacture depends so much on the skill and artistry of individual craftsmen.

Slight variations and tiny imperfections in glassware pieces are actually a confirmation of craftsmanship and individual artistry. Most customers who appreciate good glassware understand this. For those who don't, here is a series of questions and answers that a salesperson can use to promote better understanding of the product.

Does a "seed" or bubble in glassware constitute a flaw?

No. One of these tiny "seeds" or bubbles the size of a pinpoint may sometimes be observed in a piece of glassware when it is examined closely against a strong light.

The bubble is formed by gases when chemicals are united in the fusing or melting of the raw ingredients. It does not affect the quality of the beauty of the glass.

Should all pieces in a set be exactly alike?

No. There are almost always slight variations in diameter, height, and other dimensions in any group of tumblers, goblets, plates, or other articles of glass. These variations are usually so slight that they can be detected only with a micrometer, rarely by the naked eye. This is the hallmark of fine hand craftsmanship.

What is a cord?

A cord is an almost invisible difference in density in the glass which occurs during the fusing of the molten glass. It is visible only by reason of the fact that it reflects light. When a goblet with a cord in it is filled with water, no light is reflected and the cord becomes invisible.

Is a mold mark a sign of imperfection?

No. A mold mark is merely a ridge on a molded glassware piece that indicates the point at which the mold that formed the item was separated for removal of the finished ware. If it is overly prominent, however, it may be an indication of careless workmanship.

What is a shear mark?

A shear mark is a slight puckering of the glass caused when the artisan snips off excess molten glass when shaping the piece, as for example the end of the handle of a pitcher. It is a normal characteristic of glass and should not be considered a flaw.

Is hand-made glassware really made by hand, or merely hand-finished?

The production of hand-made glassware is indeed a hand process. The skilled hands and eyes of many men, working in teams, go into the making of every piece. The amazing thing is that such a high degree of excellence can be attained; that piece after piece coming from any individual or group of glass blowers or pressers is so nearly and accurately a duplicate of every other piece.

Why can't small irregularities be entirely eliminated from hand-made glass?

For the very reason that the glass is hand-made. No matter how deft the touch of the sensitive hands of glass craftsmen, it is impossible to eliminate completely small variations. These should not, therefore, be considered flaws. Glass is one of the trickiest materials to work with. Even machine-made glassware cannot be made absolutely perfect. But consider this: even the finest diamond, examined under a jeweler's loupe, rarely reveals absolute perfection.

How can the salesperson and the customer judge the quality of glassware?

There are certain simple tests and guides. Look for clarity and luster by holding the piece against a pure white background. Good glassware is quite clear, while inferior grades show a cloudy bluish or greenish tinge.

Quality glassware is also marked by a permanent polish or luster that results from fire-polishing.

Look for smooth edges. Glassware edges should be even, never rough and scratchy. In hand-cut ware, the design should be sharp and accurate. In etched ware, each tiny detail should be distinct and clearly defined.

Fine handblown glass frequently contains lead, which improves its clarity and adds to its weight. If a piece of stemware rings with a clear musical tone when struck lightly, this indicates lead content. Lime glass, on the other hand, does not have this resonance, but this does not make it any less desirable. The lime in such glass adds to its toughness and strength.

Reprinted from
CHINA GLASS & TABLEWARES

Tiara Exclusives SUGGESTED SELLING PRICE

DUNKIRK, INDIANA 47336

NO.	DESCRIPTION	COST	NO.	DESCRIPTION	COST
10001	Classique Urn, Sunset	$11.50	10208	Sandwich Goblets, Gold - 4 pcs.	$12.50
10002	Leaf Compote, Sunset	10.90	10209	Sandwich Place Setting, Gold - 4 pcs.	12.50
10003	Leaf 8'' Bowl, Sunset	13.50	10210	Sandwich Starter Set, Gold - 16 pcs.	34.90
10005	Basket Handled, Blue	13.50	10212	Sandwich Sugar/Cream Set, Gold	9.50
10006	Mugs 3½ oz., Frosted Crystal - 6 pcs.	7.50	10213	Sandwich Pitcher, Gold	10.90
10008	Tankards 12 oz, Frosted Crystal - 4 pcs.	9.50	10216	Sandwich Candlestick, Gold - pr.	8.50
10011	Leaf Candleholders, Sunset - pr.	9.90	10217	Sandwich Console Bowl, Gold	8.50
10012	Leaf Sherbets, Sunset - 4 pcs.	17.90	10219	Sandwich Serving Platter, Gold - 13'' dia.	8.50
10013	Honey Dish and Cover, Gold	10.50	10220	Sandwich Butter Dish & Cover, Gold	10.50
10014	South Seas Soap Dish, Black	6.50	10221	Sandwich Basket Handled, Gold	13.50
10020	Colonial Water Bottle, Blue	7.50	10226	Sandwich Snack Set, Gold - 8 pcs.	14.50
10021	Eagle Ash Tray, Lime	8.90	10227	Sandwich Salt and Pepper, Gold	9.90
10022	Eagle Ash Tray, Gold	8.90	10228	Sandwich Berry Set, Gold - 5 pcs.	10.90
10023	Eagle Ash Tray, Crystal Etched	8.90	10229	Sandwich Puff Box & Cover, Gold	6.50
10025	Smoker Set, Frosted Crystal - 6 pcs.	9.50	10230	Sandwich Tiered Ensemble, Gold	11.50
10027	Lord's Supper Plate, Sunset	9.90	10231	Sandwich Bridge Set, Gold - 4 pcs.	4.90
10028	Jar & Cover Sunset	14.50	10233	Sandwich Ftd. Sherbet, Gold - 4 pcs.	9.50
10030	Basket Handled, Sunset	13.50	10235	Sandwich Platter, Gold - 16'' dia.	12.50
10031	Sugar & Cream Set, Blue	9.50	10237	Sandwich Golden Glo Lamp	7.90
10032	Egg & Cover, Blue	13.50	10238	Sandwich Celery Tray, Gold	7.90
10034	Colonial Vase, Sunset	8.50	10239	Sandwich 7'' Bread/Butter Plate, Gold - 4 pcs.	9.90
10035	Pitcher 64 oz, Frosted Crystal	8.90	10319	Art Deco Hld. Relish, Black	10.50
10036	Patio Beverage Set, Frosted Crystal - 5 pcs.	14.90	10322	Art Deco 12 oz. Tumbler, Black - 4 pcs.	16.50
10039	Weiss Candy Box/Cover, Black	12.50	10323	Art Deco 8½'' Center Bowl, Black	7.50
10040	Baluster Zombie Mug, Black - pr.	9.50	10324	Art Deco 4¾'' Dessert Bowl, Black - pr.	6.50
10044	Demijohn, Blue	34.50	10325	Art Deco Salad Service, Black - 5 pcs.	11.50
10045	Demijohn, Gold	34.50	10409	Collector Bottle - Satchmo, smoke	18.50
10046	Egg & Cover, Lime	13.50	10411	Collector Bottle - Miller, Pink	18.50
10047	Flowered Paper Weight, Multicolor	7.50	10419	Monarch 8½'' Bowl, Black	12.90
10048	Crimped Paper Weight, Multicolor	7.50	10420	Monarch Cream & Sugar, Black	10.50
10049	Large Vase, Sunset	29.50	10421	Collector Bottle III, Sports, Lead Crystal	18.50
10050	Large Vase, Lemon	29.50	10422	Monarch Large Pitcher, Black	11.50
10051	Sweet Pear Pitcher, Lemon	12.90	10423	Monarch Butter & Cover, Black	10.50
10052	Sweet Pear Tumblers, Lemon - 4 pcs.	14.50	10524	Aquarius Goblet, Blue	6.50
10053	Sweet Pear Beverage Set, Lemon - 5 pcs.	22.50	10525	Pisces Goblet, Lime	6.50
10100	Mountaineer Decanter, Etched Blue	10.50	10526	Aries Goblet, Red	6.50
10101	Mountaineer Decanter, Lime	10.50	10527	Taurus Goblet, Cream	6.50
10102	Rose Vase, Lime	11.90	10528	Gemini Goblet, Yellow	6.50
10105	Rose Vase, Amethyst	11.90	10529	Cancer Goblet, Cherry	6.50
10200	Sandwich 12 oz. Tumblers, Gold - 4 pcs.	15.50	10530	Leo Goblet, Orange	6.50
10201	Sandwich 3 oz. Juice, Gold - 4 pcs.	10.50	10531	Virgo Goblet, Gold	6.50
10202	Sandwich 6'' Deep Nappy, Gold - pr.	9.50	10532	Libra Goblet, Pink	6.50
10203	Sandwich 11 pc. Wine Set, Gold	34.90	10533	Scorpio Goblet, White	6.50
10204	Sandwich Wine Goblets, Gold - 4 pcs.	12.50	10534	Sagittarius Goblet, Turquoise	6.50
			10535	Capricorn Goblet, Green	6.50

Tiara 1979 Catalog Contents

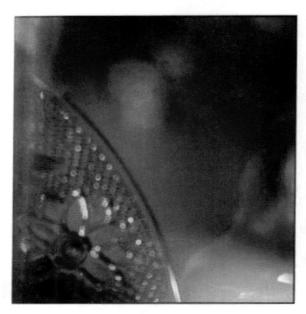

Tiara
Exclusives

The history of glass

Over 4,000 years ago, perhaps on the Sands of Egypt, Syria, or Babylonia, the manufacturing of glass began. Since then mankind has added, little by little, to the glassmaker's art. The skill of the glassmaker has been a source of beauty treasured by all people.

Making glassware by hand is the oldest industry in America, it started in the Jamestown Colony in 1608.

In the manufacture of Tiara Exclusives many of the techniques and tools of the early days are used. It is natural that you, a Tiara Customer, should want to know something about the way the line is created. Much of it is hand made, either pressed or blown, and in molds dating back many, many years. Each item is exclusive with Tiara, and will not be found in any other line.

Glass is made of Silica, Soda Ash, Lime, and Feldspar. Small amounts of various other chemicals such as Copper, Selenium, Manganese, Cadmium, etc. are added to make a "batch." After careful mixing of the selected ingredients, a quantity of broken glass — called cullet — is often added to the "batch" mixture to speed up the melting process. Glass is truly the product of earth and fire! The tank into which the glassworker shovels the "batch" has been pre-fired to an intense heat of about 2700°F. In about 18 hours the glass is ready to be gathered and blown. It takes a shop of 6 to 18 skilled workers to make one item.

A blowpipe is a hollow tube of steel with a special "head" which the gatherer slips into the tank of molten glass. Turning it in the glass, he gathers just the right "gob" on the end of the pipe. He hands it to the blower after first shaping on a marveling plate. The blower then shapes the "ball" with apple wood tools and paddles, and with carefully controlled puffs, forms a hollow bulb. His tools are varied and adapted for each item, and include the Pucellas, often called just the "tool." Like a huge pair of tweezers, the "tool" becomes a set of additional fingers for the skilled craftsman.

Now the piece is ready to be removed from the blowpipe and turned over to the stick-up boy, who picks it up and takes it to the "glory-hole", a reheating furnace kept at about 2500°F. Here the glass is reheated and taken to the finisher for further shaping. He, with the skilled touch of practiced hands, forms the decanter, bowl, pitcher, etc. When the item is to have a handle, or requires additional work, it is handed to a second finisher.

As this finisher completes the piece, a carry-in boy appears with a special fork, snaps the piece from the punty and carries it to an annealing oven or "lehr." Here it travels on a slowly moving, endless chain through several hours of diminishing heat, emerging at the end ready to be inspected. It is then labeled with Tiara Exclusive's sticker, boxed, and put in stock.

Since many Tiara Exclusives are blown and shaped by hand, variations in size, shape, and color lend real individuality to each item.

Reprinted from
CHINA GLASS & TABLEWARES

Index

Tiara Exclusives

EXECUTIVE OFFICES

DUNKIRK, INDIANA 47336 PHONE: 317-768-7821
OUT of STATE - 800-428-6586

Roger W. Jewett
National Sales
Leader

Ronald A. Kratz
National Sales
Coordinator

Ralph Salisbury
Order Processing
Manager

Southwestern Zone Leader

Robert Hatfield
224 N. Story Rd. Suite #134
Irving, TX 75061
(214-254-9112)

Ralph Waddell
General Manager

Wendell Williams
Customer Service
Manager

William Johnson
Warehouse and Shipping
Manager

Southeastern Zone Leader

Robert Hnath
681 Mountainbrooke Circle
Stone Moutain, GA 30087
(404-449-3809)

a masculine touch..

These pieces can only be described as the perfect blend of beautiful traits with a masculine air. Frosty, cool, and refreshing.

(A) 10040 "Powder Horn Tumblers", 4 Pcs. - The unique design of the 8" tumbler recaptures a part of American history. Any man will appreciate these 9 oz. horns.

(B) 10046 Tankards Frosted Crystal, Pair - The frosted pattern of these 10 oz. tankards accents the rugged handle. The 4½" high tankard is ideal for your cold beverages.

(C) 10025 Crystal Etched Smoker Set - The beauty of satin is featured in this 6-piece set (lighter, cigarette urn, and 4 ash trays.) The set accents any room or office.

2

Delicate smooth textured items that blend with any decor. The perfect gift for a favorite host or hostess. These lovely gifts make any good time better. (A) 10008 Tankards - set of 4 - These 5 5/8" tankards offer 12 ozs. of good times. Their classic design and unique finish make them unforgettable gifts.
(B) 10006 Mugs - set of 6 - Children love these 3½ oz. mugs. They are great for juice, milk, or soft drinks.
(C) 10037 Patio Pitcher 50 oz., - 10038 Patio Tankards, 12 oz., 4 pcs. - 10039 Patio Beverage Set - This five piece set is ideal for any gathering, men appreciate the generous capacity.

Frosted Crystal by *Tiara*

the experience of black...

Mystery, beauty, contrast, and elegance. The Cameo Black gift captures the delicate flowers, gleaming grapes, and colorful hues of the contemporary home.
Black glass has historically experienced limited production because of the difficulties in forming. Tiara craftsmen are proud to offer you the exclusive Cameo Black experience.
(A) 10317 Cameo Candy Box & Cover - 12" high, 2½" deep, 6" dia. - An ideal container for your candies, fruits, or flowers.
(B) 10300 Cameo Chalice & Cover - 15¾" high, 5" deep, 6" dia. - The beautiful design of this stately Chalice makes it a conversation piece.
(C) 10316 Cameo Handled Basket - 10" high. - Delicate curves of handcrafted glass highlight this gift.
(D) 10315 Cameo Ash Tray - 5½" dia., Pair - The Cameo ash tray is both beautiful and functional.

(A) 10301 Cameo Sugar/Creamer Set - This 4½" set is perfect for dinners or coffee breaks.

(B) 10303 Cameo Crimped Candleholder, Pair - These unusual candleholders set off any table. The 3" tall holders are 3½" in diameter.

(C) 10302 Cameo Console Bowl - Fruits, party mixes, or flowers arranged in this 9½" bowl brighten your table or room. The 4" deep bowl is 4¾" high.

(D) 10304 Cameo Console Set (Console Bowl & 2 Candleholders) - Highlight a shelf or special corner of a room with the Console Set.

(E) 10311 Cameo Butter & Cover - The beautiful 5" tall cover protects your butter while giving the table a touch of elegance. The tray is 6" by 9".

(F) 10312 Cameo Salt & Pepper Set - These 4" high beauties are sure to be appreciated by guests and family alike.

Cameo Black
by
Tiara

5

Dazzling drinkware in Black Cameo lets you host any gathering.

(A) 10309 Cameo Pitcher - 8" high, 6½" deep, 5½" dia. - This stylish pitcher holds 65 ozs. of cool refreshment.
(B) 10308 Cameo Goblets - 12 oz., 4 pcs., 6½" high - These elegant goblets are the perfect addition to your Cameo collection.
(C) 10310 Cameo Beverage Set, 5 pcs. (Cameo Pitcher & 4 Cameo Goblets) - Your guests will enjoy their mixed drinks or other cold beverages when served in style.
(D) 10307 Cameo Wine Goblets - 6 oz., 4 pcs., 4½" high - Friends and family will savor the wine and the beauty of your wine service.
(E) 10305 Cameo Tankards - 10 oz., 4 pcs., 4½" high - Guests will appreciate this rugged and beautiful tankard.

Impress guests with your Cameo Collection of Tumblers, Ice Teas and Salad Bowls. They will make you the perfect host or hostess.

Cameo Black
by
Tiara

(A) 10313 Cameo Hostess Set - 8 pcs., six 9 oz. Tumblers, Ice Tub & Cover, 11 7/8" high. 5½" dia. - Convenience is the word for this impressive set.
(B) 10306 Cameo Ice-Teas - 16 oz., 4 pcs., 5⅝" high - Ice crystals sparkle on the Cameo Ice-Teas. Great for your warm weather entertaining.
(C) 10314 Cameo Salad Bowl - 4 pcs., 2" high, 1⅞" deep, 5" dia. - Your salads will look greener in a Cameo Salad Bowl.

special friends...

Enter the make believe world of special friends and special parties. A magical moment sparks the imagination and with childish bubbling laughter you are off to a beautiful land of friends and fun. A Child's Bowl, Plate, Tumbler, or Mug can be a lasting reminder of those times.

Little One's Group by *Tiara*

(A) 10052 Child's Milk Tumblers, Pair - Storybook characters come alive on these 6 oz. tumblers. The 4" tall tumblers make the perfect "first glass" for your little one.
(B) 10017 Child's Plate - This 8½" diameter plate with dividers makes mealtime easier for your special little one.
(C) 10041 Child's Mug, Pair - These delightful 8 oz. mugs will become your little one's pride and joy. The 3½" mugs are perfect for juice or milk.
(D) 10042 Child's Cereal Bowl - This 6" diameter bowl is a storybook in itself.
(E) 10090 Child's Service Set, (Child's Mug, Bowl, and Plate) - Start a family tradition with this beautiful 3-piece set. A treasured gift sure to be remembered and cherished forever. (featured on page 8)

Tiara's Sandwich Collection recaptures the glamour and romance of Early America. On a gold tablecloth the rich color speaks elegance. No color is so flattering to the wood tones of the dining room, and no color can compare to the beauty of Golden Amber in a sunny window. To the best of our knowledge, Sandwich Glass dinnerware has never been produced in the Golden Amber color.

Sandwich Glass was originally named after Sandwich, Massachusetts, on Cape Cod. This beautiful glass is one of the most famous of early American glass styles. It was first made in 1825 by Deming Jarves. Jarves perfected the process of pressing glass. Handcut molds of iron were used to produce the beautiful patterns in Sandwich. The star scroll design was described by early writers as "sparkling like dew-moistened leaves." Despite the lacy quality of Sandwich Glass it is extremely durable. Each piece of the Tiara Sandwich Collection can be machine washed.

Most of the gifts in the Tiara Sandwich Collection are reproduced in the original molds. This enhances their value as collector's items and makes them ideal gifts. Every conceivable item for the table is available to Tiara customers, or will be in the near future. Tiara's collection is perfect for year round gift giving. The giver chooses shower, wedding, birthday, anniversary, or special occasion presents from a complete line of beautiful glass gifts. The Sandwich Glass Collection . . . exclusively yours from Tiara.

golden days of the past...

Set off your Sandwich dinnerware beautifully with these functional gifts in Golden Amber. Each piece adds a special touch to dining.

(A) 10262 Starter Set, 16 Pcs. - A perfect way to introduce yourself or someone else to Sandwich Glass.

(B) 10261 Place Setting, 4 Pcs. - Setting includes the 10" dinner plate, 8" salad plate, 6½ oz. cup and 6" saucer.

(C) 10217 Napkin Holder - The individuality of the craftsmen make each of these 4" holders truly unique.

(D) 10256 Dinner Bell - Revive an early American custom with an inviting ring of the dinner bell.

(E) 10227 Salt & Pepper Set - Season your food with a touch of elegance. These twin beauties are 4¾" tall.

(F) 10220 Butter Dish & Cover - Rounded balls of butter were formed on early American Farms and this unusual dish was designed to protect the fresh churned butter. The 6" tall dish is used by many for Eggs Benedict or other elegant covered dishes.

Romatic glows of golden Sandwich create a magical mood for you.

(A) 10258 Tall Candleholders - Pair - Elegance is the mood created by these 8½" tall holders. Lovely but difficult to produce, Tiara craftsmen are proud to offer this stunning pair.
(B) 10240 Glo Lamp - Decorated Ruby - The Sandwich pattern is highlighted by the candlelight. A great accent piece for any occasion. (5¾" high)
(C) 10237 Golden Glo Lamp - Warm patterns of flickering light will dance through your home. This beautiful Golden Glo is 5¾" high.
(D) 10216 Candlestick, Pair - Dining delight . . . These 3¾" high are ideal for a special candlelight dinner.

Add flair to food with the Sandwich collection of plates, platters, and trays.

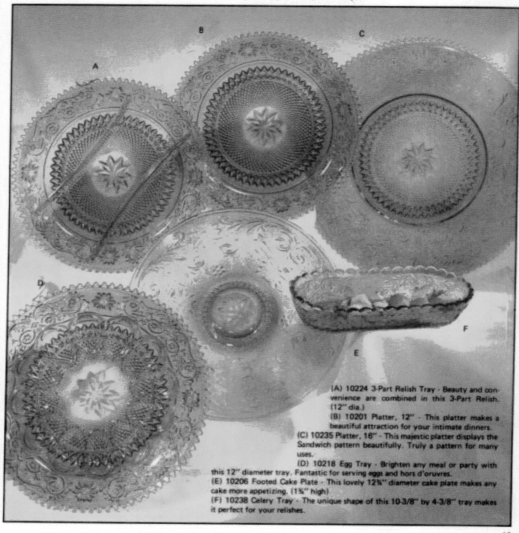

(A) 10224 3-Part Relish Tray - Beauty and convenience are combined in this 3-Part Relish. (12" dia.)

(B) 10201 Platter, 12" - This platter makes a beautiful attraction for your intimate dinners.

(C) 10235 Platter, 16" - This majestic platter displays the Sandwich pattern beautifully. Truly a pattern for many uses.

(D) 10218 Egg Tray - Brighten any meal or party with this 12" diameter tray. Fantastic for serving eggs and hors d'oruvres.

(E) 10206 Footed Cake Plate - This lovely 12¾" diameter cake plate makes any cake more appetizing. (1¾" high)

(F) 10238 Celery Tray - The unique shape of this 10-3/8" by 4-3/8" tray makes it perfect for your relishes.

Any wine has extra sparkle when enjoyed from this elegant Sandwich Server.

(A) 10208 Water Goblet Set, 8 Oz., 4 Pcs. - Your table will radiate formal elegance with these goblets.
(B) 10203 Wine Set, 11 Pcs. - Eight Wine Goblets surround this graceful 10" high Handblown Decanter. The set rests on a 10" diameter serving tray. A truly exquisite set worthy of the many compliments it will receive.
(C) 10204 Wine Goblets, 4 Pcs. - This beautiful set of 3½ oz. goblets adds a special touch to your Sandwich Wine Service.

Beautiful Sandwich serving pieces beckons guests to your beverages.

(A) 10219 Coaster Set, 4 Pcs. - The Sandwich Coasters are designed for the protection of your furniture. These 4½" coasters are the perfect addition to your Sandwich Beverage Service.
(B) 10200 Tumblers,10 Oz., 4 Pcs. - This stunning tumbler is perfect for iced-teas, sodas, or other cold beverages. (6½" high)
(C) 10213 Pitcher, 68 oz. - This pitcher adds its full measure to the formal tablesetting. (8" high)
(D) 10231 Bridge Set, 4 Pcs. - These trays are great for card parties. The 4½" by ¾" trays are quick conversation starters.

Tiara's Sandwich Collection Offers You a Bowl for any occasion.

(A) 10243 Center Bowl - The hand formed crimping of this beautiful bowl adds a new dimension to your dinner service. (4½" high), 10½" diameter).

(B) 10207 Crimped Vase - Add that extra touch of elegance to your Sandwich service with this mini-crimped vase. This 3½" high vase is perfect for flowers or candies. (6½" diameter)

(C) 10202 Deep Nappy, 2 Pcs. - Soups, salads, vegetables, and a host of other foods are just right for the Nappy. (6" dia.)

(D) 10228 Berry Set, 5 Pcs. - This set is perfect for berries, potatoes, vegetables, or ice cream. The 8" bowl makes a great server, while the four 4" Nappies are perfect for individual portions.

Parties are perfect when you use these beautiful Sandwich serving pieces.

(A) 10212 Sugar/Creamer Set - The 3-1/8" high pieces are suitable for formal or informal dining.

(B) 10226 Snack Set 8 Pc. - This super Sandwich Snack Set is the hit of any coffee or tea party. The 8½" by 6¾" oval plate makes this beautiful set truly unique.

(C) 10214 Punch Set, 14 Pcs. - Please your guests with this impressive 9-quart punch bowl. Perfect for your party punches. (Bowl 6¾" high, 13" dia.)

Grace your home with a golden touch of elegance.

(A) 10205 Mini-Basket - Delicate curves of Sandwich Glass make this 7¾" high basket a beautiful conversation piece.

(B) 10209 Wall Clock - Time will be the secondary thought as guests admire your 12" diameter Sandwich Wall Clock. The warmth of Golden Amber highlights this beautiful cordless clock.

(C) 10223 Wall Sconce - Dramatically set the mood of your home with this unique wall sconce. Placed on either side of your Sandwich Wall Clock they will create a spectacular appearence. Each sconce is 8" high.

(D) 10229 Puff Box & Cover - This delightful gift is a relic of Early America. The 1-7/8" high by 3-5/8" diameter box will make a "special place" for your treasures.

(E) 10221 Handled Basket - A Sandwich bowl is hand shaped into a basket with a beautifully curved handle attached. Brightens any table or mantle. (10" high)

What is a flaw in glass?

Is a small bubble in a fine piece of stemware a flaw? How about a cord, or a mold mark? The answer is definitely no, but it's sometimes difficult to convince a customer of this.

Most dinnerware and glassware departments and specialty shops have had trouble at one time or another with customers who seek flawless perfection in the tableware merchandise they buy.

Such perfection can be achieved only in assembly-line products, of course. It is not possible or even desirable in quality ware whose manufacture depends so much on the skill and artistry of individual craftsmen.

Slight variations and tiny imperfections in glassware pieces are actually a confirmation of craftsmanship and individual artistry. Most customers who appreciate good glassware understand this. For those who don't here is a series of questions and answers that a salesperson can use to promote better understanding of the product.

Does a "seed" or bubble in glassware constitute a flaw?

No. One of these tiny "seeds" or bubbles the size of a pinpoint may sometimes be observed in a piece of glassware when it is examined closely against a strong light.

The bubble is formed by gases when chemicals are united in the fusing or melting of the raw ingredients. It does not affect the quality or the beauty of the glass.

Should all pieces in a set be exactly alike?

No. There are almost always slight variations in diameter, height, and other dimensions in any group of tumblers, goblets, plates, or other articles of glass. These variations are usually so slight that they can be detected only with a micrometer, rarely by the naked eye. This is the hallmark of fine hand craftsmanship.

What is a cord?

A cord is an almost invisible difference in density in the glass which occurs during the fusing of the molten glass. It is visible only be reason of the fact that it reflects light. When a goblet with a cord in it is filled with water, no light is reflected and the cord becomes invisible.

Is a mold mark a sign of imperfection?

No. A mold mark is merely a ridge on a molded glassware piece that indicates the point at which the mold that formed the item was separated for removal of the finished ware. If it is overly prominent, however, it may be an indication of careless workmanship.

What is a shear mark?

A shear mark is a slight puckering of the glass caused when the artisan snips off excess molten glass when shaping the piece, as for example the end of the handle of a pitcher. It is a normal characteristic of glass and should not be considered a flaw.

Is hand-made glassware really made by hand, or merely hand-finished?

The production of hand-made glassware is indeed a hand process. The skilled hands and eyes of many men, working in teams, go into the making of every piece. The amazing thing is that such a high degree of excellence can be attained; that piece after piece coming from any individual or group of glass blowers or pressers is so nearly and accurately a duplicate of every other piece.

Why can't small irregularities be entirely eliminated from hand-made glass?

For the very reason that the glass is hand-made. No matter how deft the touch of the sensitive hands of glass craftsmen, it is impossible to eliminate completely small variations. These should not, therefore, be considered flaws. Glass is one of the trickiest materials to work with. Even machine-made glassware cannot be made absolutely perfect. But consider this: even the finest diamond, examined under a jeweler's loupe, rarely reveals absolute perfection.

How can the salesperson and the customer judge the quality of glassware?

There are certain simple tests and guides. Look for clarity and luster by holding the piece against a pure white background. Good glassware is quite clear, while inferior grades show a cloudy bluish or greenish tinge.

Quality glassware is also marked by a permanent polish or luster that results from fire-polishing.

Look for smooth edges. Glassware edges should be even, never rough and scratchy. In hand-cut ware, the design should be sharp and accurate. In etched ware, each tiny detail should be distinct and clearly defined.

Fine handblown glass frequently contains lead, which improves its clarity and adds to its weight. If a piece of stemware rings with a clear musical tone when struck lightly, this indicates lead content. Lime glass, on the other hand, does not have this resonance, but this does not make it any less desirable. The lime in such glass adds to its toughness and strength.

the charm
of yesterday...

The good old days . . . visits to grandmother's house and her ginger scented kitchen. Tiara is happy to join grandma in offering charming gifts.

[A] 10034 Sweet Pear Beverage Set, 5 Pcs. (Pitcher & 4 Tumblers) - Let this set highlight a memorable evening. Frosty cool cider or fruit juices really sparkle in Burnt Honey. (Shades Vary)

[B] 10032 Sweet Pear Pitcher - Beautiful sweet pears grace this 50 oz. pitcher. (9-1/8" high)

[C] 10033 Sweet Pear Tumblers, 4 Pcs. - These handsome 9 oz. tumblers are perfect for fruit juices. (5½" high)

[D] 10008 Colonial Water Bottle, Burnt Honey - The Colonial Water Bottle, a unique gift giving idea. Each bottle is handblown in a turn of the century mold. In Colonial times the bottle, filled with water, graced the table. Today the delicate lines of the 8" high bottle holds its own in style. (Shades vary)

[E] 10006 Grandpa Decanter - Grandpa's favorite! This merry gentleman twinkles with delight when filled to his generous 37 oz. His rotund shape and hat makes him a party favorite. (10" high)

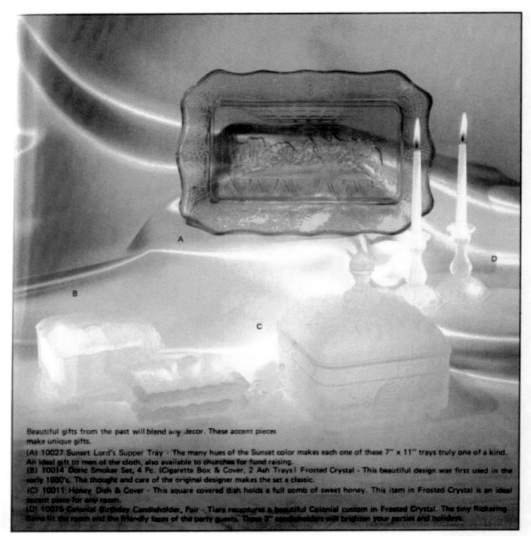

Beautiful gifts from the past will blend any decor. These accent pieces make unique gifts.

(A) 10027 Sunset Lord's Supper Tray - The many hues of the Sunset color makes each one of these 7" x 11" trays truly one of a kind. An ideal gift to men of the cloth, also available to churches for fund raising.

(B) 10014 Doric Smoker Set, 4 Pc. (Cigarette Box & Cover, 2 Ash Trays) Frosted Crystal - This beautiful design was first used in the early 1900's. The thought and care of the original designer makes the set a classic.

(C) 10011 Honey Dish & Cover - This square covered dish holds a full comb of sweet honey. This item in Frosted Crystal is an ideal accent piece for any room.

(D) 10075 Colonial Birthday Candleholder, Pair - Tiara recaptures a beautiful Colonial custom in Frosted Crystal. The tiny flickering flame lit the room and the friendly faces of the party guests. These 3" candleholders will brighten your parties and holidays.

Beautiful shades of blue highlight these exceptional gifts.

(A) 10009 Decorator Vase - The simple design of this contemporary vase will enhance your flower arrangements. (7½" high, 5½" top diameter)

(B) 10002 Hurricane Pitcher - A lovely addition to any room. This 51 oz. pitcher was made from a mold that produced actual hurricane lamps in the 1920's. A beautiful accent piece, great for flowers. (9½" high)

(C) 10103 Blue Bird Oval Bowl - The beautiful engraving of the "Blue Bird of Happiness" bowl is an exceptional example of craftsmenship of the early 1900's. Perfect for candies, nuts, or fresh flowers. (8½" diameter)

Vases for any mood or occasion.

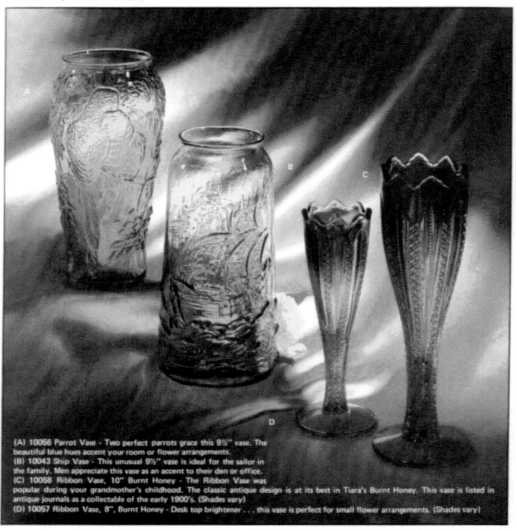

(A) 10056 Parrot Vase - Two perfect parrots grace this 9½″ vase. The beautiful blue hues accent your room or flower arrangements.

(B) 10043 Ship Vase - This unusual 9½″ vase is ideal for the sailor in the family. Men appreciate this vase as an accent to their den or office.

(C) 10058 Ribbon Vase, 10″ Burnt Honey - The Ribbon Vase was popular during your grandmother's childhood. The classic antique design is at its best in Tiara's Burnt Honey. This vase is listed in antique journals as a collectable of the early 1900's. (Shades vary)

(D) 10057 Ribbon Vase, 8″, Burnt Honey - Desk top brightener . . . this vase is perfect for small flower arrangements. (Shades vary)

sparkling color complements...

Brighten any room with these colorful and functional gifts. An array of colors that complement any decor. Perfect mood setters, accent pieces, or memorable gifts.

(A) 10026 Lotus Ash Tray - The beautiful floral design of this tray is appreciated by smokers and non-smokers alike. The lovely Horizon Blue tray is 9½" in diameter.

(B) 10023 Crystal Eagle Ash Tray - The exceptional art work of this massive tray makes it a favorite of collectors of Early Americana. The Crystal tray blends with any decor. It is 10½" in diameter.

(C) 10022 Gold Eagle Ash Tray - Woodtones are complemented by the rich golden hues of the Eagle Ash Tray. Perfect for the executive decor. The beautiful eagle tray is 10½" in diameter.

(D) 10001 Smoker Set, 6 Pc. (Lighter, Cigarette Urn, 4 Ash Trays) - This elegant set graces any room or office. A practical gift for that special someone.

Warm moods come naturally in a room displaying these golden gifts. Handcrafted items stand out impressively in your home. Each glass creation generates conversation.

(A) 10044 Demijohn, Burnt Honey - This 20" demijohn is perfect for tall dried flower arrangements. (shades vary)
(B) 10049 Terrarium, Burnt Honey - The golden hues of this 15" terrarium accent your greenery. (shades vary)
(C) 10070 Aquarius Pitcher, Burnt Honey - The brilliance of the stars is reflected in Tiara's own "water bearer". The 15" high vessel features a fragile decorative handle that can not be used to pick up the pitcher. (shades vary)
(D) 10048 Hob-Nail Vase, Burnt Honey - This 8½" vase captures a classic American design. (shades vary)

Craftsmenship and beauty make these gifts everyday favorites . . . . .

(A) 10419 Monarch 8½" Bowl - This elegant bowl enhances flowers and fruits.
(B) 10063 Kahlua Mug, Pair - Palm trees and warm breezes come to mind as your guests sip their mai tais or other cool drinks from these 6-1/8" tall mugs.
(C) 10422 Monarch Large 47 oz. Pitcher - Craftsmenship at its best makes this impressive 8" tall pitcher a work of art.
(D) 10424 Monarch 8 Oz. Goblets, 4 Pcs. - The beautiful deep cut pattern of these 6¼" goblets sparkles in any light.

Beautiful modern accents with good old fashioned usefulness

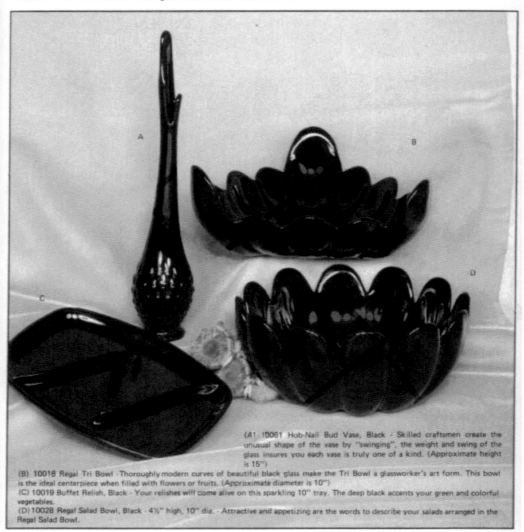

(A) 10061 Hob-Nail Bud Vase, Black - Skilled craftsmen create the unusual shape of the vase by "swinging", the weight and swing of the glass insures you each vase is truly one of a kind. (Approximate height is 15")

(B) 10018 Regal Tri Bowl - Thoroughly modern curves of beautiful black glass make the Tri Bowl a glassworker's art form. This bowl is the ideal centerpiece when filled with flowers or fruits. (Approximate diameter is 10")

(C) 10019 Buffet Relish, Black - Your relishes will come alive on this sparkling 10" tray. The deep black accents your green and colorful vegetables.

(D) 10028 Regal Salad Bowl, Black - 4½" high, 10" dia. - Attractive and appetizing are the words to describe your salads arranged in the Regal Salad Bowl.

Perfect Party Pleasers For Your Formal Or Informal Gatherings

(A) 10107 Provincial Punch Set - This 8 quart
bowl keeps any party going in style. Twelve cups,
12 duracite hooks, and a duracite ladle complete
the set. (7½" , 13" dia.)
(B) 10108 Provincial 5 Oz. Punch Cups - 1 doz. - Large gatherings make these cups essential. (3-3/8" high)
(C) 10080 Hob-Nail Pitcher - Classic American design makes the 56 oz. pitcher a decorative as well as a functional gift. (pitcher is 8¼" high)
(D) 10081 Hob-Nail Tumblers, 4 pcs., - These 9 oz. tumblers are perfect for juice, or soft drinks. (5" high)
(E) 10082 Hob-Nail Set, 5 pcs. (Hob-Nail Pitcher & 4 Tumblers) - This unique crystal beverage set will capture the fancy of your friends.

catch the sunset.

Flaming clouds and brilliant orange, red, and golden rays of color paint the skies. Tiara has captured these warm hues in their Sunset Collection. Each handcrafted gift reflects its own special hue of beautiful color. No two pieces of the beautiful glass are exactly the same color.

(A) 10072 Constellation Cake Plate 1½" high - Like the sun itself this 13½" diameter footed cake plate brightens your home.

(B) 10087 Constellation Ftd. Candleholders, Pair - Flames come alive in these 5" tall candleholders. These fiery sunsets breath takingly accent any room.

(C) 10073 Constellation Console Bowl, 3¾" high - Beauty and craftsmenship make this 11½" diameter bowl perfect for fruits, flowers, or other uses.

(D) 10086 Constellation Mini - Basket - Delicate curves of fiery glass make this 6¾" high gift an ideal window accent.

SUNSET by Tiara

29

touch the stars..

Sprinkle some starlight into your gift giving with these goblets from the Zodiac. Bright vibrant colors capture the personality of your sign. An ideal gift for the star of special occasions.

10524 Aquarius - Blue, 10525 Pisces - Lime, 10526 Aries - Red, 10527 Taurus - Cream, 10528 Gemini - Yellow, 10529 Cancer - Cherry, 10530 Leo - Orange, 10531 Virgo - Gold, 10532 Libra - Pink, 10533 Scorpio - White, 10534 Sagittarius - Turquoise, 10535 Capricorn - Green

ZODIAC by *Tiara*

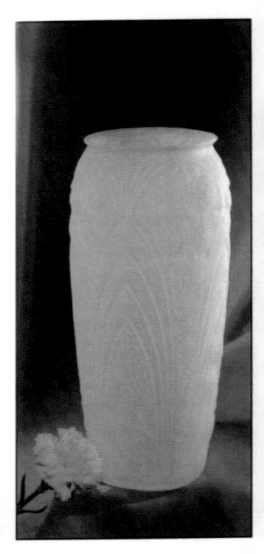

preferred hostess plan

A Preferred Hostess is one selected by a Counselor, who agrees to hold three or more Giftaramas, in her home, in a calendar year. There is NO requirement for a certain amount of sales.

Being a member of our Preferred Hostess Club affords you many extras! First, you can rebook, and not hold it within two weeks, and still receive your $3.00 dating credit. Secondly, your name will be entered on our Computer, enabling us to keep you informed of new products, prices, and specials on a timely basis. Thirdly, when the total sales of your three or more Giftaramas reach $500 in a calendar year, you will be entitled to a FREE gift! The 1978 Limited Edition item pictured - - The Frosted Crystal 12" Vase, #10111 - - can be yours!

Sign up NOW as a Preferred Hostess, and earn one or more of these antique reproductions! Your Counselor will award you one for every $500 in sales you account for in the calendar year!

Appreciatively,

Roger W. Jewett
National Sales Leader

December 1, 1978

As Tiara Exclusives continues to expand into out 9th year, I want to take this opportunity to thank all of our Assocates, our Preferred Hostesses, our regular hostesses, and all our Tiara customers for their loyalty and support this past year!

It has been very gratifying to receive numerous complimentary comments and letters this year recognizing our efforts to give total support to all involved in Tiara's success!

We have added 3 extra hand shops, several top executives in our Tiara office, and have increased our inventory to over twelve million dollars worth of finished products. We are doing everything possible to make 1979 an OUTSTANDING year for all concerned, and we pledge our continued support to our field sales force and our loyal customers throughout the year ahead!

J. E. Hooffstetter
President

December 1, 1978

When Tiara was founded in 1970 we mapped out a 10 year building program, and thanks to the tremendous acceptance of Tiara's gifts in glass by our customers, we will far surpass our 10th year goal in this our 9th year!

We certainly appreciate the tremendous acceptance of the Tiara line by the thousands of hostesses and customers all over America. Throughout 1979 we pledge to keep the line exciting, and to make available unusual extra gifts of the month for our hostesses.

Our thousands of Preferred Hostesses, the back bone of our business, mean a great deal to us, and we certainly hold them in high esteem. Now that we have computorized that plan, we have great expectations for 1979.

Roger W. Jewett
National Sales Leader

Do you know?

That Tiara Counselors have an opportunity to use all the ability they possess, and all they can acquire?

That Tiara Counselors have NO investment in samples, and receive over $325 worth FREE when they sign up?

That Tiara Counselors get paid every day they work, with NO waiting for their profits?

That Tiara Counselors do NO packing and sacking, or delivering? That everything they sell is delivered for them by UPS, at no cost to them?

That Tiara Counselors have NO reports to fill out, and no record keeping?

That Tiara Counselors are FIELD TRAINED by Sales Leaders with hundreds of years of party plan experience behind them?

That Tiara Counselors are promoted as rapidly as they meet specified levels of achievement, so they can earn profits on what other people sell?

That Tiara Counselors, in many cases, are husband and wife teams that are building fine businesses for themselves, and a new way of life for their families?

That Tiara Couselors need more help to service the thousands of customers who are anxious to avail themselves of Tiara Gifts throughout America, and that they would LOVE to have you join them?

NOW THAT YOU DO KNOW — won't you get in touch with us, so that we can help you help yourself to the riches you deserve? Simply write our National Sales Leader, giving your name, address, phone, and a simple statement of your personal goals!

WRITE: Roger W. Jewett, 9440 Holliday Dr., Indianapolis, Indiana, 46260. You'll be GLAD you did!

GUARANTEE

All Tiara Gifts are guaranteed to be of fine quality, and craftsmanship, within the limits of the arts represented.

All products are guaranteed for life, and should breakage occur, either accidental or otherwise, or any other damage, replacement will be made at fifty percent (50%) of the prevailing price, provided this receipted shopping guide is sent to Tiara Exclusives as proof of purchase. The receipted shopping card will be returned to you along with your replacement merchandise.

A fee of one dollar ($1.00) to cover packing, shipping and indemnity must be included with each order for replacement.

There shall be no limitation upon this guarantee, and replacement policy, except in the case of discontinued items, in which event, the company will no longer be responsible, or liable, for replacement.

Flowers, candles, fruit and beverage are used as props in the photographs of this catalog. These are not available through Tiara Exclusives.

Your Tiara Associate

CREDITS: Photography — Photo Craft, Muncie, Ind. Separations — Color Separations, Dayton, Ohio.
Art & Production — Colony Printing, Eaton, Indiana.   1978 By Tiara Exclusives

Tiara Exclusives SUGGESTED SELLING PRICE

DUNKIRK, INDIANA 47336

NO.	DESCRIPTION	COST	NO.	DESCRIPTION	COST
10001	Smoker Set, Black, -6 pcs.	$16.50	10209	Sandwich Wall Clock, Gold	$39.90
10002	Hurricane Pitcher, Blue	$16.50	10212	Sandwich Sugar/Creamer Set, Gold	$11.90
10003	Colonial Water, Bottle, Burnt Honey	$12.90	10213	Sandwich Pitcher, Gold	$19.50
10006	Mugs 3½ oz., Frosted Crystal, -6pcs.	$10.90	10214	Sandwich 14pc. Punch Set, Gold	$39.90
10008	Tankards 12 oz., Frosted Crystal, -4pcs.	$14.50	10216	Sandwich Candlestick, Gold -pr.	$10.90
10009	Decorator Vase, Blue	$10.90	10217	Sandwich Napkin Holder, Gold	$ 9.90
10011	Honey Dish & Cover, Frosted Crystal	$14.90	10218	Sandwich Egg Hors D'Oeuvre Tray, Gold	$10.90
10014	Doric Smoke Set, 4 pcs, Frosted Crystal	$11.90	10219	Sandwich Coaster Set, 4pcs., Gold	$ 9.90
10017	Child's Plate, Gold	$ 5.50	10220	Sandwich Butter Dish & Cover, Gold	$14.50
10018	Regal Tri Bowl, Black	$12.90	10221	Sandwich Basket Handled, Gold	$21.50
10019	Buffet Relish, Black	$ 5.90	10223	Sandwich Wall Sconce, Gold	$17.50
10022	Eagle Ash Tray, Gold	$12.90	10224	Sandwich 3 part Relish, Gold	$10.90
10023	Eagle Ash Tray, Frosted Crystal	$12.90	10226	Sandwich Snack Set, Gold -8pcs.	$15.90
10025	Smoker Set, Frosted Crystal, -6pcs.	$16.50	10227	Sandwich Salt & Pepper Set, Gold	$12.50
10026	Lotus Ash Tray, Blue	$11.50	10228	Sandwich Berry Set, Gold -5pcs.	$13.90
10027	Lord's Supper Plate, Sunset	$13.50	10229	Sandwich Puff Box & Cover, Gold	$ 8.90
10028	Regal Salad Bowl, Black	$12.90	10231	Sandwich Bridge Set, Gold -4pcs.	$ 8.50
10032	Sweet Pear Pitcher, Burnt Honey	$24.90	10235	Sandwich Platter, Gold -16" dia.	$18.50
10033	Sweet Pear Tumbler, Burnt Honey, -4pcs.	$27.50	10237	Sandwich Golden Glo Lamp	$ 9.90
10034	Sweet Pear Bev. Set, Burnt Honey, -5pcs.	$39.90	10238	Sandwich Celery Tray, Gold	$10.50
10037	Patio Pitcher 50 oz., Frosted Crystal	$12.90	10240	Sandwich Glo Lamp, Ruby	$ 9.90
10038	Patio Tankard 12 oz., Frosted Crystal, -4pcs.	$14.90	10243	Sandwich Console Crimped Bowl, Gold	$13.90
10039	Patio Bev. Set, Frosted Crystal, -5pcs.	$21.90	10256	Sandwich Dinner Bell, Gold	$10.90
10040	Powder Horn Tumblers, Frosted Crystal, -4pcs.	$13.90	10258	Sandwich Tall Candleholders, Gold -pr.	$15.50
10041	Child's Mug, Gold -pr.	$ 8.50	10261	Sandwich Place Setting, Gold -4pcs.	$14.90
10042	Child's Cereal Bowl, Gold	$ 5.50	10262	Sandwich Starter Set, Gold -16pcs.	$39.90
10043	Ship Vase, Gold	$15.50	10300	Cameo Chalice & Cover, Black	$ 9.90
10044	Demijohn, Burnt Honey	$49.90	10301	Cameo Sugar/Creamer Set, Black	$ 7.90
10046	Tankards 10 oz., Frosted Crystal, -pr.	$ 8.50	10302	Cameo Console Bowl, Black	$16.50
10048	Hob Nail Vase, Burnt Honey	$15.50	10303	Cameo Crimped Candleholder, Black -pr.	$ 6.50
10049	Terrarium, Burnt Honey	$49.90	10304	Cameo Console Set, Black -3pcs.	$19.90
10052	Child's Milk Tumbler, Gold -pr.	$ 8.50	10305	Cameo Tankard, 10 oz., Black -4pcs.	$11.90
10056	Parrot Vase, Blue	$12.90	10306	Cameo Ice Tea, 15 oz., Black -4pcs.	$11.90
10057	Ribbon Vase, 8", Burnt Honey	$12.50	10307	Cameo Wine Goblet, 6 oz., Black -4pcs.	$10.90
10058	Ribbon Vase, 10", Burnt Honey	$14.50	10308	Cameo Goblet, 12oz., Black -4pcs.	$14.50
10061	Hob Nail Bud Vase, Black	$12.90	10309	Cameo Pitcher, 65 oz., Black	$11.90
10063	Kahlua Mug, Black -pr.	$13.90	10310	Cameo Beverage Set, Black, -5pcs.	$21.50
10070	Aquarius Pitcher, Burnt Honey	$59.90	10311	Cameo Butter & Cover, Black	$ 8.50
10072	Constellation Cake Plate, Sunset	$15.90	10312	Cameo Salt & Pepper Set, Black	$ 8.50
10073	Constellation Console Bowl, Sunset	$15.90	10313	Cameo Hostess Set, Black -8pcs.	$19.90
10075	Colonial Birthday Candleholder, pr., Fst. Cry.	$ 8.90	10314	Cameo Salad Bowl, Black -4pcs.	$10.90
10080	Hob Nail Pitcher, Crystal	$17.50	10315	Cameo Ash Tray, Black -2pcs.	$ 5.50
10081	Hob Nail Tumblers, Crystal, -4pcs.	$20.90	10316	Cameo Basket Handled, Black	$22.50
10082	Hob Nail Bev. Set, Crystal, -5pcs.	$32.90	10317	Cameo Footed Compote and Cover, Black	$ 8.50
10086	Constellation Mini Basket, Sunset	$12.90	10419	Monarch 8½" Bowl, Black	$16.50
10087	Constellation Ftd., Candleholders, Sunset, -pr.	$14.90	10422	Monarch Large Pitcher, Black	$18.50
10090	Child's Set, Gold -3pcs.	$11.90	10424	Monarch Goblet, Black, -4pcs.	$21.90
10103	Blue Bird Oval Bowl,	$10.90	10524	Aquarius Goblet, Blue	$ 8.90
10104	Mountaineer Decanter, Gold	$15.90	10525	Pisces Goblet, Lime	$ 8.90
10107	Provincial Punch Set, Frosted Crystal	$37.90	10526	Aries Goblet, Red	$ 8.90
10108	Provincial Punch Cup, Frosted Crystal, -12pcs.	$17.50	10527	Taurus Goblet, Cream	$ 8.90
10200	Sandwich 10 oz. Tumbler, Gold -4pcs.	$19.90	10528	Gemini Goblet, Yellow	$ 8.90
10201	Sandwich 12" Platter, Gold	$ 9.50	10529	Cancer Goblet, Cherry	$ 8.90
10202	Sandwich 6" Deep Nappy, pr., Gold	$12.90	10530	Leo Goblet, Orange	$ 8.90
10203	Sandwich 11pc. Wine Set, Gold	$39.90	10531	Virgo Goblet, Gold	$ 8.90
10204	Sandwich Wine Goblet, Gold -4pcs.	$14.50	10532	Libra Goblet, Pink	$ 8.90
10205	Sandwich Mini Basket, Gold	$12.90	10533	Scorpio Goblet, White	$ 8.90
10206	Sandwich Footed Cake Plate, Gold	$13.50	10534	Sagittarius Goblet, Turquoise	$ 8.90
10207	Sandwich Crimped Vase, Gold	$10.50	10535	Capricorn Goblet, Green	$ 8.90
10208	Sandwich Goblets, Gold -4pcs.	$14.90			

TE-118 REV. 1/79

Tiara Exclusives SUGGESTED SELLING PRICE

DUNKIRK, INDIANA 47336

NO.	DESCRIPTION	COST	NO.	DESCRIPTION	COST
10001	Smoker Set, Black, -6 pcs.	$16.50	10207	Sandwich Crimped Vase, Gold	$10.50
10002	Hurricane Pitcher, Blue	$16.50	10208	Sandwich Goblets, Gold -4 pcs.	$14.90
10003	Colonial Water, Bottle, Burnt Honey	$12.90	10209	Sandwich Wall Clock, Gold	$39.90
10006	Mugs 3½ oz., Frosted Crystal, -6 pcs.	$10.90	10212	Sandwich Sugar/Creamer Set, Gold	$11.90
10008	Tankards 12 oz., Frosted Crystal, -4 pcs.	$14.50	10213	Sandwich Pitcher, Gold	$19.50
10009	Decorator Vase, Blue	$10.90	10214	Sandwich 14 pc. Punch Set, Gold	$39.90
10011	Honey Dish & Cover, Frosted Crystal	$14.90	10216	Sandwich Candlestick, Gold -pr.	$10.90
10016	Hunter's Horn Mug, Cry. pr.	$13.90	10217	Sandwich Napkin Holder, Gold	$ 9.90
10017	Child's Plate, Gold	$ 5.50	10218	Sandwich Egg Hors D'Oeuvre Tray, Gold	$10.90
10018	Regal Tri Bowl, Black	$12.90	10219	Sandwich Coaster Set, 4 pcs., Gold	$ 9.90
10019	Buffet Relish, Black	$ 5.90	10220	Sandwich Butter Dish & Cover, Gold	$14.50
10022	Eagle Ash Tray, Gold	$12.90	10221	Sandwich Basket Handled, Gold	$21.50
10023	Eagle Ash Tray, Frosted Crystal	$12.90	10223	Sandwich Wall Sconce, Gold	$17.50
10025	Smoker Set, Frosted Crystal, -6 pcs.	$16.50	10224	Sandwich 3 part Relish, Gold	$10.90
10026	Lotus Ash Tray, Blue	$11.50	10226	Sandwich Snack Set, Gold -8 pcs.	$15.90
10027	Lord's Supper Plate, Sunset	$13.50	10227	Sandwich Salt & Pepper Set, Gold	$12.50
10028	Regal Salad Bowl, Black	$12.90	10228	Sandwich Berry Set, Gold -5 pcs.	$13.90
10031	Hob Nail Mini Basket, Black	$12.90	10229	Sandwich Puff Box & Cover, Gold	$ 8.90
10033	Sweet Pear Tumbler, Burnt Honey, -4 pcs.	$27.50	10230	Sand. Juice Tmblr. Gold	$15.90
10034	Sweet Pear Bev. Set, Burnt Honey, -5 pcs.	$39.90	10231	Sandwich Bridge Set, Gold -4 pcs.	$ 8.50
10037	Patio Pitcher 50 oz., Frosted Crystal	$12.90	10235	Sandwich Platter, Gold -16" dia.	$18.50
10038	Patio Tankard 12 oz., Frosted Crystal, -4 pcs.	$14.90	10237	Sandwich Golden Glo Lamp	$ 9.90
10039	Patio Bev. Set, Frosted Crystal, -5 pcs.	$21.90	10238	Sandwich Celery Tray, Gold	$10.50
10040	Powder Horn Tumblers, Frosted Crystal, -4 pcs.	$13.90	10239	Sandwich Salad Bowl, Gold	$ 9.90
10041	Child's Mug, Gold -pr.	$ 8.50	10240	Sandwich Glo Lamp, Ruby	$ 9.90
10042	Child's Cereal Bowl, Gold	$ 5.50	10243	Sandwich Console Crimped Bowl, Gold	$13.90
10043	Ship Vase, Gold	$15.50	10244	Sand. Two-Tier Tidbit, Gold	$14.90
10044	Demijohn, Burnt Honey	$49.90	10245	Sand. Ftd. Candleholder, Gold -pr.	$10.90
10046	Tankards, 10 oz., Frosted Crystal, -pr.	$ 8.50	10256	Sandwich Dinner Bell, Gold	$10.90
10047	Mountaineer Decanter, Blue	$15.90	10258	Sandwich Tall Candleholders, Gold -pr.	$15.50
10048	Hob Nail Vase, Burnt Honey	$15.50	10261	Sandwich Place Setting, Gold -4 pcs.	$14.90
10049	Terrarium, Burnt Honey	$49.90	10262	Sandwich Starter Set, Gold -16 pcs.	$39.90
10051	Hob Nail Pitcher, Blue	$17.50	10300	Cameo Chalice & Cover, Black	$ 9.90
10052	Child's Milk Tumbler, Gold -pr.	$ 8.50	10301	Cameo Sugar/Creamer Set, Black	$ 7.90
10053	Lord's Supper Plate, Pink	$14.50	10303	Cameo Crimped Candleholder, Black -pr.	$ 6.50
10056	Parrot Vase, Blue	$12.90	10305	Cameo Tankard, 10 oz., Black -4 pcs.	$11.90
10058	Ribbon Vase, 10", Burnt Honey	$14.50	10306	Cameo Ice Tea, 15 oz., Black -4 pcs.	$11.90
10061	Hob Nail Bud Vase, Black	$12.90	10307	Cameo Wine Goblet, 6 oz., Black -4 pcs.	$10.90
10062	Duchess Basket Hld. Pink	$19.50	10308	Cameo Goblet, 12 oz., Black -4 pcs.	$14.50
10063	Kahlua Mug, Black -pr.	$13.90	10309	Cameo Pitcher, 65 oz., Black	$11.90
10070	Aquarius Pitcher, Burnt Honey	$59.90	10310	Cameo Beverage Set, Black, -5 pcs.	$21.50
10072	Constellation Cake Plate, Sunset	$15.90	10311	Cameo Butter & Cover, Black	$ 8.50
10073	Constellation Console Bowl, Sunset	$15.90	10312	Cameo Salt & Pepper Set, Black	$ 8.50
10075	Colonial Birthday Candleholder, pr., Fst. Cry.	$ 8.90	10313	Cameo Hostess Set, Black -8 pcs.	$19.90
10086	Constellation Mini Basket, Sunset	$12.90	10314	Cameo Salad Bowl, Black -4 pcs.	$10.90
10087	Constellation Ftd., Candleholders, Sunset, -pr.	$14.90	10315	Cameo Ash Tray, Black -2 pcs.	$ 5.50
10090	Child's Set, Gold -3 pcs.	$11.90	10316	Cameo Basket Handled, Black	$22.50
10092	Child's Nrsy. Rhym Pl. Gld 4 pcs.	$ 9.90	10317	Cameo Footed Compote and Cover, Black	$ 8.50
10103	Blue Bird Oval Bowl	$10.90	10524	Aquarius Goblet, Blue	$ 8.90
10107	Provincial Punch Set, Frosted Crystal	$37.90	10525	Pisces Goblet, Lime	$ 8.90
10108	Provincial Punch Cup, Frosted Crystal, -12 pcs.	$17.50	10526	Aries Goblet, Red	$ 8.90
10120	Hob Nail Pitcher, Pink	$18.90	10527	Taurus Goblet, Cream	$ 8.90
10121	Hob Nail Tumblers, Pink -4 pcs.	$22.90	10528	Gemini Goblet, Yellow	$ 8.90
10122	Hob Nail Bev. Set, Pink - 4 pcs.	$34.90	10529	Cancer Goblet, Cherry	$ 8.90
10200	Sandwich 10 oz. Tumbler, Gold -4 pcs.	$19.90	10530	Leo Goblet, Orange	$ 8.90
10201	Sandwich 12" Platter, Gold	$ 9.50	10531	Virgo Goblet, Gold	$ 8.90
10202	Sandwich 6" Deep Nappy, pr., Gold	$12.90	10532	Libra Goblet, Pink	$ 8.90
10203	Sandwich 11 pc. Wine Set, Gold	$39.90	10533	Scorpio Goblet, White	$ 8.90
10204	Sandwich Wine Goblet, Gold -4 pcs.	$14.50	10534	Sagittarius Goblet, Turquoise	$ 8.90
10205	Sandwich Mini Basket, Gold	$12.90	10535	Capricorn Goblet, Green	$ 8.90
10206	Sandwich Footed Cake Plate, Gold	$13.50			

Tiara 1981 Catalog Contents

Tiara Exclusives

1981

INDEX

Tiara Exclusives

EXECUTIVE OFFICES

DUNKIRK, INDIANA 47336
PHONE: 317-768-7821
OUT OF STATE: 800-428-6586

J.E. Hooffstetter
President

Ronald A. Kratz
National Sales Coordinator

Paul N. Mills
Director of Sales Promotion

Roger W. Jewett
National Sales Leader

Ralph Salisbury
Order Processing Manager

Carolyn Street
Accounting Supervisor

Ralph Waddell
General Manager

Jim Whiteman
Warehouse and Shipping Manager

Wendell Williams
Customer Service Manager

ZONE LEADERS

Rocky Mountain Zone
Jerry Tripp
7100 Broadway, Suite #1-L
Watervliet Bus. Pkwy.
Denver, CO 80221
(303-427-3913)

Northwestern Zone
Hal Scott
6978 Pampas Way
Fair Oaks, CA 95628
(916-966-8508)

Western Zone
Vicki & Bob Kurtz
2882 Pelican Dr.
Union City, CA 94587
(415-471-9734)   (213-862-9465)

Southwestern Zone
Robert Hatfield
224 N. Story Rd., Suite #134
Irving, TX 75061
(214-254-9113)

Midwestern Zone
Jerry Maynard
470 E. 9 Mile Rd.
Ferndale, MI 48220
(313-543-2121)

Atlantic Coast Zone
Gloria Hall
7803 Strathdon Ct.
Alexandria, VA 22310
(703-922-7136)

Southeastern Zone
Robert Hnath
6350 McDonough Dr., Suite G & H
Norcross, GA 30093
(404-449-3809)

North Central Zone
Judy Fiala
4338 N. Judd Ave.
Schiller Park, IL 60176
(312-678-8351)

(A) **10153 Constellation Footed Candle Holders — Pair —** Romanticize your table top with the romantic warmth of candlelight with these 5" tall candle holders.

(B) **10151 Constellation Console Bowl —** Beauty in its line design and the craftsmanship of the glass worker makes this 11½" diameter bowl an ideal centerpiece for fruits, flowers or other uses. (3¾")

(C) **10150 Constellation Cake Plate —** The star pattern of this 13½" diameter cake plate will highlight a variety of blue and green tones when on display. Your cakes and pastries will have an added touch of elegance when served on this plate.

(D) **10154 Constellation 6" Nut Bowl —** A complementary touch to any table in your room. Assorted candies will be most tempting and your favorite flower arrangement will be the perfect accent in this bowl.

(E) **10152 Constellation Mini Basket —** The design of this 6 ¾" high basket lends itself as the unusual serving piece for tea cookies, nuts, or mints.

Constellation

1

Ponderosa Pine

(A) **10105 Leaf Relish — 11¾" x 9¼"** — The striking pattern of this three-part relish will add a touch of the outdoors to your buffet or formal dining table.

(B) **10160 Ponderosa Pine Plate — 10" dia., 4 pcs.** — Introduced for the first time by Tiara in the United States is this original design of the Ponderosa Pine pattern. The ideal breakfast and luncheon service. Your friends will envy you when your brunches are served using this new line of glassware.

(C) **10162 Ponderosa Pine Juice — 4¾" high, 4 pcs.**

(D) **10161 Ponderosa Pine Mug — 4¾" high, 4 pcs.**

2

Designer Selection

(A) **10070 Aquarius Pitcher, Burnt Honey** — The brilliance of the stars is reflected in Tiara's own "water bearer." The 15" high vessel features a fragile decorative handle that cannot be used to pick up the pitcher. (Shades vary)

(B) **10044 Demijohn, Burnt Honey** — This 20" demijohn is perfect for tall dried flower arrangements. (Shades vary)

(C) **10049 Terrarium, Burnt Honey** — The golden hues of this 15" terrarium accent your greenery. (Shades vary)

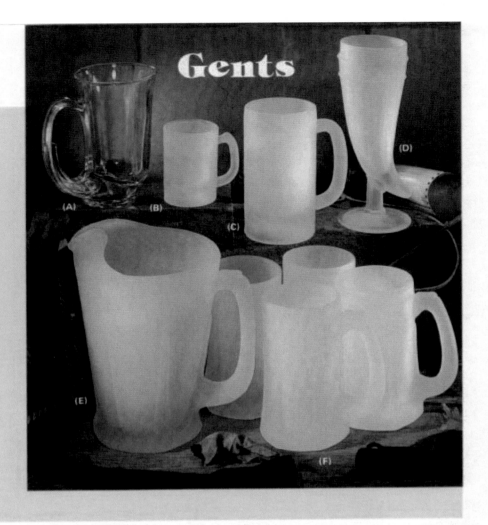

Gents

(A) **10016 Hunter's Horn Mug — 12-oz. pair —** After the fox hunt or any gala event, your favorite beverage served in this unique mug will capture the mood of any celebration. (5½" high)

(B) **10006 Mugs — set of 6 —** Children love these 3½-oz. mugs. They are great for juice, milk or soft drinks.

(C) **10008 Mugs — set of 4 —** These 5 5/8" mugs offer 12-oz. of good times. Their classic design and unique finish make them unforgettable gifts.

(D) **10040 Powder Horn Tumblers — 4 pcs. —** The unique design of the 8" tumbler recaptures a part of American history. Any man will appreciate these 9-oz. horns.

(E) **10039 Patio Beverage Set — 5 pcs. —** The 50-oz. pitcher and the four 12-oz. tankards are ideal for any gathering. Men appreciate the generous capacity for their favorite beverage.

(F) **10038 Patio Tankards — 12-oz., 4 pcs. —** Children take delight when sodas and sundaes are served in this multiple use tankard.

The History Of Glass

Over 4,000 years ago, perhaps on the Sands of Egypt, Syria, or Babylonia, the manufacturing of glass began. Since then mankind has added, little by little, to the glassmaker's art. The skill of the glassmaker has been a source of beauty treasured by all people.

Making glassware by hand is the oldest industry in America, it started in the Jamestown Colony in 1608.

In the manufacture of Tiara Exclusives many of the techniques and tools of the early days are used. It is natural that you, a Tiara Customer, should want to know something about the way the line is created. Much of it is hand made, either pressed or blown, and in molds dating back many, many years. Each item is exclusive with Tiara, and will not be found in any other line.

Glass is made of silica, soda ash, lime, and feldspar. Small amounts of various other chemicals such as copper, selenium, manganese, cadmium, etc. are added to make a "batch." After careful mixing of the selected ingredients, a quantity of broken glass — called cullet — is often added to the "batch" mixture to speed up the melting process. Glass is truly the product of earth and fire! The tank into which the glassworker shovels the "batch" has been pre-fired to an intense heat of about 2700°F. In about 18 hours the glass is ready to be gathered and blown. It takes a shop of six to 18 skilled workers to make one item.

A blowpipe is a hollow tube of steel with a special "head" which the gatherer slips into the tank of molten glass. Turning it in the glass, he gathers just the right "gob" on the end of the pipe. He hands it to the blower after first shaping on a marveling plate. The blower then shapes the "ball" with apple-wood tools and paddles, and with carefully controlled puffs, forms a hollow bulb. His tools are varied and adapted for each item, and include the Pucellas, often called just the "tool." Like a huge pair of tweezers, the "tool" becomes a set of additional fingers for the skilled craftsman.

Now the piece is ready to be removed from the blowpipe and turned over to the stick-up boy, who picks it up and takes it to the "glory-hole," a reheating furnace kept at about 2500°F. Here the glass is reheated and taken to the finisher for shaping. He, with the skilled touch of practiced hands, forms the decanter, bowl, pitcher, etc. When the item is to have a handle, or requires additional work, it is handed to a second finisher.

As this finisher completes the piece, a carry-in boy appears with a special fork, snaps the piece from the punty and carries it to an annealing oven or "lehr." Here it travels on a slowly moving, endless chain through several hours of diminishing heat, emerging at the end ready to be inspected. It is then labeled with a Tiara Exclusive's sticker, boxed and put in stock.

Since many Tiara items are blown and shaped by hand, variations in size, shape and color lend real individuality to each item.

Historical Collector Items

(A) **10047 Mountaineer Decanter** — Another addition to your decanter collection — introduction of our most honored guest in his blue attire. Your favorite beverage or mouthwash will put a gleam in his eye. (10" high)

(B) **10051 Hob-Nail Pitcher** — Truly Early American in appearance. This 56-oz. pitcher enhances any selected cool beverage. (8¼" high)

(C) **10060 Aloha Bowl** — Capture the excitement of a South Seas aloha luau serving your fresh fruit or salad in this 9½" diameter bowl.

6

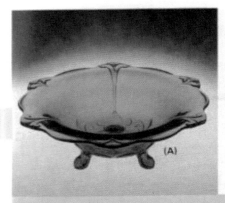

(A) 10069 Duchess 3-Toed Bowl — 12" dia. — A complementary touch when displayed with our Duchess Basket. This bowl is reminiscent of generations past.

(A)

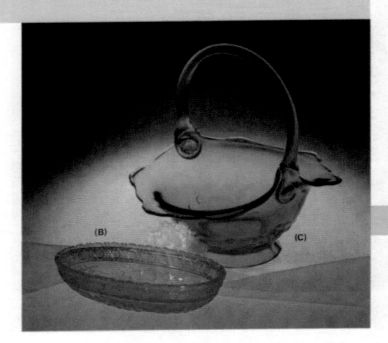

(B)

(C)

(B) 10103 Blue Bird Oval Bowl — The beautiful engraving of the "Blue Bird of Happiness" bowl is an exceptional example of craftsmanship of the early 1900's. Perfect for candies, nuts or fresh flowers. (8½" dia.)

(C) 10059 Duchess Handled Basket — The elegance of yesteryear puts this handcrafted basket in a class by itself. Its blue color complements the fruits and flowers of your artistic arrangements.

7

The Little One's Group

(A)   (B)   (C)

D—Set

(A) **10042 Child's Cereal Bowl** — This 6" diameter bowl is a storybook in itself.

(B) **10017 Child's Plate** — This 8½" diameter plate with dividers make mealtime easier for your special little one.

(C) **10041 Child's Mug — pair** — These delightful 8-oz. mugs will become your little one's pride and joy. The 3½" mugs are perfect for juice or milk.

(D) **10090 Child's Service Set — (Child's Mug, Bowl, and Plate)** — Start a family tradition with this beautiful 3-pc. set. A treasured gift sure to be remembered and cherished forever.

(A) **10091 Little Piggy Snack Set — 4 pc.** — Tray — 10¼" x 6½" inches; cup — 2½" high. The little ones will be delighted when lunches are served on the original Little Piggy Snack Tray.

(B) **10052 Child's Milk Tumblers — pair** — Storybook characters come alive on these 6-oz. tumblers. These 4" tumblers make the perfect "first glass" for your little one.

(C) **10092 Child's Nursery Rhyme Plate — 4 pcs.** — Reintroduced after a 60 year absence, these 6½" diameter plates will be a joyous gift for any little one.

Decorator Items

(A) **10079 Hurricane Pitcher** — Rural Americana is captured when the glass technician formed a lip and attached a handle to this hurricane chimney that was originally manufactured in the 1920's. A very functional 51-oz. pitcher for your favorite cool beverages or an ideal container for an abstract arrangement of fresh cut flowers.

(A)

(B) **10003 Colonial Water Bottle, Burnt Honey** — A unique gift giving idea. Each bottle is hand-blown in a turn-of-the-century mold. In Colonial times the bottle, filled with water, graced the table. Today the delicate lines of the 8" high bottle holds your favorite beverage in style. (Shades vary)

(C) **10064 Lord's Supper Tray** — The many hues of the burnt honey color make each one of these 7" x 11" trays truly one of a kind. An ideal gift to men of the cloth, also available to churches for fund raising. (Shades vary)

(D) **10058 Ribbon Vase — 10" Burnt Honey** — The Ribbon Vase was popular during grandmother's childhood. The classic antique design is at its best in Tiara's burnt honey. This vase is listed in antique journals as a collectible of the early 1900's. (Shades vary)

(B)

(C)

(D)

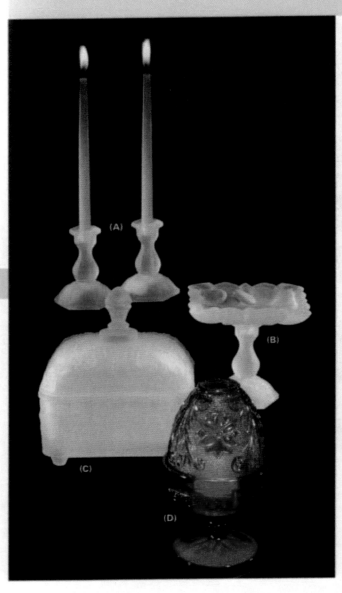

(A) **10075 Colonial Birthday Candle Holder** — pair — Tiara recaptures a beautiful Colonial custom in frosted crystal. The tiny flickering flame from these holders lit the friendly faces of Colonial party goers as they graced each place setting. These 3" candle holders will brighten your parties and holidays with an elegant touch of the past.

(B) **10065 Colonial Footed Tray** — Frosted Crystal — Stunning — When combined with the Colonial Birthday Candle holder to form a miniature console set. The footed tray also adds an elegant touch to your bath when used as a footed soap dish. (3½" high)

(C) **10011 Honey Dish and Cover** — This square covered dish holds a full comb of sweet honey. The honeycomb and bee pattern adds a perfect touch of nostalgia to any room.

(D) **10240 Glo Lamp** — Decorated Ruby — The Sandwich pattern is highlighted by candlelight. A great accent piece for any occasion. (5¾" high)

11

Sandwich
Collection
by

Tiara recaptures the glamour and romance of Early America. On a gold table-cloth the rich color speaks elegance. No color is so flattering to the wood tones of the dining room, and no color can compare to the beauty of Golden Amber in a sunny window.

Sandwich Glass was originally named after Sandwich, Massachusetts, on Cape Cod. This beautiful glass is one of the most famous of early America glass styles. It was first made in 1825 by Deming Jarves. Jarves perfected the process of pressing glass. Handcut molds of iron were used to produce the beautiful patterns in Sandwich. The star scroll design was described by early writers as "sparkling like dew-moistened leaves." Despite the lacy quality of Sandwich Glass it is extremely durable. Each piece of the Tiara Sandwich Collection can be machine washed.

Every conceivable item for the table is available to Tiara customers, or will be in the near future. Tiara's collection is perfect for year-round gift giving. The giver chooses shower, wedding, birthday, anniversary, or special occasion presents from a complete line of beautiful glass gifts. The Sandwich Glass Collection . . . exclusively yours from Tiara.

(A) **10246 Footed Sherbet Set — 4 pcs.** — Ice cream and puddings take on an elegance you'll appreciate, when served in these footed sherbets. (3½" high)

(B) **10261 Place Setting — 4 pcs.** — Setting includes the 10" dinner plate, 8" salad plate, 9-oz. cup and 6" saucer.

(C) **10262 Starter Set — 16 pcs.** — A perfect way to introduce yourself or someone else to Sandwich Glass.

(D) **10248 Dinner Plate — 4 pcs.** — These four beautiful dinner plates let you add a custom touch to your dinner service.

(E) **10216 Candlestick — pair** — Dining delight — these 3¾" high holders are ideal for a special candlelight dinner.

(F) **10204 Wine Goblet — 4 pcs.** — This beautiful set of 3½-oz. goblets adds a special touch to your Sandwich wine service.

(G) **10208 Water Goblet Set — 8-oz., 4 pcs.** — Your table will radiate formal elegance with these goblets.

(H) **10256 Dinner Bell** — Revive an Early American custom with an inviting ring of the dinner bell.

(A) 10279 Sandwich Classic Lamp — A home owners dream, the 18″ high classic lamp with the use of our exclusive wine decanter is an attractive addition to any room in your home.

(B) 10253 Sandwich Mini Vase — A breakfast tray would not be complete without a mini vase, 3¾″ high, decorated with a small bouquet of fresh-cut flowers.

(C) 10202 Deep Nappy — 2 pcs. — Soups, salads, vegetables and a host of other foods are just right for the Nappy. (6″ dia.)

14

(A) **10243 Center Bowl** — The hand formed crimping of this beautiful bowl adds a new dimension to your dinner service. (4½" high, 10½" dia.)

(B) **10245 Footed Candle Holders — pair** — Accent the bliss and royalty of dining pleasure with candlelight. A thoughtful gift for friends or family. (3¼" high)

(C) **10207 Crimped Vase** — Add that extra touch of elegance to your Sandwich service with this mini-crimped vase. This 3½" high vase is perfect for flowers or candies. (6½" dia.)

(D) **10237 Golden Glo Lamp** — Warm patterns of flickering light will dance through your home. This beautiful Golden Glo is 5¾" high.

(E) **10203 Wine Set — 11 pcs.** — Eight wine goblets surround this graceful 10" high handblown decanter. The set rests on a 10" diameter serving tray. A truly exquisite set worthy of the many compliments it will receive.

(A) **10281 Sandwich Canister** — 7¼″ high — A very versatile addition to the Sandwich Collection because of its multiple uses. This canister will sparkle on the counter top of every kitchen.

(B) **10205 Mini-Basket** — Delicate curves of Sandwich Glass make this 7¾″ high basket a beautiful conversation piece.

(C) **10228 Berry Set** — **5 pcs.** — This set is perfect for berries, potatoes, vegetables or ice cream. The 8″ bowl makes a great server, while the four 4″ Nappies are perfect for individual portions.

(D) **10238 Celery Tray** — The unique shape of this 10 3/8″ by 4 3/8″ tray makes it perfect for your relishes.

(E) **10211 Salad Bowl — Crimped** — Six perfect crimps give this universal serving bowl an added elegance. This 10″ diameter bowl is perfect for salads, fruits, vegetables and desserts. (4¾″ high, 10″ dia.)

(A) **10209 Wall Clock** — Time will be the secondary thought as guests admire your 12" diameter Sandwich Wall Clock. The warmth of golden amber highlights this beautiful cordless clock.

(B) **10223 Wall Sconce** — Dramatically set the mood of your home with this unique wall sconce. Placed on either side of your Sandwich Wall Clock, they will create a spectacular appearance. Each sconce is 8" high.

(C) **10221 Handled Basket** — A Sandwich bowl is hand-shaped into a basket with a beautifully curved handle attached. Brightens any table or mantle. (10" high)

(D) **10258 Tall Candle Holders** — pair — Elegance is the mood created by these 8½" tall holders. Lovely but difficult to produce, Tiara craftsmen are proud to offer this stunning pair.

(E) **10229 Puff Box and Cover** — This delightful gift is a relic of Early America. The 1 7/8" high by 3 5/8" diameter box will make a "special place" for your treasures.

17

(A) **10220 Butter Dish and Cover** — Rounded balls of butter were formed on Early American farms and this unusual dish was designed to protect the fresh-churned butter. The 6" tall dish is used by many for Eggs Benedict or other elegant covered dishes.

(B) **10244 Two-Tier Tidbit** — Elevate your special cookies, candies, or hors d'oeuvres with this elegant serving piece; adds prestige to any table setting or tea service. (9½" high)

(C) **10226 Snack Set — 8 pcs.** — This super Sandwich Snack Set is the hit of any coffee or tea party. The 8½" by 6¾" oval plate makes this beautiful set truly unique.

(D) **10231 Bridge Set — 4 pcs.** — These trays are great for card parties. The 4½" by ¾" trays are quick conversation starters.

(A) 10224 3-Part Relish Tray — Beauty and convenience are combined in this 3-Part Relish. (12" dia.)

(B) 10214 Punch Set — 14 pcs. — Please your guests with this impressive 9-quart punch bowl. Perfect for your party punches. (Bowl 6¾" high, 13" dia.)

(C) 10247 5-Part Relish Tray — Convenience is the word for this 10" tray. Its many divisions make it perfect for individual relish services as well as your holiday assortments of nuts and fruits.

(D) 10201 Platter — 12" — This platter makes a beautiful attraction for your intimate dinners.

(E) 10218 Egg Tray — Brighten any meal or party with this 12" diameter tray. Fantastic for serving eggs or hors d'oeuvres.

19

Sandwich Footed Compote — The perfect accent piece for any room in the home, including your dining table. Fresh fruits and candies will alure the beholder when viewed. The perfect gift for the person of your choice.

(A) 10239 Salad Bowl — The ability to serve as a universal serving bowl makes this item perfect for salads, fruits, vegetables and desserts. (4¾" high, 10" dia.)

(B) 10230 Tumblers — 8-oz., 4 pcs. — This 8-oz. tumbler is an ideal addition to our Sandwich collection. Suited for juice, milk or other cold beverages.

(C) 10213 Pitcher — 68-oz. — This pitcher adds its full measure to the formal tablesetting. (8" high)

(D) 10200 Tumblers — 10-oz., 4 pcs. — This stunning tumbler is perfect for ice tea, sodas or other cold beverages. (6½" high)

(E) 10260 Sandwich 5" Salad Bowl — 4 pcs. — Designed as a complementary piece to be used with our large salad bowl, this 5" salad bowl is ideally suited for individual salads, fruits or desserts of your choice.

(A) 10254 Sandwich Sugar/Creamer Set — Created to add a distinguished touch of elegance to your formal dining table, this 5" cream and sugar set is an ideal bridal gift.

(B) 10227 Salt and Pepper Set — Season your food with a touch of elegance. These twin beauties are 4¾" tall.

(C) 10280 Sandwich 4-Part Relish — A serving piece, 10" diameter, suited for your special cut wedges of assorted cheese and hors d'oeuvres.

(D) 10219 Coaster Set — 4 pcs. — The Sandwich Coasters are designed for the protection of your furniture. These 4½" diameter coasters are the perfect addition to your Sandwich beverage service.

(E) 10217 Napkin Holder — The individuality of the craftsmen makes each of these 4" holders truly unique.

What is a flaw in glass?

Is a small bubble in a fine piece of stemware a flaw? How about a cord, or a mold mark? The answer is definitely no, but it's sometimes difficult to convince a customer of this.

Most dinnerware and glassware departments and specialty shops have had trouble at one time or another with customers who seek flawless perfection in the tableware merchandise they buy.

Such perfection can be achieved only in assembly-line products, of course. It is not possible or even desirable in quality ware whose manufacture depends so much on the skill and artistry of individual craftsmen.

Slight variations and tiny imperfections in glassware pieces are actually a confirmation of craftsmanship and individual artistry. Most customers who appreciate good glassware understand this. For those who don't here is a series of questions and answers that a salesperson can use to promote better understanding of the product.

Does a "seed" or bubble in glassware constitute a flaw?

No. One of these tiny "seeds" or bubbles the size of a pinpoint may sometimes be observed in a piece of glassware when it is examined closely against a strong light.

The bubble is formed by gases when chemicals are united in the fusing or melting of the raw ingredients. It does not affect the quality or the beauty of the glass.

Should all pieces in a set be exactly alike?

No. There are almost always slight variations in diameter, height, and other dimensions in any group of tumblers, goblets, plates or other articles of glass. These variations are usually so slight that they can be detected only with a micrometer, rarely by the naked eye. This is the hallmark of fine hand craftsmanship.

What is a cord?

A cord is an almost invisible difference in density in the glass which occurs during the fusing of the molten glass. It is visible only by reason of the fact that it reflects light. When a goblet with a cord in it is filled with water, no light is reflected and the cord becomes invisible.

Is a mold mark a sign of imperfection?

No. A mold mark is merely a ridge on a molded glassware piece that indicates the point at which the mold that formed the item was separated for removal of the finished ware. If it is overly prominent, however, it may be an indication of careless workmanship.

What is a shear mark?

A shear mark is a slight puckering of the glass caused when the artisan snips off excess molten glass when shaping the piece, as for example the end of the handle of a pitcher. It is a normal characteristic of glass and should not be considered a flaw.

Is hand-made glassware really made by hand, or merely hand-finished?

The production of hand-made glassware is indeed a hand process. The skilled hands and eyes of many men, working in teams, go into the making of every piece. The amazing thing is that such a high degree of excellence can be attained; that piece after piece coming from any individual or group of glass blowers or pressers is so nearly and accurately a duplicate of every other piece.

Why can't small irregularities be entirely eliminated from hand-made glass?

For the very reason that the glass is hand-made. No matter how deft the touch of the sensitive hands of glass craftsmen, it is impossible to eliminate completely small variations. These should not, therefore, be considered flaws. Glass is one of the trickiest materials to work with. Even machine-made glassware cannot be made absolutely perfect. But consider this: Even the finest diamond, examined under a jeweler's loupe, rarely reveals absolute perfection.

How can the salesperson and the customer judge the quality of glassware?

There are certain simple tests and guides. Look for clarity and luster by holding the piece against a pure white background. Good glassware is quite clear, while inferior grades show a cloudy bluish or greenish tinge.

Quality glassware is also marked by a permanent polish or luster that results from fire-polishing.

Look for smooth edges. Glassware edges should be even, never rough and scratch. In hand-cut ware, the design should be sharp and accurate. In etched ware, each tiny detail should be distinct and clearly defined.

Fine handblown glass frequently contains lead, which improves its clarity and adds to its weight. If a piece of stemware rings with a clear musical tone when struck lightly, this indicates lead content. Lime glass, on the other hand, does not have this resonance, but this does not make it any less desirable. The lime in such glass adds to its toughness and strength.

Reprinted from
China Glass & Tablewares

Zodiac

Sprinkle some starlight into your gift giving with these goblets from the zodiac. Bright vibrant colors capture the personality of your sign. An ideal gift for the star of special occasions.

10524 Aquarius — Blue, 10525 Pisces — Lime, 10526 Aries — Red, 10527 Taurus — Cream, 10528 Gemini — Yellow, 10529 Cancer — Cherry, 10530 Leo — Orange, 10531 Virgo — Gold, 10532 Libra — Pink, 10533 Scorpio — White, 10534 Sagittarius — Turquoise and 10535 Capricorn — Green.

Party Pleasers

(A) **10019 Buffet Relish** — Your relishes will come alive on this sparkling 10" tray. The deep black accents your green and colorful vegetables.

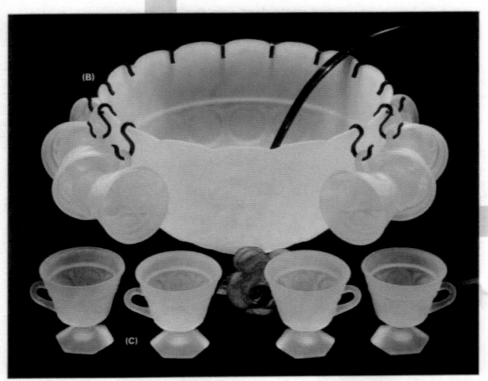

(B) **10107 Provincial Punch Set** — This 8-quart bowl keeps any party going in style. Twelve cups, duracite hooks and a duracite ladle complete the set. (7½" tall, 13" dia.)

(C) **10108 Provincial 5-oz. Punch Cups — 1 doz.** — Large gatherings make these cups essential. (3 3/8" high)

Office And Home Accents

(A) **10025 Crystal Etched Smoker Set** — The beauty of satin is featured in this 6-piece set (lighter, cigarette urn and four ashtrays). The set accents any room or office.

(B) **10001 Smoker Set** — **6 pcs.** — **(Lighter, Cigarette Urn, 4 Ashtrays).** — This elegant set graces any room or office. A practical gift for that special someone.

(C) **10818 German Drinking Stein** — **pair** — The deep cut pattern of these striking 11-oz. steins captures the spirit of the Old World taverns. (6" tall) (Not recommended for hot drink)

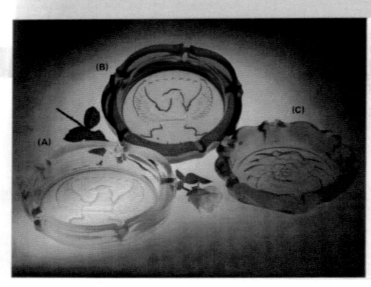

(A) **10023 Crystal Eagle Ashtray** — The exceptional artwork of this massive tray makes it a favorite of collectors of Early Americana. The crystal tray blends with any decor. It is 10½" in diameter.

(B) **10022 Gold Eagle Ashtray** — Wood-tones are complemented by the rich golden hues of the Eagle Ashtray. Perfect for the executive desk. The beautiful eagle tray is 10½" in diameter.

(C) **10026 Lotus Ashtray** — The beautiful floral design of this tray is appreciated by smokers and non-smokers alike. The lovely horizon blue tray is 9½" in diameter.

(A) **10135 Sweet Pear Sugar/Creamer — 3½" high** — A classic look complementing your table service will be enhanced with the unusual Sweet Pear design Sugar and Creamer.

(B) **10131 Sweet Pear Sherbet — pair** — The beautiful Sweet Pear design is captured on these 3½" tall sherbets. Perfect for collecting and an elegant way to serve nuts, candies, puddings or frozen desserts.

(C) **10130 Sweet Pear Plate — pair** — A collector's dream come true. These matched plates are produced from the original molds and make great additions to our previously released Sweet Pear Items. (6" dia.)

The burnt honey color will cause the shades to vary in the production of each piece of glass.

The Sweet Pear Collection

26

(A) **10133 Sweet Pear 8" Plate** — The perfect hostess selection for snacks or luncheon dishes and the envy of all collectors.

(B) **10132 Sweet Pear 6" 3-Toed Nappy** — Recreated after many years of absence from the market, this nappy, when used as a candy dish, will cause conversation because of its unusual design.

(C) **10134 Sweet Pear Pickle — 8"** — A complementary touch when used for pickle service, relish service or your favorite fruit. This item is produced from the original equipment and also listed in numerous antique journals.

27

(A) **10317 Cameo Candy Box and Cover** — 12" high, 2½" deep, 6" dia. — An ideal container for your candies, fruits or flowers.

(B) **10300 Cameo Chalice and Cover** — 15¾" high, 5" deep, 6" dia. — The beautiful design of this stately chalice makes it a conversation piece.

(C) **10315 Cameo Ash Tray** — 5½" dia., pair — The Cameo ashtray is both beautiful and functional.

The Cameo Flair

(A) **10306 Cameo Ice Teas** — 15-oz., 4 pcs., 5⅝" high — Ice crystals sparkle on the Cameo ice teas. Great for your warm weather entertaining.

(B) **10307 Cameo Wine Goblets** — 6-oz., 4 pcs., 4½" high — Friends and family will savor the wine and the beauty of your wine service.

(C) **10308 Cameo Goblets** — 12-oz., 4 pcs., 6½" high — These elegant goblets are the perfect addition to your Cameo collection.

(D) **10310 Cameo Beverage Set** — 5 pcs. (Cameo pitcher and 4 Cameo goblets) — Your guests will enjoy their mixed drinks or other cold beverages when served in style.

(A) **10311 Cameo Butter and Cover** — The beautiful 5" tall cover protects your butter while giving the table a touch of elegance. The tray is 6" x 9".

(B) **10312 Cameo Salt and Pepper Set** — These 4" high beauties are sure to be appreciated by guests and family alike.

(C) **10303 Cameo Crimped Candle Holder** — pair — These unusual candle holders set off any table. The 3" tall holders are 3½" in diameter.

(D) **10313 Cameo Hostess Set** — 8 pcs. (six 9-oz. tumblers, ice tub and cover, 11 7/8" high, 5 3/4" dia.). Convenience is the word for this impressive set.

30

Flowers, candies, fruit and beverage are used as props in the photographs of this catalog. These are not available through Tiara Exclusives.

Preferred Hostess Plan

A preferred Hostess is one selected by a Counselor, who agrees to hold three or more Giftaramas, in her home, in a calendar year. There is NO requirement for a certain amount of sales.

Being a member of our Preferred Hostess Club affords you many extras! First, you can rebook, and not hold it within two weeks, and still receive your $3 dating credit. Secondly, your name will be entered on our computer, enabling us to keep you informed of our new products, prices and specials on a timely basis. Thirdly, when the total sales of your three or more Giftaramas reach $500 in a calendar year, you will be entitled to a FREE gift! The 1981 Limited Edition item pictured — the Sandwich Butter and Cover, #10113 — can be yours!

Sign up NOW as a Preferred Hostess and earn one or more of these antique reproductions! Your Counselor will award you one for every $500 in sales you account for in the calendar year!

Appreciatively,

Roger W. Jewett
National Sales Leader

Tiara Exclusives

HOSTESS PLAN

Tiara Hostesses are treated to a premium incentive program that is almost unbelievable! It certainly pays well to be a Hostess at a Tiara Giftarama!

Simply invite a Tiara Associate to conduct a Giftarama at your home some morning, afternoon, or evening and you will have unfolded before your eyes a myriad of exclusive gifts that can be yours FREE!

For holding the Giftarama within two weeks, you will receive $3 and you can add $3 more for every $20 in orders accepted! That means that an average Giftarama of $200 would allow the Hostess $33 in gifts of her own choosing. But that isn't all — if three Giftaramas are arranged at a Giftarama, the Hostess would receive another $12 in gifts! Thus, a $200 Giftarama with three bookings, pays the Hostess $45 in Tiara gifts!

In addition, the gifts of the month are given to all Hostesses whose Giftaramas reach specified levels of sales, making it possible for the average Hostess to earn 40% or more of the total value of sales in free gifts!

GUARANTEE

All Tiara Gifts are guaranteed to be of fine quality and craftsmanship within the limits of the arts represented. All products are guaranteed for life, and should breakage occur, either accidental or otherwise, or any other damage, replacement will be made at fifty percent (50%) of the current price, provided the receipted shopping guide is sent to Tiara Exclusives as proof of purchase. The receipted shopping card will be returned to you along with your replacement merchandise.

A fee of two dollars and fifty cents ($2.50) to cover packing, shipping and indemnity must be included with each order for replacement.

There shall be no limitation upon this guarantee, and replacement policy, except in the case of discontinued items, in which event, the company will no longer by responsible, or liable, for replacement.

Credits: Photography — Photo Craft, Muncie, Ind. — Color Separations — Color Separations, Dayton, Ohio. Design — R. Kratz. Production & Typesetting — Colony Printing and Labeling, Inc. Eaton, Ind.

Tiara 1983 Catalog Contents

Tiara EXCLUSIVES

1983

Tiara Exclusives ®

As we ring in a new year, Tiara is taking the initiative to REDUCE many of our prices! During this past year we have made an all out effort to cut costs in every conceivable manner and to perfect our production efforts to eliminate waste and time. We have also researched several modern methods to bring our internal operation to a point where it is extremely efficient and therefore cost effective.

As a result of all these implementations we are extremely proud to be able to pass on these savings to a public that has been so loyal, and so supportive of our efforts! Tiara continues to lead the field and we dedicate ourselves to maintain the pace throughout 1983!

My sincere thanks to all our loyal preferred hostesses who have been so helpful and supportive. We appreciate all that you have done and look forward to serving you again in the coming year!

James E. Hooffstetter
James E. Hooffstetter
President

1982 was a year of transition for Tiara and it was a GOOD year! With this new catalog we greet 1983 with tremendous excitement and high expectations! It is unheard of in these times for a national company to LOWER prices! Only by dedication and hard work have we been able to improve our manufacturing methods, our office procedures, and our shipping facilities to the point where lowering prices can be a reality.

Tiara will leap to a new plateau of business in the coming year, because we have an outstanding sales force, a fantastic group of over 21,000 preferred hostesses, and the faith and confidence of the American buying public! Our marketing plan is second to none and allows any person with enthusiasm and purpose to make good and make money quickly and continuously. The ladders of free enterprise are STILL UP in Tiara! We invite you to join our team! Please write me now! BELIEVE AND ACHIEVE!

Roger W. Jewett
Roger W. Jewett
National Sales Leader
1717 W. 86th St., Suite #180
Indianapolis, IN 46260

"We recognize the individuality of man and respect his right to achieve his own dreams, in his own time!"

Index

Tiara Exclusives.

EXECUTIVE OFFICES
DUNKIRK, INDIANA 47336-9737
PHONE: 317-768-7821
OUT OF STATE: 800-428-6586

J. E. Hooffstetter
President

Roger W. Jewett
National Sales Leader

Ralph Waddell
General Manager

Ronald A. Kratz
Director of Sales Promotion

ZONE LEADERS

Northwestern Zone
Hal Scott
6978 Pampas Way
Fair Oaks, CA 95628
(916-966-6508)

Midwestern Zone
Jerry Maynard
411 S. Lafayette
Royal Oak, MI 48067
(313-543-2121)

Southeastern Zone
Robert Hnath
6350 McDonough Dr.
Suite G & H
Norcross, GA 30093
(404-449-3809)

Western Zone
Jeannine Reaves (Section)
15600 Tetley St.
Hacienda Heights, CA 91745
(213-336-4844)

North Central Zone
Judy Rustia (Section)
4336 N. Judd Ave.
Schiller Park, IL 60176
(312-678-8351)

Atlantic Coast Zone
Gloria Hall
8607 Mt. Vernon Hwy.
Alexandria, VA 22309
(703-360-0724)

Rocky Mountain Zone
Jerry Tripp
7000 Broadway
Suite #202, Bldg. #2
Denver, CO 80221
(303-427-3913)

Southwestern Zone
Robert Hatfield
224 N. Story Rd.
Suite #134
Irving, TX 75061
(214-254-9113)

New York Zone
Rory O'Connor (Acting)
148 Regent St.
Saratoga Springs, NY 12866
(518-584-2442)

Chantilly
Green Sandwich

(A) **10343 Large Basket** — Skilled glass artisans have gently shaped this basket and delicately added the curved handle for a truly graceful look. This basket is functional as a container in the kitchen or dining area for fresh fruits and snacks or elegant as an accent piece. (10" high)

(B) **10345 Tall Candleholders** — The warm glow of candlelight will shimmer romantically when these graceful candleholders are used to enhance your meal. Makes an appropriate gift for any special occasion. (8½" high)

(C) **10308 Goblets — 4 pcs.** — Dinner guests will admire your exceptional taste when your table is graced with these lovely goblets. (8 oz.)

(D) **10351 Starter Set — 16 pcs.** — Tiara's chantilly green dinnerware helps to bring the fresh, clean look of spring to any meal service! Guaranteed to brighten your cabinets and kitchen without remodeling! (4 each: 10" dinner plates, 8" salad plates, 6" saucers and 9 oz. cups)

(E) **10353 Wine Goblets — 6 pcs.** — Just the 'right' size in the right setting for the 'right' toast at the right time! Allows you to serve additional guests with your wine set too! (4 1/4" high)

(A)
(B)
(C)
(E)
(D-Starter Set)

2

(A) 10344 Wine Set — 9 pcs. — House guests will appreciate your discriminating taste as they admire this unique and exclusive wine set. In addition to six delicate goblets the set includes a 10" high, hand-blown decanter and a 10" diameter serving tray.

(B) 10306 Salad Bowls — The most popular size for your special salad, these four bowls can be used for cereal, soup and popcorn. (5" dia.)

(C) 10305 Tumblers — A style and size so popular, we now offer a set of four in our beautiful new chantilly green. (6½" high)

(D) 10352 Pitcher — Tiara's craftsmen have created this beauty to provide you with the opportunity to match your table setting completely! (8" high)

(E) 10557 Snack Set — Treat your guests to something special by utilizing our eight piece snack set at your next get-together. (8½" x 6¾" dia.)

3

(A) 10341 Egg Tray — Dress up your deviled eggs by serving them on this versatile tray, which dinner guests are sure to admire. (12" dia.)

(B) 10342 Relish Tray — An ideal service for large relishes, the delicate hue of chantilly green makes this tray the perfect addition to your holiday buffet table. (12" dia.)

(C) 10340 Sandwich Platter — Create an appetizing array of your favorite hors d'oeuvres and serve them on our 12" platter to add a distinctive touch to your buffet.

(D) 10347 Canister — (5 5/8" high)   **(E) 10348 Canister** — (7¼" high)   **(F) 10349 Canister** — (8 7/8" high)

Refresh and brighten your kitchen countertop with our chantilly green canister set. Whether used individually or as a set, these canisters are perfect for storing flour, sugar, coffee or any food staples. Use one as a tobacco humidor and brighten a den, or enhance your bathroom by storing cotton balls and other bath essentials in one of these decorative containers.

Designer's Choice

(A) 10516 Demijohn — This masterfully crafted vessel makes a truly unusual gift for that very special occasion. Will make flowers look even better in any season! (20" high)

(B) 10354 Peacock Vase — A hand blown collector's creation which marks this a "Gift of Distinction"! (15" high)

(C) 10028 Terrarium — Brought to life by the breath of craftsmen to create a treasure you'll love! Beautiful with flowers or a candle to accent any home or office. (15" high)

(D) 10379 Rustic Vase — This elegantly styled vase will delight even the most sophisticated decorator. A unique accent piece for any home. (16" high)

5

(A) 10185 Constellation Ftd. Candleholders — Reflects the demands for the return of understated elegance! (5" tall)

(B) 10180 Constellation Console Bowl — Enduring quality is reflected in this centerpiece. Made entirely by hand! (3¾" high, 11½" dia.)

(C) 10186 Constellation Cookie Jar and Cover —Springtime comes indoors as its many facets capture the morning light! (9" high)

(A)

(B)

(C)

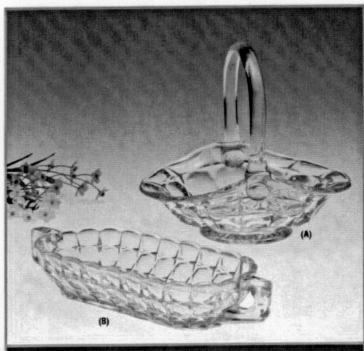

(A) 10183 Constellation Mini Basket —
The design of this delicate basket lends
itself as an unusual serving piece for almost anything as well as a "kitchen
pick-me-up" with fresh flowers. (6¾"
high)

(B) 10184 Constellation Pickle Dish —
Not to be overlooked for its other imaginative (ahh, banana split) uses! (10¼"
long)

(C) 10181 Constellation Cake Plate —
What better way to serve special cakes
and pastries than on this beautiful handmade platter! (13½" dia.)

(D) 10182 Constellation Nut Bowl —
Limited only by your imagination! Float a
candle or your favorite flower. Makes a
marvelous catchall for snacks such as
pretzels or peanuts! (6" high)

(E) 10188 Bon Bon and Cover — Beauty
and function are combined in Tiara's
handmade Bon Bon and Cover. A delightful accent and a perfect hostess
gift! (6" high)

The Creation of Glass

Over 4,000 years ago, perhaps on the sands of Egypt, Syria or Babylonia, the creation of glass began. Since then mankind has added, little by little, to the glassmaker's art. The skill of the glassmaker has been a source of beauty, treasured by all.

It is natural that you, a Tiara Customer, should want to know something about the way the line is created. Making glassware by hand is the oldest industry in America, started in the Jamestown Colony in 1608. Many of the techniques and tools of the early days are used in the manufacture of Tiara Exclusives. Each item is exclusive with Tiara, and will not be found in any other line.

Glass is truly the product of earth and fire! Made of silica, soda ash, lime and feldspar, small amounts of various other chemicals such as copper, selenium, manganese and cadmium are added to make a "batch." After careful mixing of the selected ingredients, a quantity of broken glass — called cullet — is often added to the "batch" to speed up the melting process. The tank into which the glassworker shovels the "batch" has been pre-fired to an intense heat of about 2700°F. In about 18 hours the glass is ready to be gathered and blown.

A blowpipe is a hollow tube of steel with a special "head" which the gatherer slips into the tank of molten glass. Turning it in the glass, he gathers just the right "gob" on the end of the pipe. He hands it to the blower after first shaping on a marveling plate. The blower then shapes the "ball" with apple-wood tools and paddles, and with carefully controlled puffs, forms a hollow bulb. His tools are varied and adapted for each item, and include the Pucellas, often called just the "tool." Like a huge pair of tweezers, the "tool" becomes a set of additional fingers for the skilled craftsman.

Now the piece is ready to be removed from the blowpipe and turned over to the stick-up boy, who picks it up and takes it to the "glory-hole," a reheating furnace kept at about 2500°F. Here the glass is reheated and taken to the finisher for shaping. He, with the skilled touch of practiced hands, forms the decanter, bowl, pitcher, etc. When the item is to have a handle, or requires additional work, it is handed to a second finisher.

As this finisher completes the piece, a carry-in boy appears with a special fork, snaps the piece from the punty and carries it to an annealing oven or "lehr." Here it travels on a slowly moving, endless chain through several hours of diminishing heat, emerging at the end ready to be inspected. It is then labeled with a Tiara Exclusive's sticker, boxed and put in stock.

It takes a shop of six to 18 skilled workers to make just one item in Tiara's line. Since many are blown and shaped by hand, variations in size, shape and color lend real "individuality" to the items you select for yourself or as gifts for friends and family.

Sandwich Collection

The original Sandwich Glass was named after Sandwich, Massachusetts, on Cape Cod. It is one of the most famous of all Early American glass styles. Glass Collectors treasure it. Museums display any pieces they can get. It was first made in 1825 by Deming Jarves, who developed the ability to press glass by hand. The beautiful patterns were cut in iron molds by hand!

The star and scroll design was described by the early writers as "sparkling like dew-moistened leaves." In spite of its lacy quality it has tremendous sturdiness and durability and can be machine washed.

Every conceivable item for the table is available to Tiara customers now, or will be in the near future. To the best of our knowledge, Sandwich Glass dinnerware has never before been made in the Golden Amber color. On a gold tablecloth the rich color speaks quality, and marks the owner of it as a discriminating homemaker!

The use of the exclusive line of shower gifts, wedding gifts, birthday and anniversary gifts, and for Christmas affords the giver a continuity unmatched in beautiful glass!

The Sandwich Glass Collection . . . exclusively yours from Tiara.

Sandwich Collection

(A) 10208 Goblets — 4 pcs. — A must for every formal dinner service. (8 oz.)

(B) 10245 Ftd. Candleholders — Dining delights — these holders help accent that special occasion with just the right mood. They are attractive with fresh flowers "planted" in the base! (3¼" high)

(C) 10256 Bell — You'll love the old-time charm brought to your table with the ringing of our dinner bell!

(D) 10283 Table Wines — 4 pcs. — Insure your vintage choice coming to the table elegantly. (8½ oz.)

(E) 10262 Starter Set — 16 pcs. — Whether the menu offers filet mignon or the simplest fare, the service will be absolutely perfect with our Sandwich Starter Set! (4 each: 10" dinner plates, 8" salad plates, 6" saucers and 9 oz. cups)

9

(A) 10237 Glo Lamp — Warm patterns of flickering light will dance throughout the evening when you place a few of these lamps around the room. (5¾" high)

(B) 10253 Mini Vase — Ideal for that one special flower or a handful of violets. (3¾" high)

(C) 10202 Nappy — 2 pcs. — Complement any home with these highly decorative and beautifully functional bowls. They are a gift giving item! (6" dia.)

(D) 10222 Ash Tray — A smartly appealing ash tray to grace your dinner table or side table. (7 3/8" dia.)

(A) 1026D Salad Bowls — A complementary piece to our large salad bowl, these four bowls can be used for cereal, soup or popcorn. (5" dia.)

(B) 1021F Salad Bowl Crimped — Six crimps give this universal bowl a subtle richness making it perfect for any serving need. (4¾" high x 10" dia.)

(C) 1020I Platter — Cold cuts, cheese and crackers will gain importance when served on this platter. (12" dia.)

(D) 10224 3 Part Relish — Ample space in each section makes this unusual tray just the right serving piece for a variety of relishes. (12" dia.)

(E) 1021B Egg Tray — Serve hors d'oeuvres and deviled eggs to your guests in style on this handy tray. (12" dia.)

(A) 10223 Wall Sconce — Dramatically set the mood in your home with this exclusive sconce. Placed on either side of your favorite picture, they will create a spectacular appearance. (8" high)

(B) 10243 Console Crimped Bowl — The hand-formed crimping of this bowl adds a dramatic glamour even Cleopatra would envy! (4½" high, 10½" dia.)

(C) 10278 Ftd. Compote — A striking accent for any room! Don't keep this one to yourself — give one to a friend too! (8" high)

(D) 10205 Mini Basket — Create a lovely tabletop, or enhance a dark shelf with this little gem which is worthy of a most important spot in one's home and will be ready to serve while entertaining. This basket will hold your soaps in the bath, or where a splash of color would help, just add a dried arrangement! (7¾" high)

(A)

(B)

(C)

(D)

12

(A) 10258 Tall Candle Holders — These holders will add grace and formality in a traditional manner to your table! (8½" high)

(B) 10210 Jewel Box — One of life's simple treasures . . . this stunning jewel box will serve you beautifully on a coffee table, dresser or vanity! (1¾" high x 2 5/8" x 3 5/8")

(C) 10221 Basket — Made entirely by hand and always the delight of those with an eye for design. Its many uses include fruits, flowers, breads, biscuits or vegetables. (10" high)

(D) 10209 Clock — Time will be the secondary thought as guests admire your Sandwich Wall Clock. The warmth of golden amber high-lights this extraordinary cordless timepiece. (12" dia.)

(E) 10229 Puff Box and Cover — This useful reproduction makes the perfect gift for any age or occasion — equally at home in any room! (1-7/8" high x 3 5/8" dia.)

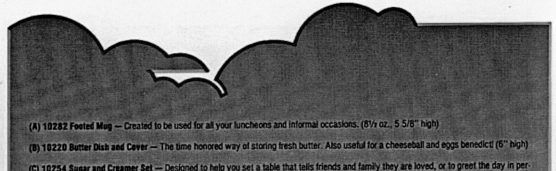

(A) 10282 Footed Mug — Created to be used for all your luncheons and informal occasions. (8½ oz., 5 5/8" high)

(B) 10220 Butter Dish and Cover — The time honored way of storing fresh butter. Also useful for a cheeseball and eggs benedict! (6" high)

(C) 10254 Sugar and Creamer Set — Designed to help you set a table that tells friends and family they are loved, or to greet the day in perfect unison as you serve coffee in our footed mug. (5" high)

(D) 10227 Salt and Pepper — There is no doubt these twin beauties will "spice" up your table. (4¾" high)

(E) 10273 Gravy Boat — At last! In response to customer requests, we have designed our own Sandwich Gravy Boat to help you serve sauces over desserts, salad dressings or gravies. (3" high)

(A)
(B)
(C)
(D)

(A) 10233 Canister — (5 5/8")
(B) 10281 Canister — (7¼")
(C) 10234 Canister — (8 7/8")
These canisters combine style with versatility. As a set they afford a classic way to coordinate the storage of coffee, tea, flour, sugar, rice, beans, etc. Individually, these canisters have multiple uses. Use the large one for cookies, the middle size for a humidor and the small size for a candy box. Stackable for limited counter space.

(D) 10215 Tall Handled Basket — Each is unique and of COLLECTOR quality. The ageless appeal of this design and form makes an important statement in any decor! (10¼" high, 4¾" dia.)

(E)
(F)

(E) 10241 Wine Set — 9 pcs. — Six delicate wine goblets surround this graceful 10" high, hand blown decanter. The entire set rests on a 10" diameter serving tray. A truly exclusive set worthy of the many compliments it will receive.

(F) 10236 Large Domed Candle Holder — A romantic mood set aglow by the graceful good looks of the sandwich pattern. The ultimate in decorative lighting for you or a friend.

(A) 10213 Pitcher — This handsome 68 oz. pitcher adds a full measure of success to the most glittering get-together or the most intimate sit down dinner! (8" high)

(B) 10200 Tumblers — These four 10 oz. tumblers are a refreshing way to satisfy even the thirstiest of the bunch. Be sure to have extras on hand for company. (6½" high)

(C) 10228 Berry Set — This is perhaps our most popular five piece service set for fruit, vegetables, desserts or snacks. (8" bowl, 4" nappy)

(A) 10244 Two Tiered Tidbit — Have great fun and great results when serving simple snacks — especially nice when used in pairs. (9½" high)

(B) 10226 Snack Set — 8 pcs. — Very important guests deserve this special snack service. The sandwich pattern offers just a perfect setting in an elegant and traditional manner! (8½" x 6¾" dim.)

(C) 10217 Napkin Holder — Both charming and functional. One of these holders deserves to be at each end of your table, not to mention the bath for guest towels, the desk top for mail and by the door for business cards! (4" high)

What is a Flaw in Glass?

Is a small bubble in a fine piece of stemware a flaw? How about a cord, or a mould mark? The answer is definitely no, but it's sometimes difficult to convince a customer of this.

Most dinnerware and glassware departments and specialty shops have had trouble at one time or another with customers who seek flawless perfection in the tableware merchandise they buy.

Such perfection can be achieved only in assembly-line products, of course. It is not possible or even desirable in quality ware whose manufacture depends so much on the skill and artistry of individual craftsmen.

Slight variations and tiny imperfections in glassware pieces are actually a confirmation of craftsmanship and individual artistry. Most customers who appreciate good glassware understand this. For those who don't, here is a series of questions and answers that a salesperson can use to promote better understanding of the product.

Does a "seed" or bubble in glassware constitute a flaw?

No. One of these tiny "seeds" or bubbles the size of a pinpoint may sometimes be observed in a piece of glassware when it is examined closely against a strong light.

The bubble is formed by gases when chemicals are united in the fusing or melting of the raw ingredients. It does not affect the quality or the beauty of the glass.

Should all pieces in a set be exactly alike?

No. There are almost always slight variations in diameter, height, and other dimensions in any group of tumblers, goblets, plates or other articles of glass. These variations are usually so slight that they can be detected only with a micrometer, rarely by the naked eye. This is the hallmark of fine hand craftsmanship.

What is a cord?

A cord is an almost invisible difference in density in the glass which occurs during the fusing of the molten glass. It is visible only by reason of the fact that it reflects light. When a goblet with a cord in it is filled with water, no light is reflected and the cord becomes invisible.

Is a mould mark a sign of imperfection?

No. A mould mark is merely a ridge on a molded glassware piece that indicates the point at which the mould that formed the item was separated for removal of the finished ware. If it is overly prominent, however, it may be an indication of careless workmanship.

What is a shear mark?

A shear mark is a slight puckering of the glass caused when the artisan snips off excess molten glass when shaping the piece, as for example the end of the handle of a pitcher. It is a normal characteristic of glass and should not be considered a flaw.

Is handmade glassware really made by hand, or merely hand-finished?

The production of handmade glassware is indeed a hand process. The skilled hand and eyes of many men, working in teams, go into the making of every piece. The amazing thing is that such a high degree of excellence can be attained; that piece after piece coming from any individual or group of glass blowers or pressers is so nearly and accurately a duplicate of every other piece.

Why can't small irregularities be entirely eliminated from handmade glass?

For the very reason that the glass is handmade. No matter how deft the touch of the sensitive hands of glass craftsmen, it is impossible to eliminate completely small variations. These should not, therefore, be considered flaws. Glass is one of the trickiest materials to work with. Even machine-made glassware cannot be made absolutely perfect. But consider this: Even the finest diamond, examined under a jeweler's loupe, rarely reveals absolute perfection.

How can the salesperson and the customer judge the quality of glassware?

There are certain simple tests and guides. Look for clarity and luster by holding the piece against a pure white background. Good glassware is quite clear, while inferior grades show a cloudy bluish or greenish tinge.

Quality glass is also marked by a permanent polish or luster that results from fire-polishing.

Look for smooth edges. Glassware edges should be even, never rough and scratch. In hand-cut ware, the design should be sharp and accurate. In etched ware, each tiny detail should be distinct and clearly defined.

Fine handblown glass frequently contains lead, which improves its clarity and adds to its weight. If a piece of stemware rings with a clear musical tone when struck lightly, this indicates lead content. Lime glass, on the other hand, does not have the resonance, but this does not make it any less desirable. The lime in such glass adds to its toughness and strength.

Reprinted from China Glass & Tablewares

Ponderosa Pine

(A) 10160 Dinner Plates — 4 pcs. — Just right for breakfast and luncheon service or to complement any occasion. (10" dia.)

(B) 10166 Salad Plates — 4 pcs. — Just the right size to complete a luncheon service in this popular design! Use anytime, in formal dining or when sandwiches are served. (8" dia.)

(C) 10164 Salad Bowl — This refreshing design was specially selected for beauty and value and is sure to be a favorite among your serving pieces. (9½" dia.)

(D) 10165 Individual Salad Bowls — 4 pcs. — The perfect size for whatever you serve — salad, soups, vegetables or desserts. (5" dia.)

(E) 10163 Goblet — 4 pcs. — Use these goblets to complete your Ponderosa Pine service in style! (6½" high)

(F) 10161 Mug — 4 pcs. — A great look for that relaxing cup of coffee any time of day. (4¾" high)

(G) 10162 Juice — 4 pcs. — Any juice will taste better when served in this special glass! Also nice with a candle and ring during the holidays. (4¾" high)

Zodiac

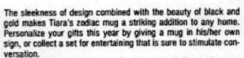

The sleekness of design combined with the beauty of black and gold makes Tiara's zodiac mug a striking addition to any home. Personalize your gifts this year by giving a mug in his/her own sign, or collect a set for entertaining that is sure to stimulate conversation.

10387 Capricorn	10393 Cancer
10388 Aquarius	10394 Leo
10389 Pisces	10395 Virgo
10390 Aries	10396 Libra
10391 Taurus	10397 Scorpio
10392 Gemini	10398 Saggitarius

The
Masculine
Touch

(A)

(B)

(C)

(D-Set)

(A) 10040 Powderhorn Tumblers — set of four — A reminder of our glorious heritage that any man would appreciate for "high spirits" in these 9 oz. tumblers. (8" high)

(B) 10015 Hunter's Horn Mug — Toast friends and associates as you recapture the mood of the hunt with this handsome pair of 12 oz. mugs. They make a sporting gift which is appealing to masculine tastes. (5½" high)

(C) 10038 Patio Tankards — set of four — The perfect companion for our Patio Beverage Set — you'll want several extra sets of these 12 oz. tankards on hand for guests! (5¾" high)

(D) 10039 Patio Beverage Set — The 50 oz. pitcher and four 12 oz. tankards are ideal for any gathering of family or friends. The permanent frosty color adds a cool, zesty appearance to your favorite beverage. (5 pcs.)

21

(A) 10025 Smoker's Set — Let your imagination run. This set may be used for coasters, individual treats at the card table or stacked with a candle ring when smokers aren't around. The urn doubles as a mini-vase to display your spring violets. (6 pcs.)

(B) 10432 Colonial Candy Box and Cover — A charming reminder of another era — this candy box and cover, in black, is a splendid container for your favorite sweets! (5¾" high)

(C) 10085 Colonial Candy Box and Cover — The crystal twin!

(D) 10022 Eagle Ash Tray — The majesty of our nation's symbol is captured in this distinctive gift item. The golden hues complement any home or executive office. It's quite functional — even for pipes and cigars! (10½" dia.)

(E) 10026 Lotus Ash Tray — The horizon-blue floral design of this tray will be appreciated by smokers and non-smokers alike. (9½" dia.)

(A)

Home & Office Accents

(D)

(C)

(B)

(E)

(A)

(A) **10818 German Drinking Stein — pair** — The deeply etched design of these striking 11 oz. steins captures the spirit of the Old World Taverns. (6" high) (NOT RECOMMENDED FOR HOT DRINKS)

(B) **10190 Ribbon Vase** — The gently fluted neck of this early 1900 COLLECTIBLE allows your buds to bloom freely. Remember mothers and grandmothers alike with this ideal gift! (8" high)

(C) **10321 Birthday Plate** — Create a lasting memory of your loved one's birthday by giving them this original plate. Beautiful and perfectly usable for any occasion. (8" dia.)

(D) **10323 Three French Hens Plate** — The tradition continues as Tiara proudly releases the 1983 Collector's plate in time for the new year! (8" dia.)

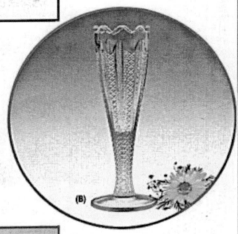

(B)

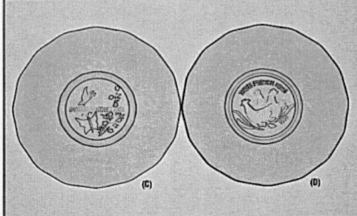

(C)   (D)

Party Pleasers

(A) 10010 Pineapple Bowl — Clearly outstanding! The pineapple, symbol of hospitality, is beautifully displayed on this versatile bowl. It is a great look for happy hostessing with fresh fruits or salads! (10" x 12" dia.)

(B) 10107 Provincial Punch Set — Whatever the beverage, this punch set will make it particularly appealing. The 8-quart capacity keeps your party going in style! The set is completed with 12 matching cups, 12 duracite hooks and a ladle. (7½" high x 13" dia.)

(C) 10105 Leaf Relish — Complement your service when entertaining with this 3-part relish. (11¾" x 9¼")

Accent Group

(A)

(B)

(E)

(D)

(C)

(A) 10065 Colonial Footed Tray — This crystal etched tray forms a miniature console set when displayed with the Colonial Birthday Candleholders. You can add a luxurious touch to your bathroom when this tray is used as a soap dish. (3½" high)

(B) 10075 Colonial Birthday Candleholders — pair — Tiara recaptures a wonderful colonial custom in etched crystal. These tiny holders graced each place setting, lighting the friendly faces of colonial party-goers with miniature flames. (3" tall)

(C) 10380 Colonial Water Bottle — A unique gift-giving idea, each bottle is hand blown in a turn-of-the-century mold. In colonial times the bottle, filled with water, graced the table. Today, the delicate lines of the 8" bottle makes it a perfect companion for beautiful blossoms!

(D) 10469 Lord's Supper Plate — Tiara has faithfully reproduced the delicate surface designs of this nostalgic plate in ever popular ice blue to create a versatile piece for your bread service or gift giving needs. This is one of several popular items we recommend for your club's fund raising events. (7" x 11" long)

(E) 10468 Chalice — Centuries of tradition are reflected in the unique form and grace of Tiara's newest work of art! It makes a perfect companion for the Lord's Supper Plate and is sure to be cherished when received as a gift. (7" high)

Back Yard Fun

(A) 10008 Maxi-Mugs — 4 pcs. — Serve your favorite brew or beverage in these uniquely finished mugs. The heavy weighted bottom discourages overturning. Who do you know that loves to entertain at home? (5 5/8" high, 12 oz.)

(B) 10006 Mini-Mugs — 6 pcs. — A must for every "pint-size" member of the group. Children love being "grown-up" with these 3½ oz. mugs just their size! They're also great stick-in-the closet gifts for birthdays, Easter baskets or "get well" juices for your special girls and boys.

(C) 10093 Large Pig Plate — A uniquely versatile plate! At party time it becomes an attractive serving piece for hams, sausages or cold cuts. Any other time use it as a centerpiece or tote tray for supplies to an outside barbecue. (13 1/8" long)

(D) 10091 Piggy Snack Set — The young and the "young at heart" will be delighted with their meals when served on the original Piggy Snack tray. Great for outdoor barbecues as well as a dieter's salad. (tray 10¼" x 6¼", cup 2½" high)

The Little One's Service

(A) 10090 Child's Service Set — Start a family tradition with this adorable 3 pc. set. A treasured gift which will be cherished forever. (8 oz. mug, 6" dia. bowl, 8½" dia. plate)

(B) 10052 Child's Tumblers — The nursery rhyme characters come alive on this pair of 6 oz. glasses. The 4" diameter makes the perfect "first glass" for little hands!

(A) 10059 Duchess Handled Basket — Bring the essence of days gone by into your home with this delicately simple, handcrafted basket! (10" high)

(B) 10047 Jolly Mountaineer Decanter — "Lift your spirits" with the magic of this COLLECTORS item. Guaranteed to amuse and entertain your friends whether it holds liquor, candy, coins, mouth wash or detergent in the kitchen. (10" high)

(C) 10009 Duchess Candlesticks — 2 pcs. — The colonial design of these candlesticks make them perfect complementary pieces to our Duchess Bowl and Basket, creating a centerpiece that is sure to be admired! (8½" high)

(D) 10103 Blue Bird Oval Bowl — The precise engraving of the "Blue Bird of Happiness" bowl is an example of the exacting standards developed nearly a century ago and lovingly maintained through the ages by the proud artisans of this art! Deserving of collecting for generations to come! (8½" dia.)

(E) 10069 Duchess 3 Toed Bowl — This classic look reminiscent of generations past is equally as elegant in use as it is on display! (12" dia.)

(F) 10494 Honey Dish and Cover — The honeycomb and bee pattern in this covered dish adds a wistful touch of nostalgia to your home. (6" high)

(A)

(B)

(C)

(D)

(E)

(F)

(A) 10375 Rose Pillow Vase — A remarkable value, as well as classic styling, are features of this newest COLLECTORS item! It will be the focal point of conversation when used as a decorative holder for flowers, business cards, game cards or cigarettes. (3¾" high)

(B) 10377 Empress Mint Dish — The exotic design of this dish is truly a deserving gift for royalty! Use it to add that touch of elegance when you entertain your special friends. (6" dia.)

(C) 10378 Duck Ash Tray — This unique item is a COLLECTORS TREASURE dating back to the early 1920's! A great gift idea for smokers and non-smokers alike. Why not place this item on your sportman's desk or dresser? (9½" long)

(D) 10376 Empress Jewell Box and Cover — From a period rich in gracious and romantic designs, this delicate box needs only the addition of your personal treasures! Hand pressed in beautiful coral glass, it also serves as an attractive container for paper clips, stamps, pins, etc. (5½" x 3½" x 1 7/8" dim.)

Sweet Pear Collection

(A) 10191 Sweet Pear Creamer and Sugar — The perfect companion to complete your meal. Don't overlook the benefits of this beauty for beverage service or a centerpiece display. (3½" high)

(B) 10192 Sweet Pear Olive — A dainty dish that looks great anywhere! For candies, nuts, etc. (7" x 5" dim.)

(C) 10193 Sweet Pear Cup and Saucer — Be sure to acquire a number of these sets to round out your collection! (cup 2¾" high, saucer 6" dia.)

(A)

(B)

(C)

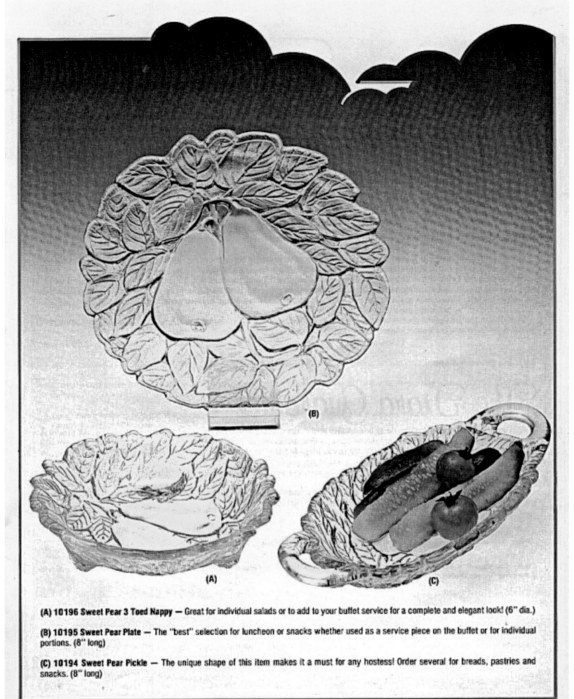

(B)

(A)

(C)

(A) 10196 Sweet Pear 3 Toed Nappy — Great for individual salads or to add to your buffet service for a complete and elegant look! (6" dia.)

(B) 10195 Sweet Pear Plate — The "best" selection for luncheon or snacks whether used as a service piece on the buffet or for individual portions. (8" long)

(C) 10194 Sweet Pear Pickle — The unique shape of this item makes it a must for any hostess! Order several for breads, pastries and snacks. (8" long)

Hostess Plan

Tiara Hostesses are treated to a premium incentive program that is almost unbelievable! It certainly pays well to be a Hostess at a Tiara Giftarama!

Simply invite a Tiara Associate to conduct a Giftarama in your home some morning, afternoon, or evening and you will have unfolded before your eyes a myriad of exclusive gifts that can be yours FREE!

For holding the Giftarama within two weeks, you will receive $3 and you can add $3 more for every $20 in orders accepted! That means that an average Giftarama of $200 would allow the Hostess $33 in gifts of her own choosing. But that isn't all — if three Giftaramas are arranged at a Giftarama, the Hostess would receive another $12 in gifts! Thus, a $200 Giftarama with three bookings pays the Hostess $45 in Tiara gifts!

In addition, the gifts of the month are available to all Hostesses whose Giftaramas reach specified levels of sales, making it possible for the average Hostess to earn 40% or more of the total value of sales in free gifts!

The Tiara Guarantee

All Tiara Gifts are guaranteed to be of fine quality and craftsmanship within the limits of the arts represented. All products are guaranteed for life, and should breakage occur, either accidental or otherwise, or any other damage, replacement will be made at fifty percent (50%) of the current price, provided the receipted shopping guide is sent to Tiara Exclusives as proof of purchase. The receipted shopping card will be returned to you along with your replacement merchandise.

A fee of two dollars and seventy-five cents ($2.75) to cover packing, shipping and indemnity must be included with each order for replacement.

There shall be no limitation upon this guarantee, and replacement policy, except in the case of discontinued items, in which event, the company will no longer be responsible, or liable, for replacement.

Flowers, candles, fruit and beverage are used as props in the photographs of this catalog. These are not available through Tiara Exclusives.

Credits: Coordinator - R. Kratz — Photography - Photocraft, Muncie, Ind. — Color Separation - Color Separation, Inc., Dayton, Ohio — Production & Typesetting - Colony Printing and Labeling, Inc., Eaton, Ind.

Do You Know

That Tiara Associates . . .

- have an opportunity to use all the ability they possess, and all they can acquire?

- have NO investment in samples, and receive over $200 worth FREE when they sign up?

- get paid every day they work, with NO waiting for their profits?

- Do NO packing and sacking or delivering? That everything they sell is delivered for them by United Parcel Service, at no cost to them?

- have NO reports to fill out, and no record keeping?

- are FIELD-TRAINED by Sales Leaders with hundreds of years of party plan experience?

- are promoted as rapidly as they meet specified levels of achievement, so they can earn profits on what other people sell?

- in many cases, are husband and wife teams that are building fine businesses for themselves, and a new way of life for their families?

- need more help to service the thousands of customers who are anxious to avail themselves of Tiara Gifts throughout America, and that they would LOVE to have you join them?

NOW THAT YOU DO KNOW — won't you get in touch with us, so that we can help you help yourself to the riches you deserve? Simply write our National Sales Leader, giving your name, address, phone and a simple statement of your personal goals! WRITE: Roger W. Jewett, 1717 W. 86th St., Suite 180, Indianapolis, Indiana 46260. You'll be GLAD you did!

Preferred Hostess Plan

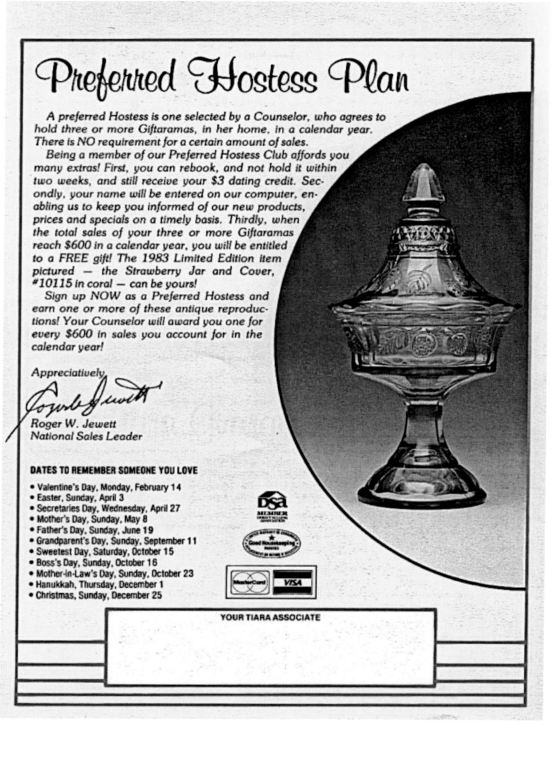

   A preferred Hostess is one selected by a Counselor, who agrees to hold three or more Giftaramas, in her home, in a calendar year. There is NO requirement for a certain amount of sales.

   Being a member of our Preferred Hostess Club affords you many extras! First, you can rebook, and not hold it within two weeks, and still receive your $3 dating credit. Secondly, your name will be entered on our computer, enabling us to keep you informed of our new products, prices and specials on a timely basis. Thirdly, when the total sales of your three or more Giftaramas reach $600 in a calendar year, you will be entitled to a FREE gift! The 1983 Limited Edition item pictured — the Strawberry Jar and Cover, #10115 in coral — can be yours!

   Sign up NOW as a Preferred Hostess and earn one or more of these antique reproductions! Your Counselor will award you one for every $600 in sales you account for in the calendar year!

Appreciatively,

Roger W. Jewett
Roger W. Jewett
National Sales Leader

DATES TO REMEMBER SOMEONE YOU LOVE

- Valentine's Day, Monday, February 14
- Easter, Sunday, April 3
- Secretaries Day, Wednesday, April 27
- Mother's Day, Sunday, May 8
- Father's Day, Sunday, June 19
- Grandparent's Day, Sunday, September 11
- Sweetest Day, Saturday, October 15
- Boss's Day, Sunday, October 16
- Mother-in-Law's Day, Sunday, October 23
- Hanukkah, Thursday, December 1
- Christmas, Sunday, December 25

DSA MEMBER

Good Housekeeping

MasterCard   VISA

YOUR TIARA ASSOCIATE

Tiara EXCLUSIVES

CAPRICORN
Dec. 21 — Jan. 19

1983

Suggested Selling Price

NUMBER	DESCRIPTION	RETAIL	SHIPPING FEE
10006	Mugs, 3½ oz. crystal etched, set of 6	13.90	1.25
10008	Mugs, 12 oz. crystal etched, set of 4	17.90	2.50
10009	Duchess Candlesticks, blue, pair	24.90	1.00
10010	Pineapple Salad Bowl, yellow mist	22.50	2.25
10016	Hunter's Horn Mugs, crystal, pair	12.90	1.25
10022	Eagle Ash Tray, amber	19.50	2.00
10025	Smoker's Set, crystal etched, 6 pieces	22.50	1.50
10026	Lotus Ash Tray, Blue	14.90	1.50
10028	Terrarium, blue	78.50	3.75
10038	Patio Tankards, 12 oz., crystal etched, 4 pieces	21.90	2.50
10039	Patio Beverage Set, crystal etched, 5 pieces	29.90	3.75
10040	Powderhorn Tumblers, crystal etched, 4 pieces	19.90	1.50
10047	Mountaineer Decanter, blue	31.90	1.00
10052	Child's Milk Tumblers, amber, pair	9.90	.75
10059	Duchess Handled Basket, blue	26.50	2.00
10065	Colonial Footed Tray, crystal etched	9.90	.50
10069	Duchess 3 Toed Bowl, blue	24.50	1.25
10075	Colonial Birthday Candles, crystal etched, pair	8.90	.50
10085	Colonial Candy Box & Cover, crystal	9.90	1.00
10090	Child's Set, amber, 3 pieces	11.50	1.25
10091	Little Piggy Snack Set, amber, 4 pieces	14.90	1.25
10093	Piggy Platter, amber	9.90	1.00
10103	Blue Bird Oval Bowl, blue	11.90	.75
10105	Leaf Relish Dish, crystal	14.50	1.00
10107	Provincial Punch Set, crystal etched, 26 pieces	59.90	5.50
10160	Ponderosa Pine Plates, crystal, 4 pieces	14.90	2.75
10161	Ponderosa Pine Mugs, crystal, 4 pieces	11.90	1.25
10162	Ponderosa Pine Juice Glasses, crystal, 4 pieces	9.90	1.25
10163	Ponderosa Pine Goblets, crystal, 4 pieces	15.50	2.25
10164	Ponderosa Pine Salad Bowl, 9½", crystal	14.90	1.50
10165	Ponderosa Pine Salad Bowls, crystal, 4 pieces	14.50	1.50
10166	Ponderosa Pine Salad Plates, crystal, 4 pieces	13.50	2.25
10180	Constellation Console Bowl, yellow mist	25.50	1.50
10181	Constellation Cake Plate, yellow mist	25.50	1.50
10182	Constellation 6" Nut Bowl, yellow mist	13.90	.75
10183	Constellation Mini Basket, yellow mist	17.50	1.00
10184	Constellation Pickle Dish, yellow mist	15.50	1.00
10185	Constellation Candleholders, yellow mist, pair	16.50	.75
10186	Constellation Cookie Jar & Cover, yellow mist	31.50	2.00
10188	Constellation Bon Bon & Cover, yellow mist	20.50	1.25
10190	Ribbon Vase, 8", yellow mist	15.50	.75
10191	Sweet Pear Sugar & Creamer Set, yellow mist	19.90	.75
10192	Sweet Pear Olive Dish, yellow mist	9.90	.75
10193	Sweet Pear Cup & Saucer Set, yellow mist	17.90	.75
10194	Sweet Pear 8" Pickle Dish, yellow mist	9.90	.50
10195	Sweet Pear 8" Plate, yellow mist	9.90	.75
10196	Sweet Pear 3 Toed Nappy, yellow mist	9.50	.50
10200	Sandwich 10 oz. Tumblers, amber, 4 pieces	14.90	1.50
10201	Sandwich 12" Platter, amber	9.50	1.25
10202	Sandwich 6" Deep Nappy, amber, pair	14.50	1.00
10205	Sandwich Mini Basket, amber	16.90	1.00
10208	Sandwich Goblets, amber, 4 pieces	12.50	1.25
10209	Sandwich Wall Clock, amber	39.90	2.00
10210	Sandwich Jewel Box & Cover, amber	19.90	.75
10211	Sandwich Crimped Salad Bowl, amber	9.90	1.25
10213	Sandwich Pitcher, amber	28.90	2.00
10215	Sandwich Tall Handled Basket, amber	24.90	1.00

NUMBER	DESCRIPTION	RETAIL	SHIPPING FEE
10217	Sandwich Napkin Holder, amber	15.50	.75
10218	Sandwich Egg Hors D'oeuvre Tray, amber	9.90	1.25
10220	Sandwich Butter & Cover, amber	19.50	1.00
10221	Sandwich Handled Basket, amber	29.50	2.25
10222	Sandwich Ash Tray, amber	8.50	.75
10223	Sandwich Wall Sconce, amber	17.90	1.25
10224	Sandwich 3 Part Relish Tray, amber	9.50	1.25
10226	Sandwich Snack Set, amber, 8 pieces	17.50	2.00
10227	Sandwich Salt & Pepper Set, amber	12.50	.75
10228	Sandwich Berry Set, amber, 5 pieces	14.50	1.25
10229	Sandwich Puff Box & Cover, amber	9.90	.75
10233	Sandwich Canister, amber, small	9.90	1.25
10234	Sandwich Canister, amber, large	13.90	2.00
10236	Sandwich Dining Lamp, amber	9.90	1.00
10237	Sandwich Glo Lamp, amber	9.50	.75
10241	Sandwich Wine Set, amber, 9 pieces	44.50	2.50
10243	Sandwich Crimped Console Bowl, amber	19.90	1.50
10244	Sandwich 2 Tier Tidbit Tray, amber	16.50	1.25
10245	Sandwich Footed Candleholders, amber, pair	9.50	.75
10248	Sandwich Dinner Plates, amber, 4 pieces	15.50	2.75
10253	Sandwich Mini Vase, amber	5.90	.50
10254	Sandwich Sugar & Creamer Set, amber	28.90	.75
10256	Sandwich Dinner Bell, amber	9.90	.50
10258	Sandwich Tall Candleholders, amber, pair	19.90	1.25
10260	Sandwich 5" Salad Bowls, amber, 4 pieces	9.90	1.25
10262	Sandwich Starter Set, amber, 16 pieces	47.90	5.50
10273	Sandwich Gravy Boat, amber	14.90	.75
10278	Sandwich Footed Compote, amber	12.90	1.00
10281	Sandwich Canister, amber, medium	11.90	1.50
10282	Sandwich Footed Mugs, amber, 4 pieces	12.50	1.75
10283	Sandwich Table Wine Goblets, amber, 4 pieces	12.50	1.75
10305	Sandwich 10 oz. Tumblers, chantilly green, 4 pieces	14.90	1.50
10306	Sandwich 5" Salad Bowls, chantilly green, 4 pieces	9.90	1.25
10308	Sandwich Goblets, chantilly green, 4 pieces	12.50	1.25
10321	Birthday Plate, amber	8.50	.75
10323	Three French Hens Plate, amber	8.50	.75
10340	Sandwich 12" Platter, chantilly green	9.50	1.25
10341	Sandwich Egg Hors D'oeuvre Tray, chantilly green	9.90	1.25
10342	Sandwich 3 Part Relish Tray, chantilly green	9.50	1.25
10343	Sandwich Large Basket, chantilly green	29.50	2.25
10344	Sandwich Wine Set, chantilly green, 9 pieces	44.50	2.50
10345	Sandwich Tall Candleholders, chantilly green, pair	19.90	1.25
10347	Sandwich Canister, chantilly green, small	9.90	1.25
10348	Sandwich Canister, chantilly green, medium	11.90	1.50
10349	Sandwich Canister, chantilly green, large	13.90	2.00
10351	Sandwich Starter Set, chantilly green, 16 pieces	47.90	5.50
10352	Sandwich Pitcher, chantilly green	28.90	2.00
10353	Sandwich Wine Set Goblets, chantilly green, 6 pieces	20.50	1.50
10354	Peacock Vase, chantilly green	37.50	2.00
10375	Rose Pillow Vase, coral	8.90	.50
10376	Empress Jewel Box & Cover, coral	21.90	.75
10377	Empress Mint Dish, coral	10.50	.75
10378	Duck Ash Tray, coral	16.90	1.00
10379	Optic Vase, coral	71.50	3.25
10380	Colonial Water Bottle, coral	19.90	1.00
10387	Zodiac Tankard, black, Capricorn	9.90	.75
10388	Zodiac Tankard, black, Aquarius	9.90	.75

NUMBER	DESCRIPTION	RETAIL	SHIPPING FEE
10389	Zodiac Tankard, black, Pisces	9.90	.75
10390	Zodiac Tankard, black, Aries	9.90	.75
10391	Zodiac Tankard, black, Taurus	9.90	.75
10392	Zodiac Tankard, black, Gemini	9.90	.75
10393	Zodiac Tankard, black, Cancer	9.90	.75
10394	Zodiac Tankard, black, Leo	9.90	.75
10395	Zodiac Tankard, black, Virgo	9.90	.75
10396	Zodiac Tankard, black, Libra	9.90	.75
10397	Zodiac Tankard, black, Scorpio	9.90	.75
10398	Zodiac Tankard, black, Sagittarius	9.90	.75
10432	Colonial Candy Box & Cover, black	9.90	.75
10468	Chalice, ice blue	7.50	.75
10469	Lord's Supper Plate, ice blue	15.50	1.00
10494	Honey Dish & Cover, blue	15.50	1.00
10516	Demijohn, yellow mist	85.50	3.50
10557	Sandwich Snack Set, chantilly green, 8 pieces	17.50	2.00
10818	German Drinking Stein, black, pair	12.50	1.00

*Gift Certificates are now available from your Tiara Associate!

```
                    YOUR TIARA ASSOCIATE




```

11118 REV. 1/83

© 1983
by Tiara Exclusives

Tiara 1987 Catalog Contents

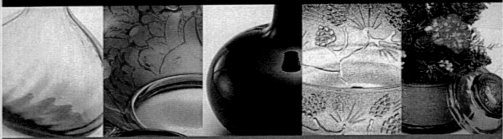

Tiara Exclusives®

1987 • CATALOGUE

INDEX

EXECUTIVE OFFICES

Tiara Exclusives

DUNKIRK, INDIANA 47336-9425   Phone 317-768-7821

Robert J. Staab
President

Ralph Waddell
General Manager

Robert Hatfield
National Sales Leader

Ronald A. Kratz
Director of Sales Promotion

NATIONAL SALES LEADERS OFFICE
Robert Hatfield
224 N. Story Rd. #138
Irving, TX 75061
214-790-2264
800-423-0160 Out of State
800-441-0907 Texas Residents

INTERNATIONAL SALES OFFICE
James F. Beitler
P.O. Box 2278, Kingshill
St. Croix, V.I. 00850
809-773-7256

FLORIDA SALES OFFICE
Phyllis & Ron Easley
1227 Parkland Ct.
Altamonte Springs, FL 32714
(305-298-7273)

GULF COAST SALES OFFICE
Tommie Hinski
709 Keith
Pasadena, TX 77504
(713-943-0868)

MID-AMERICA SALES OFFICE
Pat & Dale Malwick
8403 South 77th E. Place
Tulsa, OK 74133
(918-250-1228)

NORTH CENTRAL SALES OFFICE
Judith A. Rustia-Stojnic
2217 Romm Ct.
Shaumburg, IL 60194
(312-884-7622)

NORTHEASTERN SALES OFFICE
Marsha & Rory O'Connor
84 Ludlow St.
Saratoga Springs, NY 12866
(518-584-2442)

NORTHWESTERN SALES OFFICE
Hal Scott
6978 Pampas Way
Fair Oaks, CA 95628
(916-966-6508)

ROCKY MOUNTAIN SALES OFFICE
Sandra Tripp
7070 Zephyr Circle
Arvada, CO 80004
(303-425-6588)

SMOKEY MOUNTAIN SALES OFFICE
Glenda Carlyle
1701 Leolillie Lane
Charlotte, NC 28216
(704-394-4297)

SOUTHEASTERN SALES OFFICE
Lucia Hnath
681 Mountainbrooke Circle
Stone Mountain, GA 30087
(404-921-5922)

SOUTHWESTERN SALES OFFICE
Gail Hatfield
224 N. Story Rd. #134
Irving, TX 75061
(214-790-2245)
(214-399-0131)

WESTERN SALES OFFICE
Jeannine Reaves
15600 Tetley St.
Hacienda Heights, CA 92745
(818-336-4844)
(714-594-8009)

Can You Imagine . .

That Tiara associates have NO investments in samples, and receive more than $400 worth of glassware FREE?

That Tiara associates get paid every DAY they work, with no waiting for their profits?

That Tiara associates do NO packing and sacking and NO delivering? That everything they sell is delivered for them by U.P.S., at NO cost to them?

That Tiara associates have NO reports to fill out and NO record keeping required?

That Tiara associates are FIELD TRAINED by leaders with hundreds of years of party plan experience?

NOW YOU KNOW — Won't you please get in touch with us? We can help you to help yourself to the riches you deserve!

PLEASE WRITE FOR ADDITIONAL INFORMATION:

National Sales Office • 224 North Story Rd. • Suite #138 • Irving, TX 75061

214-790-2264 • Toll Free Out Of State Residents 1-800-423-0160 • Toll Free Texas Residents 1-800-441-0907

WATER LILY ACCENTS

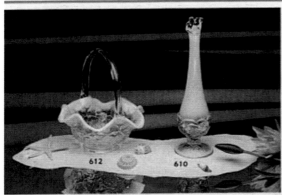

608 Fruit Bowl
Enchanting antiquity is captured for you in this footed serving bowl. An exceptional decorating piece to enhance your collection of the Water Lily Accents. (7½" high, 11" dia.) $36.90

609 Console Bowl
A unique cupped edge adds a stunning touch to this captivating design. A lovable bowl for fruits, nuts or a floral arrangement. (3" high, 9" dia.) $32.50

610 Bud Vase
An exquisite accent for any table. Alluringly sized for a single rose or your favorite fresh cut flower! (10¼" high) $18.50

611 Candlesticks
pair — Richly finished for that distinctive look on your dining table for a sparkling accent. (3" high, 5¾" dia.) $27.50

612 Basket
Finely hand sculptured by master craftsmen, use for treats, a small plant or a floral arrangement. An ideal wedding basket! (7½" high) $24.50

We Honor

2

TREASURED COLLECTION

143 Dewdrop Basket
The time spent by craftsmen paddling the molten glass to its present shape, makes this basket an outstanding value and unusual gift. (8½" high) $37.90

144 Lily Fruit Bowl
The deep rich glow of ruby warmly complements the fresh fruit or flowers you arrange as a centerpiece when important guests visit. (9½" dia., 2½" high) $27.50

148 Dewdrop Candy Box and Cover
Warm up your table with the fire-like glow of this beautiful accent piece. (6¾" high) $29.90

150 Dewdrop Mini Basket
Contoured style, hand formed by American glass craftsmen, makes this item an enchanting gift for any occasion. The crystal handle adds the perfect touch! (7" high)
                    $24.50

3

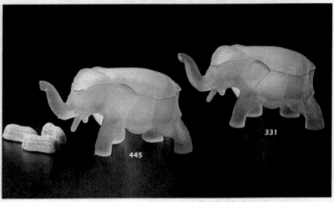

085 Colonial Candy Box and Cover
Early American in design but modern in function. This crystal container can be used in any room of your home. (5¾" high) $12.90

317 Sandwich Votives
pair - These votives in chantilly green will bring the warm glow of candlelight to brighten a corner in any room. (candles included, 3½" high) $13.90

331 Elephant
A classic symbol of good luck. Everyone will want to add this chantilly green etched elephant to their collection. This container can be used for candles or nuts and will be a conversation piece when displayed on the tabletop in any room. (4½" high) $14.90

432 Colonial Candy Box and Cover
A charming reminder of another era - this candy box and cover, in black, is a splendid container for your favorite sweets! (5¾" high) $12.90

445 Elephant
This "good luck" symbol can be used as a gift for any occasion. One of a kind . . . this unique blue etched item has multiple uses. (4½" high) $14.90

452 Leaf Candle Lamp
The soft warm glow of this pink etched lamp adds a nice touch to times that need a little romance! (4⅛" high, candle not included) .... $ 9.90

HOME AND OFFICE ACCESSORIES

326 Sandwich Ash Tray
A distinguished gift for friends, acquaintances and business associates which will be a treasured remembrance for years to come. Produced in chantilly green. (7⅜" dia.) $10.90

329 Captain's Decanter with Stopper
This unique decanter once graced the table of proud sailing ships. The wide bottom design made it stable against the rolling seas. Today, it is an ideal decorator piece or perfect container for spirits in chantilly green. (9" high, 9¼" dia.) $44.50

370 Mushroom Lamp
pink
466 Mushroom Lamp
blue
Bathe your rooms with a soft glow of romantic light from one or both of these mood setting lamps. Choose your favorite scented candle to create a relaxing atmosphere. (Includes a crystal votive cup, 4¼" high) $12.90

385 Honey Dish and Cover
This covered square dish in pink etched makes an excellent container for many things, including its original use for a full comb of honey! The honeycomb and bee pattern adds a wistful touch that is sure to "spark" all sorts of conversation. (6" high) $19.90

817 Royal Candy Box and Cover
Black glass and the deep cut design adds dignity and charm to this item. It can be used for candies, soaps and jewelry. (6¼" x 3⅛" dim.) $14.90

5

PONDEROSA PINE

This refreshing pattern in crystal was created for beauty and value to complement any decor.

160 Dinner Plates
4 pieces — The basic plate in Ponderosa Pine for formal or informal dining. (10" dia.) $19.90

161 Mug
4 pieces — Great for that relaxing cup of coffee any time of day. (9 oz. cap., 4¾" high) $14.90

162 Juice
4 pieces — When not in use for juice...add a glowing touch with a votive candle and flower ring. (9 oz. cap., 4¾" high) $12.90

166 Salad Plates
4 pieces — The perfect size plate for salad, sandwiches, dessert or children's portions. (8" dia.) $16.90

167 Salt and Pepper
"Bigger than average" for shaking your favorite spices while cooking. (Chrome Finished Tops, 4¾" high) $14.90

171 Carafe
Designed to serve wine and juice in style or complement your flowers as a vase. (46 oz. cap., 9¼" high) $26.50

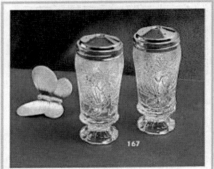

164 Salad Bowl
Popular size for serving fruits, snacks, or salad.
(9½" dia.) $16.90

165 Individual Salad Bowls
4 pieces — The perfect size for whatever you
serve — salad, soups, vegetables or desserts.
(5" dia.) $17.90

173 Vegetable Bowls
2 pieces — Serve your vegetables in style with
these footed bowls. Great for everyday use and
holiday entertaining! (7¾" dia.) $16.90

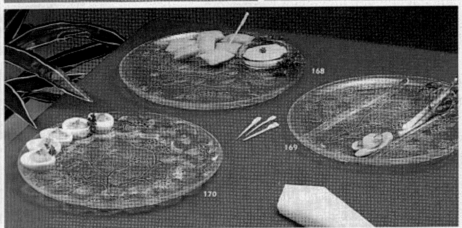

168 Serving Plate
The simplicity and versatility of this platter
makes it a "must" for any homemaker! (12⅝"
dia.) $10.90

169 Three Part Relish Tray
Sure to be a welcome addition to this popular
pattern! Use for cheese and crackers, relishes or
as an extra cold-cut platter. (12⅝" dia.) $10.90

170 Egg Tray
This unique egg tray has 18 cradles for a variety
of uses. Ideal for your tasty deviled eggs, but
imagine serving oysters on the half-shell from
this beautiful tray. A great gift that's not likely to
be duplicated. (12⅝" dia.) $10.90

159 Pitcher
A host of everyday uses for your favorite beverage service. Brighten your kitchen with an arrangement of seasonal flowers in this stylish pitcher. (68 oz. cap., 8¼" high) $16.90

163 Goblet
4 pieces — Durable yet delicate in design! (12 oz. cap., 6" high) $18.90

172 Ice Teas
4 pieces — An ideal size for your thirsty friends, and can also be used for a floral display. (18 oz. cap., 6¾" high) $18.90

174 Handled Beverage
4 pieces — The spirit of the mighty pine has been captured in glass. Use this beverage set year round as a charming touch for your favorite refreshment! (13 oz. cap., 5½" high) $19.50

8

THE CREATION OF GLASS

Over 4,000 years ago, perhaps on the sands of Egypt, Syria or Babylonia, the creation of glass began. Since then mankind has added, little by little, to the glassmaker's art. The skill of the glassmaker has been a source of beauty, treasured by all.

It is natural that you, a Tiara Customer, should want to know something about the way our glass is created. Making glassware by hand is the oldest industry in America, started in the Jamestown Colony in 1608. Many of the techniques and tools of the early days are used in the manufacture of Tiara Exclusives. Each item is a work of art and exclusive to Tiara customers.

Glass is truly the product of earth and fire! Made of silica, soda ash, lime and feldspar, small amounts of various other chemicals such as copper, selenium, manganese and cadmium are added to make a "batch." After careful mixing of the selected ingredients, a quantity of broken glass — called cullet — is often added to the "batch" to speed up the melting process. The tank into which the glassworker shovels the "batch" has been pre-fired to an intense heat of about 2700ºF. In about 18 hours the glass is ready to be gathered and blown. It takes a shop of six to eighteen skilled workers to make just one item.

A blowpipe is a hollow tube of steel with a special "head" which the gatherer slips into the tank of molten glass. Turning it in the glass, he gathers just the right "gob" on the end of the pipe. He hands it to the blower after first shaping on a marveling plate. The blower then shapes the "ball" with applewood tools and paddles, and with carefully controlled puffs, forms a hollow bulb. His tools are varied and adapted for each item, and include the Pucellas, often called just the "tool." Like a huge pair of tweezers, the "tool" becomes a set of additional fingers for the skilled craftsman.

Now the piece is ready to be removed from the blowpipe and turned over to the stick-up boy, who picks it up and takes it to the "glory-hole," a reheating furnace kept at about 2500ºF. Here the glass is reheated and taken to the finisher for shaping. He, with the skilled touch of practiced hands, forms the decanter, bowl, pitcher, etc. When the item is to have a handle, or requires additional work, it is handed to a second finisher.

As this finisher completes the piece, a carry-in boy appears with a special fork, snaps the piece from the punty and carries it to an annealing oven or "lehr." Here it travels on a slowly moving, endless chain through several hours of diminishing heat, emerging at the end ready to be inspected. It is then labeled with a Tiara Exclusive's sticker, boxed and put in stock.

Since many Tiara blown items are shaped by hand, variations in size, shape and color lend real "individuality" to the items you select for yourself or as gifts for friends and family.

Amber

The original Sandwich Glass was named after Sandwich, Massachusetts, on Cape Cod. It is one of the most famous of all Early American glass styles. Glass collectors treasure it. Museums display any pieces they can get. It was first made in 1825 by Deming Jarves, who developed the ability to press glass by hand. The beautiful patterns were cut in iron molds by hand!

The star and scroll design was described by the early writers as "sparkling like dew-moistened leaves." In spite of its lacy quality it has tremendous sturdiness and durability and can be machine washed.

Every conceivable item for the table is available to Tiara customers now, or will be in the near future. To the best of our knowledge, Sandwich Glass dinnerware has never before been made in the Golden Amber color. On a gold tablecloth the rich color speaks quality, and marks the owner of it as a discriminating homemaker!

The use of the exclusive line for shower gifts, wedding gifts, birthday and anniversary gifts, and for Christmas affords the giver a continuity unmatched in beautiful glass!

The Sandwich Glass Collection . . .exclusively yours from Tiara!

SANDWICH COLLECTION

208 Goblets
4 pieces — A must for every formal dinner service. (8 oz. cap., 5¼" high) $15.90

245 Butter Dish and Cover
Grace your dining table with this appealing rectangular butter container. (7" long) $23.90

248 Dinner Plates
4 pieces — Extras are always a good idea! Eliminate embarrassing moments when company arrives at mealtime or holiday dining increases your needs. (10" dia.) $19.90

253 Mini Vase
Ideal for a special bouquet! (3¾" high) $7.50

262 Starter Set
16 pieces — Whether the menu offers filet mignon or the simplest fare, the service will be absolutely perfect with our Sandwich Starter Set! (4 each: 10" dinner plates, 8" salad plates, 6" saucers and 9 oz. cups) $52.50

10

201 Platter
Ideally suited for serving cold cuts, cheese and crackers. (12" dia.) $12.50

218 Egg Tray
Serve hors d'oeuvres and deviled eggs to your guests in style on this handy tray. (12" dia.) $12.50

221 Basket
Made entirely by hand and always the delight of those with an eye for design. It may be used for fruits, flowers, breads, biscuits or vegetables. (10" high) $34.90

224 Relish Tray
Ample space in each section makes this unusual tray the perfect serving piece for a variety of relishes. (12" dia.) $12.50

227 Salt and Pepper
There is no doubt these twin beauties will "spice" up your table. (4¾" high) $14.90

237 Glo Lamp
Warm patterns of flickering light will dance through the evening when you place a few of these lamps around the room. An ideal gift giving item! (5¼" high) $11.90

200 Tumblers
4 pieces — These 10 oz. tumblers are a refreshing way to satisfy even the thirstiest of the bunch. Be sure to have extras for company. (6½" high) $17.90

212 Vegetable Bowl
pair — These classic bowls are perfect for your vegetable service. (8" dia.) $12.50

226 Snack Set
8 pieces — Very important guests deserve this perfect snack service! The delicate amber pattern adds grace and tradition to the occasion. (8½" x 6¾" dim., 6 oz. cup) $19.90

241 Wine Set
9 pieces — Ensure your vintage choice being served elegantly! Six delicate wine goblets surround this graceful 10" high, handblown decanter and hand ground stopper. The entire set rests on a 10" diameter serving tray. A truly exclusive gift worthy of the many compliments it will receive. $52.50

243 Pitcher
This gorgeous 64 oz. pitcher accents our Sandwich Collection. Can be truly functional for your beverage service or arranged with flowers to enhance any countertop or table in the kitchen. (8½" high) $19.90

252 Oval Trays
pair — A useful and attractive accessory to the Sandwich Collection, these oval trays will certainly serve you well. (8½" x 6¾" dim.) $ 9.50

269 Sugar and Creamer Set
Newly designed to match your Sandwich dinnerware, affords you a chance to set a distinctive table for formal and informal service. (sugar & cover 4⅞" high, creamer 3¾" high) $29.90

241 Set

252

212

269 Set

226 Set

243

200

12

209 Clock
Time will be the secondary thought as guests admire your Sandwich Wall Clock! The warmth of golden amber highlights this extraordinary battery operated timepiece. (12" dia.) $54.50

211 Salad Bowl Crimped
Six crimps add a subtle richness to this universal bowl, making it perfect for any serving need. (4¾" high x 10" dia.) $12.50

233 Canister
To create an ensemble for your counter or fill with your favorite goodies, this small canister is a must for your home. (5⅝" high) $12.50

234 Canister
This size is just perfect for cookies and donuts. Can also be used as a humidor for someone special. (8⅝" high) $16.90

246 Votive
pair — Now is the time to start your Sandwich Collection or add to your existing one with this favorite piece that includes a 10 hour votive candle. (3½" high) $13.90

260 Salad Bowls
4 pieces — A complement to our large salad bowl, these four bowls can be used for cereal, soup or popcorn. (5" dia.) $12.50

270 Champagne/Sherbet
pair — Any beverage or dessert will look majestic when served in this Sandwich stemware. (5¼" high) $16.90

281 Canister
Combine style and versatility to coordinate the storage of your countertop necessities. Stackable for limited space. (7½" high) $14.50

103 Snack Plate
4 pieces — Serve your snacks on these plates at any social gathering for a personal statement of style. (7½" dia.) $13.50

104 Tray
This magnificent tray was created with sheet cakes in mind but designed for multiple uses. (14½" x 10½" dim.) $27.50

110 Serving Bowl
pair — Pleasing for dinner and party service of salads, fruits and snacks. (9" x 3½" dim.) $16.90

111 Party Bowl
Handsomely complements any setting alone or can be teamed with other Celebration serving pieces. (7" dia.) $ 9.90

CELEBRATION
PARTY PLEASERS
IN CRYSTAL

109 Coasters
4 pieces — Designed to be useful, yet elegant, these coasters will be a stylish addition to any decor. (3¾" dia.)
$ 9.90

113 Punch Set
14 pieces — Celebrate any special occasion in style with this functional set. The size and versatility of this punch set allows you to serve anything from punch to desserts and variety foods for a large group with elegance. (6 oz. cup, 5 quart bowl) $39.90

15

CROWN DINNERWARE
IN IMPERIAL BLUE

780

785

784

782

781

783

786

787

780 Dinner Plate
4 pieces — The traditional appearance of these plates accented by the grandeur of color will create an air of gracious living in your dining service. (10" dia.) $18.50

781 Salad/Dessert/Bread Plate
4 pieces — A delightful way to serve snacks and dessert to your special guests! (8" dia.) $15.50

782 Cup
4 pieces — The stylish regal design of this cup will be a sparkling addition to your dining or tea service. (6 oz.)
                                                                                                                    $12.90

783 Saucer
4 pieces — A necessary item to complete your coffee and tea service for that formal table. (6" dia.) $12.50

784 Goblet
4 pieces — Complete your place setting with the elegance of this 8 ounce goblet. (5½" high) $16.90

785 Cocktail
4 pieces — A charming addition to the standard dining service for the pleasant after-dinner cocktail. (3 oz.) $14.90

786 Platter
Just the right size for the service of those tasteful appetizers, hors d'oeuvres and finger foods. (14" dia.) $14.90

787 Console Bowl
Beautify a carefully prepared salad in this classic bowl. (9" dia.) $14.90

774 Genie Water Bottle
Exquisitely crafted and handblown with an optic, this is a unique table service item for water or milk. A perfect accent for any decor in the home. (7½" high) $26.50

775 Sandwich Jewel Box
One of life's simple treasures...this stunning jewel box is beautiful on a coffee table, dresser or vanity! (1¾" high, 2⅝" x 3⅝" dim.) $16.90

UNUSUAL GIFT COLLECTION
IN PLATINUM

772 Smoker's Set
6 pieces — Let your imagination run. This set may be used for coasters, individual treats at the card table, or stacked with a candle ring when smokers aren't around. The urn doubles as a mini-vase to display your fresh cut or silk flowers. $25.90

776 Rose Pillow Vase
The remarkable value and classic styling are features of this COLLECTOR'S item! It will be the focal point of conversation when used as a decorative holder for flowers, business cards or cigarettes. (3¾" high) $13.50

18

EMPRESS
IN DUSTY ROSE

758 Basket
Lovely to look at, delightful to own! Imagine it in a favorite spot with tiny blossoms. (7½" high)
$24.50

759 Jewel Box and Cover
From a period rich in gracious and romantic designs, this delicate box needs only the addition of your personal treasures! Hand pressed, this item can also serve as an attractive container for paper clips, stamps, pins, etc. (5½" x 3½" x 1⅞" dim.)
$24.90

760 Tray
Special guests deserve your best hospitality — and our Empress Tray is just the beginning. Place this item in a bedroom or bath to help keep personal items organized. Also a perfect companion to our Empress Jewel Box. (7¼" x 11½" dim.)
$23.90

761 Oval Bowl
The proud heritage of Oriental art brings us this stunning oval bowl. This delicate color adds a designer's touch to your fruits, flowers or salads. (4" high, 13" long)
$29.90

758

760

759

761

19

THE FOSTORIA STORY

Samuel Butler once wrote, "Every man's work is always a portrait of himself." That philosophy has prevailed at the Fostoria Glass Company since its inception in 1887. For almost a century the name Fostoria has been synonymous with high quality glassware. Recently, Fostoria was acquired by the Lancaster Colony Corporation, the parent of Tiara Exclusives! This gives Tiara the rare opportunity to have lead crystal gifts manufactured EXCLUSIVELY for them by Fostoria!

Fostoria originated in Fostoria, Ohio, because of the vast amount of natural gas available in that locality. Unfortunately, four years later the gas ran out. The city of Moundsville, West Virginia, attracted the glass company to their city. 1986 was the third move of Fostoria to Lancaster, Ohio, for economic reasons.

In its earliest days, Fostoria made pressed tableware, stationers' glass (inkwells and paperweights) and such miscellaneous items as candelabrums, dresser sets and shades, beautifully hand-painted and decorated. These proved so popular that at one time there were as many as 200 different lamps in the line! Fostoria had established its reputation as a producer of fine quality handblown glassware!

By then there was a brisk business in bar bottles and stemware. Elegant blown crystal decanters with elaborate cuttings contributed a touch of class to many a Victorian saloon! Several fine hotels, restaurants, and railroads relied on Fostoria for crystal tableware. Even today, the company makes crystal for a small number of exclusive restaurants! All items made for Tiara are EXCLUSIVE in pattern and design.

Much of the satisfaction of owning "Tiara by Fostoria" derives from the fact that each piece is unique. Each has its own peculiar ring when you tap it. Today, the artist-designer is a specialist on a team of specialists. Working with researchers, lab technicians, mold and model workers, and the glass workers themselves, they strive to develop designs that are both practical and appealing. Increasingly casual lifestyles, for example, have led to several new molded giftware and tableware patterns.

In fact, Fostoria is the very special gift choice of some of our most celebrated Americans. Fostoria gifts are today given by many senators and congressmen. U.S. presidents including Eisenhower, Kennedy, Johnson, Nixon, Ford, and Reagan have given Fostoria gift items. Ronald Reagan has chosen Fostoria drinkware to be used in Air Force One, the Presidential aircraft; he is currently using Fostoria drinkware as a special personal gift bearing the Presidential Seal.

As you examine the gifts presented here in lead crystal, be assured that "Tiara by Fostoria" carries the same hallmark of quality that Fostoria has enjoyed for a century! The rich tradition is perpetuated and a new dimension has been added to the Tiara gifts in glass!

082

082 Egg and Cover
Deep cut prisms will catch every ray of light reflecting the diamond like sparkle of our Egg and Cover. An elegant accessory for any table in the home. (3" x 3¼" x 4⅜" dim.) $17.90

ACCENTS ON ELEGANCE

Tiara by **Fostoria**
in authentic lead crystal

046 Venetian Candlelamp
A sparkling lamp that's sure to cast a soft glow of warm candlelight for a wealth of uses in the home. The lamp is made with a lead crystal base, the shade and adaptor are crystal with a 5" candle included. (14¼" high) $29.90

065 Heart Paperweight
This specially designed paperweight gives a useful touch to a universal phrase for a gift to someone you LOVE! (3¾" dia.) $11.50

078 Venetian Candle Holder
(5½" high) $14.90

079 Venetian Candle Holder
(7⅝" high) $19.90

Enhance any room with the soft, romantic glow of candlelight, illuminating the mantel, end table or piano.

081 Love Paperweight
An attractive gift in crystal for the home or office. This item was designed to capture the heart of the recipient! Picture a loved one in the letter "O" for a personal touch. (5" high) $11.90

100 Inspirational Paperweight
Give the gift of motivation with Tiara's Inspirational Paperweight in crystal. Its message "What You Dare to Dream — Dare to Do" is ideal for graduates, executives and business people. (3" high) $11.50

21

EXCLUSIVELY YOURS

in authentic lead crystal

056 Pitcher
32 oz. $19.50

070 Double Old Fashion
pair, 11 oz. $17.90

071 Beverage/Highball
pair, 13 oz. $17.90

072 Goblet
pair, 9 oz. $22.90

073 Wine/Juice
pair, 7 oz. $22.90

074 Ice Tea
pair, 12 oz. $22.90

Extraordinary beauty is captured in this exclusive Tiara design! Be prepared to add that special touch of elegance by having several pairs of these sparkling items on hand for "short notice gifts" or special guests.

Tiara by Fostoria

22

SUZANNE
in authentic lead crystal

Tiara by Fostoria

075 Vase
This distinctive design will add a subtle elegance to any room in your home! (7¼" high) $14.90

076 Vase
An exquisite design in modern cut, magnificently made by master craftsmen! (5½" high) $12.90

080 Candy Box and Cover
The purity of lead crystal reflects the colors of your candies, flowers and bath soaps! Create an exciting ensemble of exquisite style by using the Suzanne Vase and Candy Box and Cover to complement each other. (5¼" high, 5½" dia.) $19.90

084 Salt and Pepper Set
This sparkling lead crystal design is accented with chrome metal tops. Ideally suited as a gift for weddings or anniversaries. (4" high) $15.90

WHAT IS A FLAW IN GLASS

Is a small bubble in a fine piece of stemware a flaw? How about a cord, or a mould mark? The answer is definitely no, but it's sometimes difficult to convince a customer of this.

Most dinnerware and glassware departments and specialty shops have had trouble at one time or another with customers who seek flawless perfection in the tableware merchandise they buy.

Such perfection can be achieved only in assembly-line products, of course. It is not possible or even desirable in quality ware whose manufacture depends so much on the skill and artistry of individual craftsmen.

Slight variations and tiny imperfections in glassware pieces are actually a confirmation of craftsmanship and individual artistry. Most customers who appreciate good glassware understand this. For those who don't, here is a series of questions and answers that a salesperson can use to promote better understanding of the product.

Does a "seed" or bubble in glassware constitute a flaw?

No. One of these tiny "seeds" or bubbles the size of a pinpoint may sometimes be observed in a piece of glassware when it is examined closely against a strong light.

The bubble is formed by gases when chemicals are united in the fusing or melting of the raw ingredients. It does not affect the quality or the beauty of the glass.

Should all pieces in a set be exactly alike?

No. There are almost always slight variations in diameter, height, and other dimensions in any group of tumblers, goblets, plates or other articles of glass. These variations are usually so slight that they can be detected only with a micrometer, rarely by the naked eye. This is the hallmark of the fine hand craftsmanship.

What is a cord?

A cord is an almost invisible difference in density in the glass which occurs during the fusing of the molten glass. It is visible only by reason of the fact that it reflects light. When a goblet with a cord in it is filled with water, no light is reflected and the cord becomes invisible.

Is a mould mark a sign of imperfection?

No. A mould mark is merely a ridge on a molded glassware piece that indicates the point at which the mould that formed the item was separated for removal of the finished ware. If it is overly prominent, however, it may be an indication of careless workmanship.

What is a shear mark?

A shear mark is a slight puckering of the glass caused when the artisan snips off excess molten glass when shaping the piece, as for example the end of the handle of a pitcher. It is a normal characteristic of glass and should not be considered a flaw.

Is handmade glassware really made by hand, or merely hand-finished?

The production of handmade glassware is indeed a hand process. The skilled hand and eyes of many men, working in teams, go into the making of every piece. The amazing thing is that such a high degree of excellence can be attained; that piece after piece coming from any individual or group of glass blowers or pressers is so nearly and accurately a duplicate of every other piece.

Why can't small irregularities be entirely eliminated from handmade glass?

For the very reason that the glass is handmade. No matter how deft the touch of the sensitive hands of glass craftsmen, it is impossible to eliminate completely small variations. These should not, therefore, be considered flaws. Glass is one of the trickiest materials to work with. Even machine-made glassware cannot be made absolutely perfect. But consider this: Even the finest diamond, examined under a jeweler's loupe, rarely reveals absolute perfection.

How can the salesperson and the customer judge the quality of glassware?

There are certain simple tests and guides. Look for clarity and luster by holding the piece against a pure white background. Good glassware is quite clear, while inferior grades show a cloudy bluish or greenish tinge.

Quality glass is also marked by a permanent polish or luster that results from fire-polishing. Look for smooth edges. Glassware edges should be even, never rough or scratchy. In hand-cut ware, the design should be sharp and accurate. In etched ware, each tiny detail should be distinct and clearly defined.

Fine handblown glass frequently contains lead, which improves its clarity and adds to its weight. If a piece of stemware rings with a clear musical tone when struck lightly, this indicates lead content. Lime glass, on the other hand, does not have the resonance, but this does not make it any less desirable. The lime in such glass adds to its toughness and strength.

Reprinted from China Glass & Tablewares

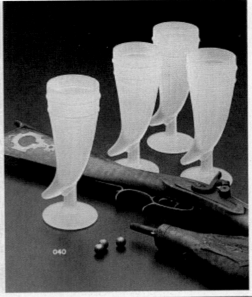

MASCULINE TOUCH

030 Hunter Horn Mugs
4 pieces — Toast friends and associates as you recapture the mood of the hunt with this handsome set of 12 ounce crystal mugs. They make a sporting gift which is appealing to masculine tastes. (5½" high) $19.90

038 Patio Tankards
4 pieces — Keep several extra sets on hand as the perfect companion to our Patio Beverage Set in crystal etched. (12 oz., 5½" high)
                                                      $24.90

039 Patio Beverage Set
5 pieces — Set the mood for fun with any gathering of your friends using this cool and zesty set in crystal etched. (50 oz. cap.)
                                                      $34.90

040 Powder Horn Tumblers
4 pieces — A reminder of our glorious heritage that any man would appreciate. (9 oz., 8" high) $24.90

We Honor

465 Set

462 Set

THE LITTLE ONE'S SERVICE

372 Set

384 Set

372 Child's Beverage Set
3 pieces — A gift to delight every little hostess you know. This pastel pink beverage set is sure to be a party pleaser with her little friends. (pitcher 5" high, tumbler 4" high) $14.90

384 Child's Service Set
3 pieces — A delicate and dainty addition for our small frys in pastel pink! (mug 8 oz., bowl 6" dia., plate 8½" dia.) $14.90

462 Child's Service Set
3 pieces — Start a family tradition with this adorable pastel blue set. Sure to be a cherished gift that will be treasured forever! (mug 8 oz., bowl 6" dia., plate 8½" dia.) $14.90

465 Child's Beverage Set
3 pieces — A unique gift for that delightful little guy and his thirsty friends in pastel blue. (pitcher 5" high, tumbler 4" high) $14.90

We Honor

CASUAL EXPRESSIONS

364

006

815

818

006 Mini Mugs
6 pieces — A must for every "pint-size" member of the group. Children love being "grown-up" with these 3½ oz. crystal etched mugs just their size! They're also great stick-in-the-closet gifts for birthdays, Easter baskets or "get well" juices for your special boys and girls. $16.90

364 Sandwich Glo Lamp
The sparkle of this chantilly green lamp and the glow of a scented candle will add homespun warmth to any room in your home. (5¾" high) $11.90

815 Adore Bud Vase
A magnificent modern design to highlight the flower of your choice. This vase in black glass offers that unusual gift for that someone you love! (8½" high) $23.50

818 German Drinking Stein
pair — The deeply etched design of these striking 11 oz. steins in black capture the spirit of the old world taverns. (6" high)
(NOT RECOMMENDED FOR HOT BEVERAGES)
                   $14.90

28

430

851

430 Tree Ornament '87
"With a sleigh full of toys" and two tiny reindeer! The delightful magic of Christmas is captured for children — young or old. on this keepsake ornament in red. (3½" dia.) $ 8.90

846 Princess Vase
This jewel-like, fashionable, and stylish vase will en-hance your floral bouquet. The premier blue color adds that elegant touch to any room. (8" high) $22.50

851 Lashea Water Bottle
Optically swirled handblown glass in premier blue adds a contemporary touch of versatility to your favorite bev-erage or freshcut flowers. (9½" high) $26.90

846

We Honor

29

DESIGNER'S CHOICE

773 Victoria Vase
The majestic curved optics of this vase adds a focal point to any room. The beauty and quiet dignity of royalty is apparent in this elegant vase in platinum. (15¼" high) $49.90

812 Branch Vase
Add an elegant touch to any room with this handblown vase. The delicate flow of design is a decorator's dream come true in black. (18¼" high) $79.90

853 Exotic Vase
Far eastern influence inspired the creation of this handblown Exotic Vase in premier blue. Complement any decor by adding fresh cut or dried flowers. (14½" high) $79.90

We Honor

020 Madonna
An extraordinary sculpture in crystal etched glass for that special accent in the home. Truly a thoughtful gift! (10" high) $29.50

770 Lord's Supper Plate
Tiara has faithfully reproduced the delicate design of this nostalgic plate in platinum to create a versatile piece for your bread service or gift-giving needs. This is one of several popular items we recommend for your club's fund raising events. (7" x 11" long) $16.90

771 Chalice
Centuries of tradition are reflected in the unique form and grace of one of Tiara's works of art! It makes a perfect companion for the Lord's Supper Plate and is sure to be cherished when received as a gift! The Chalice in platinum can be used to serve shut-ins and the elderly on sacred holidays or just to be admired with the glow of a candle on the mantel! (7" high) $ 9.50

REMEMBRANCE

TIARA'S EXCITING BOOKING PROGRAM

Free to Hostesses

When you have your giftarama and one of your friends schedules and holds a qualified giftarama (within two weeks) with $175 or more in net sales you will be sent the appreciation gift.

When two of your friends schedule and hold qualified giftaramas (within three weeks of the original giftarama) that together generate total net sales of $350 or more you can select any item listed in the two booking gift selection.

When three of your friends schedule and hold qualified giftaramas (within four weeks of the original giftarama) that together generate total net sales of $500 or more you can select any item listed in the three booking gift selection.

APPRECIATION GIFT

489 Colonial
Footed Tray
in horizon blue
(3½" high)

TWO BOOKING GIFTS

YOUR CHOICE

660 Venetian Candelamp
shade and adaptor in crystal,
base in lead crystal,
candle included
(14" high)

895 Fan Box and Cover
in chantilly green
(2⅛" x 9⅜" diam.)

149 Strawberry
Jar and Cover
in fiery ruby
(8¾" high)

813 Milady Vase
in black
(6⅝" high)

THREE BOOKING GIFTS

YOUR CHOICE

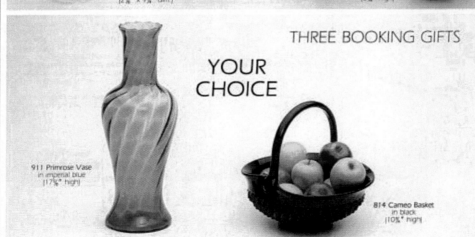

911 Primrose Vase
in imperial blue
(17⅝" high)

814 Cameo Basket
in black
(10⅜" high)

32

Hostess Plan

Tiara hostesses are treated to a premium incentive program that is almost unbelievable! It certainly pays well to be a hostess at a Tiara giftarama!

Simply invite a Tiara associate to conduct a giftarama in your home some morning, afternoon, or evening and you will have unfolded before your eyes a myriad of exclusive gifts that can be yours FREE!

For holding the giftarama within two weeks, you will receive $3 and you can add $3 more for every $20 in orders accepted! That means that an average giftarama of $200 would allow the hostess $33 in gifts of her own choosing. But that isn't all — when three giftaramas are arranged at a giftarama, the hostess would receive another $12 in gifts! Thus, a $200 giftarama with three bookings pays the hostess $45 in Tiara gifts!

In addition, the gifts of the month are available to all hostesses whose giftaramas reach specified levels of sales, making it possible for the average hostess to earn 40% or more of the total value of sales in free gifts!

Gift Certificate #545

Pictured above is Tiara's GIFT CERTIFICATE! They can be ordered in any denomination of $10 or more, in $5 increments. They are GREAT to give to loved ones when you feel they would prefer to select the items they want. Also, many hostesses use them for showers, weddings, etc.

The recipient of the GIFT CERTIFICATE merely fills in the items they desire and mails it directly to Dunkirk, Indiana. Regardless of what items are redeemed, no further shipping fee will be charged. Taxes must be paid on any amount ordered over the value of the certificate. It's THOUGHTFUL, it's EASY, it's truly an APPRECIATED gift!

The Tiara Guarantee

All Tiara gifts are guaranteed to be of fine quality and craftsmanship within the limits of the arts represented. All products are guaranteed for life, and should breakage occur, either accidental or otherwise, or any other damage, replacement will be made at fifty percent (50%) of the current price, provided the receipted shopping card is sent to Tiara Exclusives as proof of purchase. The receipted shopping card will be returned to you along with your replacement merchandise.

A fee of three dollars ($3.00) to cover packing, shipping and indemnity must be included with each order for replacement.

There shall be no limitation upon this guarantee, and replacement policy, except in the case of discontinued items, in which event, the company will no longer be responsible, or liable, for this replacement.

Shipping Fee

Tiara has established the following shipping fees for **EACH** ordering guest.

0 to $ 10.00 — Guest pays $ 1.00	$ 50.01 to $100.00 — Guest pays $ 5.00
$ 10.01 to $ 20.00 — Guest pays $ 2.00	$100.01 to $150.00 — Guest pays $10.00
$ 20.01 to $ 35.00 — Guest pays $ 3.00	$150.01 and over — Guest pays $20.00
$ 35.01 to $ 50.00 — Guest pays $ 4.00	

Tiara customers living in Alaska, Hawaii, Puerto Rico and the Virgin Islands must add 30% to the above shipping fees.

Flowers, candles, fruit and beverage are used as props in the photographs of this catalog. These are not available through Tiara Exclusives.

Credits: Coordinator - R. Kratz — Photography - Glasshouse, Muncie, IN — Propping - Pier I Imports, Muncie, IN — Color Separation - Accu-Color, Dayton, OH — Production & Typesetting - Colony Printing and Labeling, Inc., Eaton, IN.

PREFERRED HOSTESS PLAN

A preferred hostess is one selected by a counselor, who agrees to hold three or more giftaramas in her home, in a calendar year. There is NO requirement for a certain amount of sales.

Being a member of our Preferred Hostess Club affords you many extras! First, you can rebook, and not hold it within two weeks, and still receive your $3 dating credit. Secondly, your name will be entered in our computer, enabling us to keep you informed of our new products, prices and specials on a timely basis. Thirdly, when the total sales of your three or more giftaramas reach $600 in a calendar year, you will be entitled to a FREE gift! The 1987 Limited Edition Preferred Hostess Gift — #652 Lace Basket in lymon etched and handpainted (7" high) — can be yours!

Sign up NOW as a preferred hostess and earn one or more of these unique, handcrafted items! Your counselor will award you one for every $600 in sales you account for in the calendar year!

Appreciatively,

Robert E. Hatfield

Robert E. Hatfield
National Sales Leader

DATES TO REMEMBER SOMEONE YOU LOVE

Martin Luther King Day, Monday, January 12, 1987
St. Valentine's Day, Saturday, February 14, 1987
Easter, Sunday, April 19, 1987
Secretaries' Day, Wednesday, April 22, 1987
Mother's Day, Sunday, May 10, 1987
Father's Day, Sunday, June 21, 1987
Grandparent's Day, Sunday, September 13, 1987

Boss's Day, Friday, October 16, 1987
Sweetest Day, Saturday, October 17, 1987
Mother-in-law's Day, Sunday, October 25, 1987
Hanukkah, Wednesday, December 16, 1987
Christmas, Friday, December 25, 1987
New Year's Day, Friday, January 1, 1988

YOUR TIARA ASSOCIATE

Tiara 1997-98 Catalog Contents

1997-98 Gift Collection

GLASS,

CANDLES,

AND

POTPOURRI

by Tiara Exclusives

Distinctive Designs

with Contemporary Color

and Style Captures

the Essence of

Tiara Exclusives Giftware.

Trillium Collection

*Deeply cut creations with etched
highlights are combined to form
true classic designs!*

*These beautifully designed pieces
are perfect to add a touch of
elegance to any table setting!*

109   Icy Trillium Cake Plate & Dome $29.90
crystal/etch
Pastelera/Domo Icy Trillium, cristal/grabado
(10½" high, 12" dia.)

113   Icy Trillium 12" Divided Relish $12.90
crystal/etch
Platon Dividido Icy Trillium, cristal/grabado

114   Icy Trillium 12" Platter $12.90
crystal/etch
12" Platon Icy Trillium, cristal/grabado

116   Icy Trillium Chip-N-Dip $15.90
crystal/etch
*Cuenco/Fuente para Patatas Icy Trillium,
cristal/grabado*
(Includes 12" Serving Tray and 6½"
Divided Bowl.)

Index

Guarantee

All Tiara Glassware gifts are guaranteed to be of fine quality and craftsmanship within the limits of the arts represented. All glass is guaranteed for life, and should breakage occur, either accidental or otherwise, or any other damage, replacement will be made at fifty percent (50%) of the current price, provided the receipted shopping card is sent to Tiara Exclusives as proof of purchase. The receipted shopping card will be returned to you along with your replacement merchandise.

A fee of four dollars ($4.00) to cover packaging, shipping, and indemnity must be included with each order for replacement. There shall be no limitation upon this guarantee and replacement policy, except in the case of discontinued items, in which event, the Company will no longer be responsible, or liable, for this replacement.

Gift Certificate

Tiara has a terrific GIFT CERTIFICATE! This certificate can be ordered in any denomination of $10 or more, in $5 increments. It is GREAT to give to loved ones when you feel they would prefer to select their own gifts. Also, many Hostesses use them for showers, weddings, etc.

The recipient of the GIFT CERTIFICATE merely fills in the items they desire and mails it directly to Dunkirk, Indiana. Regardless of what items are selected, no further shipping fee will be charged. Taxes must be paid on any amount ordered over the value of the certificate. It's THOUGHTFUL, it's EASY, it's truly an APPRECIATED gift! Order item #20545.

We Honor

#21117

Celebrating Intimate Moments

Aromatherapy

5049 Aromatherapy $10.90
Herbal Pair
jasmine/eucalyptus
Aromaterapia Herbaceo Par
jasmin/eucalipato

5050 Aromatherapy $10.90
Natural Pair
ocean mist/peppermint
Aromaterapia Natural Par
menta/brumado

618 24 oz. Octagon Jar $12.90
spiced apple
24 onz. Tarro Llenado
fragancia manzana

3901 12 oz. Octagon Jar $9.90
spiced apple
12 onz. Tarro Llenado
fragancia manzana

4100 24 oz. Octagon Jar $12.90
fresh green apple
24 onz. Tarro Llenado
fresca manzana verde

4101 12 oz. Octagon Jar $9.90
fresh green apple
12 onz. Tarro Llenado
fresca manzana verde

Potpourri

Imagine a walk through an orchard as you enjoy the pleasing aroma of Tiara's Black Cherry Potpourri or enjoy the fresh scent of Vanilla Royale.

4002 Tiara Potpourri $5.90
vanilla royale
Popurri Tiara, vainilla real
1.5 dry quart bag

4003 Tiara Potpourri $5.90
black cherry charm
Popurri Tiara, encanto cereza
oscura
1.5 dry quart bag

A New Approach to Success

Success is a state of mind. The confident appearance and the pleasant look of successful people is a result of their ability to reach a balance between their career and their personal life. Direct sales is a path to balance in your life, and one of the most rewarding, inexpensive ways to start your own business!

Tiara products are a wonderful blend of antique design and contemporary color. The romantic and relaxing fragrances of Tiara's Lancaster Colony Candle line added to a sparkling array of dinnerware, accents, and accessories creates a product line that virtually sells itself. High pressure sales tactics aren't necessary or encouraged.

At Tiara, prosperity is based on your effort! Your age, gender, and race are, to us, not a factor. Your training is FREE. Your samples and registration fee can be *earned*. The Home Office is only as far away as your phone.

At an average of $25–$30 per hour, Tiara Associates have found a balance in their lives, and a new confidence in themselves.

Ask your Associate for details, return the postage-paid card inserted in this catalog, or call us toll free, 1-800-448-2689. We would like to help you achieve the level of success you desire!

771 Galleria Biscuit Barrel & Cover
crystal/dec. (9½" high)
*Barril Bizcocho/Tapa Galleria
cristal/dec.*

548 Wall Shelf
white (8" x 17")
Repisa de Pared, blanca

5048 Candle Combo
Combo de Vela
Includes: 24 oz. Octagon, french
vanilla; 6" Pillar, english rose;
12 pc. votives, cherry grove; and
two 8 oz. bags Shimmering Lites,
cinnamon apple.

449 Sandwich Wall Sconces, pair
spruce (8½" high)
Candelabro de Pared, abeto

955 Sandwich Wall Sconces, pair
peach (8½" high)
Candelabro de Pared, durazno

800 Classic Basket, sienna (8½" dia.)
Cesta Clásica, siena

338 Swan Oval Platter
pink/etched (14"x7½" dia.)
*Fuente Ovalada Cisne
rosado/grabado*

347 Swan Serenade Bowl
pink/etched
(9½" dia.)
*Cuenco Cisne Sereno
rosado/grabado*

021 Garden Gate Basket
aquamarine (12¼" high)
*Cesta Entrada al Jardín
aquamarina*

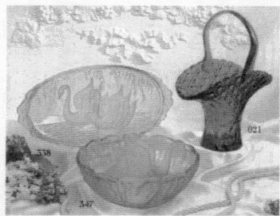
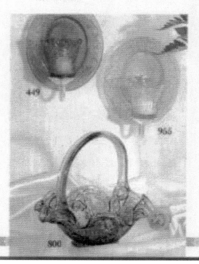

Our Hostess Treasures Program is a grouping of exclusive gifts, available only to our Hostesses!

WHEN YOUR GIFTARAMA NET SALES ARE:	$250 Level	$500 Level	$750 Level
$250 - $499	X		
$500 - $749	X	X	
$750 - $999	X	X	X

If you're not ready to make your FREE GIFT SELECTION yet, ask for a HOSTESS GOLD CERTIFICATE (#698)! These certificates can be redeemed at a later date, or combined with more HOSTESS GOLD CERTIFICATES and redeemed for a higher level! Please add $5.00 handling charge for each item selected.

$500 Level

719   Opulence Tray
24% lead crystal (13" l, 5 ¼" w)
Fuente Opulence, 24% cristal plomado

720   Opulence Ftd. Bowl
24% lead crystal (6 ¼" high)
Cuenco/Pie Opulence
24% cristal plomado

406   16 pc. Ponderosa Pine Starter Set
crystal
Vajilla Inicial 16 pzas. Ponderosa Pine
cristal

390   16 pc. Sandwich Starter Set, spruce
Vajilla Inicial 16 pzas. Sandwich, abeto

961   16 pc. Sandwich Starter Set, peach
Vajilla Inicial 16 pzas. Sandwich
Durazno

260   Diamond Lustre Basket
crystal/lustre (9" high)
Cesta Lustre Diamante, cristal/lustre

546   Swan Serenade Candle Holders, pair
pink etched (5 ¼" high)
Candeleros Cisne Serena, rosado/grabado

456   Sandwich Basket
spruce (10 ½" high) Handmade.
Cesta, abeto

061   Silhouette Two-Gallon Canister
crystal/etched
Recipiente Silhouette de 2 Galones
(12 ½" high, 8 ¾" dia.)

751 Galleria Wine Set
crystal/dec.
Juego de Vino Galleria, cristal/dec.
Includes 4 pc. 8 oz. Flutes and a 9" high,
8" dia. Wine Cooler.

062 Prestige Lamp
crystal (26" high)
Lampara Prestige, cristal

389 Royal Wedding Basket, pink
Cesta de Boda real, rosado

$750 Level

732 Empress Candy Box &
Cover
crystal/green (8" high)
*Dulcera/Tapa Empress
cristal/verde*

759 Empress Pitcher
crystal/green (64 oz.)
*Jarra Empress
cristal/verde*

058 Silhouette 2 pc. Canister
Set
crystal/etched
2 pz. Juego de Recipiente
These canisters in Tiara's
Silhouette pattern include
a one-gallon (10" high,
6 ½" dia.) and a one-half
gallon (7½" high, 5⅛" dia.).

3300	24 oz. Octagon Jar	$12.90
	24 oz. Tarro Llenado	
3301	12 oz. Octagon Jar	$9.90
	12 oz. Tarro Llenado	
3302	3" x 9" Pillar	$9.90
	Velas 3" x 9"	
3303	3" x 6" Pillar	$6.90
	Velas 3" x 6"	
094	Harmony Footed Candle Holder	$24.90
	crystal (7½" high)	
	Candelero/Pie Armonia, cristal	
208	Reflections Candle Holders	$8.90
	pair, crystal (2½" high)	
	Candeleros Reflexión, cristal	

3307	8" Taper, 12 pc.	$8.90
	unscented	
	12 pzas. 8" Velas	
3308	12" Taper, 12 pc.	$9.90
	unscented	
	12 pzas. 12" Velas	
3309	10" Formal, 12 pc.	$14.90
	unscented	
	12 pzas. 10" Velas Formal	
017	Venetian Candle Holders	$24.90
	pair, crystal (7½" high)	
	Candeleros Veneciano, cristal	
151	Bristol Candle Sticks	$49.90
	pair, crystal (9" high)	
	Candeleros Bristol, cristal	
587	Satin Daisy/Rosebud Candle Climber, spruce	$5.90
	Trepador de Vela Daisy/Rosebud de Seda, abeto	
	Flame Retardant.	

Cherry Grove

Imagine a walk through an orchard as you enjoy the pleasing aroma of Lancaster Colony Candles' Cherry Grove! The rich wine color enhances any decor. All styles are scented throughout for long-lasting fragrance with the exception of tapers and formals. (Aroma — Bosque de Cereza.)

3305	2.8" Round Ball, 6 pc.	$14.90
	6 pzas. Bolas Rendonda	
3306	12 hr. Votives, 12 pc.	$9.90
	12 pzas. Votivos	
3310	3" Carriage, 6 pc.	$9.90
	6 pzas. Velas 3" Carriage	
211	Celestial Candle Holders	$8.90
	pair, crystal (5½" dia.)	
	Candeleros Celestial, cristal	

212	Prism Votive Holders	$8.90
	pair, crystal (2" high)	
	Votivos Prisma, cristal	
219	Whitehall Candle Holders	$8.90
	pair, crystal (1½" high)	
	Candeleros Whitehall, cristal	
256	Stackable Votives, 3 pc.	$11.90
	crystal (2¼" high)	
	3 pzas. Votivos Montonables, cristal	

3500	24 oz. Octagon Jar	$12.90		6693	4" Ivy Candle Ring	$9.90
	24 onz. Tarro Llenado				4" Anillo de Vela, guia	
3501	12 oz. Octagon Jar	$9.90		208	Reflections Candle Holders	$8.90
	12 onz. Tarro Llenado				pair, crystal (2½" high)	
3502	3" x 9" Pillar	$9.90			Candeleros Reflexión, cristal	
	Velas 3" x 9"			219	Whitehall Candle Holders	$8.90
3503	3" x 6" Pillar	$6.90			pair, crystal (1½" high)	
	Velas 3" x 6"				Candeleros Whitehall, cristal	
3510	5" Carriage, 6 pc.	$9.90				
	6 pzs. Velas 5" Carriage					

Victorian Fantasy

Let your senses inhabit an English Rose Garden with the enchanting Victorian Fantasy Fragrance! English Rose is a complementary color to many settings. All styles are scented throughout with the exception of tapers and formals. (Aroma – Victoriana Fantasy.)

3507	8" Taper, 12 pc. unscented 12 pzas. 8" Velas	$8.90
3508	12" Taper, 12 pc. unscented 12 pzas. 12" Velas	$9.90
3509	10" Formal, 12 pc. unscented 12 pzas. 10" Velas Formal	$14.90
017	Venetian Candle Holders pair, crystal (7½" high) Lamparas Veneciana, cristal	$24.90
151	Bristol Candle Sticks pair, crystal (9" high) Candeleros Bristol, cristal	$49.90
6678	1" Ivy Candle Climber 1" Trepador de Vela, guia	$5.90
3505	2.8" Round Ball, 6 pc. 6 pzas. Bolas Rendonda	$14.90
3506	12 hr. Votives, 12 pc. 12 pzas. Votivas	$9.90
211	Celestial Candle Holders pair, crystal (5½" dia.) Candeleros Celestial, cristal	$8.90
212	Prism Votive Holders pair, crystal (2" high) Votivos Prisma, cristal	$8.90
256	Stackable 3 pc. Votives crystal (2½" high) 3 pzas. Votivos Montonables cristal	$11.90

Lilac Blossom

Enjoy Springtime all year long! A pleasing Lilac Blossom scent, along with the beautiful amethyst hue radiates the essence of Spring in any room. All styles are scented throughout with the exception of tapers and formals.
(Aroma — Lila Blossom.)

3407 8" Taper, 12 pc. $8.90
unscented
12 pzas. 8" Velas

3408 12" Taper, 12 pc. $9.90
unscented
12 pzas. 12" Velas

3409 10" Formal, 12 pc. $14.90
unscented
12 pzas. 10" Velas Formal

6667 1" Lilac Candle Ring $8.90
1" Anillo de Vela, lila

017 Venetian Candle $24.90
Holders
pair, crystal (7¾" high)
Candeleros Venecianos, cristal

151 Bristol Candle Sticks $49.90
pair, crystal (9" high)
Candeleros Bristol, cristal

3400 24 oz. Octagon Jar $12.90
24 onz. Tarro Llenado

3401 12 oz. Octagon Jar $9.90
12 onz. Tarro Llenado

3402 5" x 9" Pillar $9.90
Velon 5" x 9"

3403 3" x 6" Pillar $6.90
Velon 5" x 6"

3410 5" Carriage, 6 pc. $9.90
6 pzas. Velas 5" Carriage

219 Whitehall Candle $8.90
Holders
pair, crystal (1¾" high)
Candeleras Whitehall, cristal

3405 2.8" Round Ball, 6 pc. $14.90
6 pzas. Bolas Redondas

3406 12 hr. Votives, 12 pc. $9.90
12 pzas. Votivos

211 Celestial Candle $8.90
Holders
pair, crystal (5½" dia.)
Candeleros Celestial, cristal

212 Prism Votive Holders $8.90
pair, crystal (2" high)
Votivos Prisma, cristal

256 Stackable Votives $11.90
3 pc., crystal (2½" high)
3 pzas. Votivos Montonables cristal

8

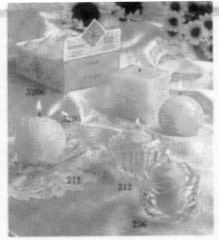

Sunburst

Create an atmosphere of warmth and sunshine with the soothing citrus fragrance of any of these candle ensembles and their cheery Sunflower color. Scented throughout from Lancaster Colony with the exception of tapers and formals. (Aroma – Citrus.)

3200	24 oz. Octagon Jar	$12.90		3210	5" Carriage, 6 pc.	$9.90
	24 onz. Tarro Llenado				*6 pzs. Velas 5" Carriage*	
3201	12 oz. Octagon Jar	$9.90		6693	4" Ivy Candle Ring	$9.90
	12 onz. Tarro Llenado				*4" Anillo de Vela, hiedra*	
3202	3" x 9" Pillar	$9.90		219	Whitehall Candle Holders	$8.90
	Velon 3" x 9"				pair, crystal (1½" high)	
3205	3" x 6" Pillar	$6.90			*Candeleros Whitehall, cristal*	
	Velon 3" x 6"					

3205 2.8" Round Ball, 6 pc. $14.90
6 pzas. Bolas Redondas

3206 12 hr. Votives, 12 pc. $9.90
12 pzas. Votivos

211 Celestial Candle Holders $8.90
pair, crystal (5⅛" dia.)
Candeleros Celestial, cristal

212 Prism Votive Holders $8.90
pair, crystal (2" high)
Votivos Prisma, cristal

256 Stackable Votives $11.90
3 pc., crystal (2¾" high)
3 pzas. Votivos Montonables cristal

3207 8" Taper, 12 pc. $8.90
unscented
12 pzas. 8" Velas

3208 12" Taper, 12 pc. $9.90
unscented
12 pzas. 12" Velas

3209 10" Formal, 12 pc. $14.90
unscented
12 pzas. 10" Velas Formal

6678 1" Ivy Candle Climber $5.90
1" Trepador de Vela, guia

017 Venetian Candle Holders $24.90
pair, crystal (7½" high)
Candeleros Venecianos, cristal

151 Bristol Candle Sticks $49.90
pair, crystal (9" high)
Candeleros Bristol, cristal

Radiant Blossoms of Sunflower Candles will brighten up your home like a summer's day! Perfect gift ideas inspired by nature itself!

Evergreen Mist

Add a touch of nature to your decor with the pine fragrance of Evergreen Mist and its elegant shade of Ivy.

(Aroma – Bruma Siempre Verde.)

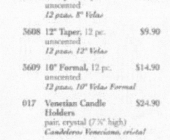

3607	8" Taper, 12 pc. unscented *12 pzas. 8" Velas*	$8.90
3608	12" Taper, 12 pc. unscented *12 pzas. 12" Velas*	$9.90
3609	10" Formal, 12 pc. unscented *12 pzas. 10" Velas Formal*	$14.90
017	Venetian Candle Holders pair, crystal (7¾" high) *Candeleros Veneciano, cristal*	$24.90
135	Kristina Candle Sticks pair, crystal (7¾" high) *Candeleros Kristina, cristal*	$49.90

3600	24 oz. Octagon Jar *24 onz. Tarro Llenado*	$12.90
3601	12 oz. Octagon Jar *12 onz. Tarro Llenado*	$9.90
3602	3" x 9" Pillar *Velas 3" x 9"*	$9.90
3603	3" x 6" Pillar *Velas 3" x 6"*	$6.90

3610	5" Carriage, 6 pc. *6 pzas. Velas 5" Carriage*	$9.90
219	Whitehall Candle Holders pair, crystal (1¾" high) *Candeleros Whitehall, cristal*	$8.90
224	4 pc. Sandwich Coasters crystal (4½" dia.) *St. Salvamanteles 4 piezas cristal*	$14.90

3605	2.8" Round Ball, 6 pc. *6 pzas. Bolas Redonda*	$14.90
3606	12 hr. Votives, 12 pc. *12 pzas. Votivos*	$9.90
211	Celestial Candle Holders pair, crystal (5½" dia.) *Candeleros Celestial, cristal*	$8.90
212	Prism Votive Holders pair, crystal (2" high) *Votivos Prisma, cristal*	$8.90
256	Stackable Votives, 5 pc. crystal *5 pzas. Votivos Montonables cristal*	$11.90

French Vanilla

Experience the romance of this warm fragrance inspired by nature and the soft ambiance of this rich creamy color.

(Aroma – French Vainilla.)

3107	8" Taper, 12 pc. unscented *12 pzas. 8" Velas*	$8.90
3108	12" Taper, 12 pc. unscented *12 pzas. 12" Velas*	$9.90
3109	10" Formal, 12 pc. unscented *12 pzas. 10" Velas Formal*	$14.90
017	Venetian Candle Holders pair, crystal (7¼" high) *Candeleros Veneciano, cristal*	$24.90
151	Bristol Candle Sticks pair, crystal (9" high) *Candeleros Bristol, cristal*	$49.90
679	1" Peach Candle Climber *Trepador de Vela de 1" durazno*	$5.90

3100	24 oz. Octagon Jar *24 onz. Tarro Llenado*	$12.90
3101	12 oz. Octagon Jar *12 onz. Tarro Llenado*	$9.90
3102	3" x 9" Pillar *Velon 3" x 9"*	$9.90
3103	3" x 6" Pillar *Velon 3" x 6"*	$6.90
3110	5" Carriage, 6 pc. *6 pzas. Velas 5" Carriage*	$9.90
208	Reflections Candle Holders pair, crystal (2¼" high) *Candeleros Reflexion, cristal*	$8.90
219	Whitehall Candle Holders pair, crystal (1¾" high) *Candeleros Whitehall, cristal*	$8.90
608	Silk Roses 5" Candle Ring, peach *Anillo de Vela Rosas de Seda 5" durazno*	$8.90

3105	2.8" Round Ball 6 pc. *6 pzas. Bolas Redonda*	$14.90
3106	12 hr. Votives 12 pc. *12 pzas. Votivos*	$9.90
211	Celestial Candle Holders pair, crystal (5½" dia.) *Candeleros Celestial, cristal*	$8.90
212	Prism Votive Holders pair, crystal (2" high) *Votivos Prisma, cristal*	$8.90
256	Stackable Votives 3 pc., crystal (2¼" high) *3 pzas. Votivos Montonables cristal*	$11.90

3007 8" Taper, 12 pc. $8.90
    unscented
    12 pzas. 8" Velas

3008 12" Taper, 12 pc. $9.90
    unscented
    12 pzas. 12" Velas

3009 10" Formal, 12 pc. $14.90
    unscented
    12 pzas. 10" Velas Formal

017 Venetian Candle $24.90
    Holders
    pair, crystal (7⅝" high)
    Candeleros Veneciana, cristal

155 Kristina Candle Sticks $49.90
    pair, crystal (7¾" high)
    Candeleros Kristina, cristal

Fragrant Gardenia

Capture the glory of Gardenias in your own home with the enchanting scent of this exclusive collection of candles. The snowy palette of Alabaster illuminates any room setting! (Aroma – Gardenia.)

3000	24 oz. Octagon Jar *24 oz. Tarro Llenado*	$12.90
3001	12 oz. Octagon Jar *12 oz. Tarro Llenado*	$9.90
3002	3" x 9" Pillar *Velas 3" x 9"*	$9.90
3003	3" x 6" Pillar *Velas 3" x 6"*	$6.90

3010	5" Carriage, 6pc. *6 pzas. Velas 5" Carriage*	$9.90
208	Reflections Candle Holders pair, crystal (2¼" high) *Candeleros Reflexion, cristal*	$8.90
219	Whitehall Candle Holders pair, crystal (1½" high) *Candeleros Whitehall, cristal*	$8.90

3005 2.8" Round Ball, 6pc. $14.90
    6 pzas. Belas Redonda

3006 12 hr. Votives, 12 pc. $9.90
    12 pzas. Votivas

3011 Tea Lights, 6 pc. $2.90
    6 pzas. Lucitas de Te'

211 Celestial Candle $8.90
    Holders
    pair, crystal (5½" dia.)
    Candeleros Celestial, cristal

212 Prism Votive Holders $8.90
    pair, crystal (2" high)
    Votivas Prisma, cristal

256 Stackable Votives $11.90
    3 pc., crystal (2½" high)
    3 pzas. Votivas Mantonables cristal

Wild Berries

In early summer nature sings a rhapsody in blue. With the Wild Berry fragrance and the Indigo color of this candle collection you're sure to hear her song! (Aroma – Moras Silvestre.)

3707	8" Taper, 12 pc. unscented *12 pzas. 8" Velas*	$8.90
3708	12" Taper, 12 pc. unscented *12 pzas. 12" Velas*	$9.90
3709	10" Formal, 12 pc. unscented *12 pzas. 10" Velas Formal*	$14.90
017	Venetian Candle Holders pair, crystal (7 ½" high) *Candeleros Venecianos, cristal*	$24.90
135	Kristina Candle Sticks Holders pair, crystal (7 ½" high) *Candeleros Kristina, cristal*	$49.90

3700	24 oz. Octagon Jar *24 onz. Tarro Llenado*	$12.90	
3701	12 oz. Octagon Jar *12 onz. Tarro Llenado*	$9.90	
3702	3" x 9" Pillar *Velon 3" x 9"*	$9.90	
3703	3" x 6" Pillar *Velon 3" x 6"*	$6.90	
3710	5" Carriage, 6 pc. *6 pzas. Velas 5" Carriage*	$9.90	
219	Whitehall Candle Holders pair, crystal (18" high) *Candeleros Whitehall, cristal*		$8.90
224	4 pc. Sandwich Coasters crystal (4½" dia.) *St. Salvamanteles 4 piezas, cristal*		$14.90
6678	1" Ivy Candle Climber *1" Trepador de Vela, guia*		$5.90

Tiara's wide array of colors and fragrances provides the discriminating consumer a large selection to choose from!

3705	2.8" Round Ball, 6 pc. *6 pzas. Bolas Redondas*	$14.90
3706	12 hr. Votives, 12 pc. *12 pzas. Votivos*	$9.90
211	Celestial Candle Holders pair, crystal (5½" dia.) *Candeleros Celestial, cristal*	$8.90
212	Prism Votive Holders pair, crystal (2" high) *Votivos Prisma, cristal*	$8.90
256	Stackable Votives 3 pc., crystal (2½" high) *3 pzas. Votivos Montonables cristal*	$11.90

6683 3" Tulip Candle Ring $9.90
wine
Anillo de Vela Tulipan, vino

608 Silk Roses 3" Candle Ring $8.90
peach
Anillo de Vela Rosas de Seda 3"
durazno

626 Silk Roses 3" Candle Ring $8.90
spruce
Anillo de Vela Rosas de Seda 3"
abeto

6681 3" Rose Candle Ring $9.90
vanilla
Anillo de Vela Rosa de 3"
vainilla

6682 3" Rose Candle Ring $9.90
mauve
Anillo de Vela Rosas de 3"
malva

008 Egg, crystal $9.90
(5½" high x 4½" length)
Huevo, cristal

009 Polar Bear Votive $7.90
crystal etched (3" high)
Votivo Oso Polar
cristal/grabado

704 Pineapple Votive $8.90
Holders, crystal
pair (4" high)
Votivos Forma Piña
cristal, par
Use with your favorite votives
or Shimmering Lites!

839 Elephant $19.90
imperial blue (4½" high)
Elefante, azul imperial

236 Lord's Supper Tray $17.90
crystal/etched (7" x 11")
Santa Cena del Señor
cristal/grabado

509 2 pc. 5" Easels $9.90
pair, clear plastic
Pintores, par, claro plastico

511 2 pc. 8" Easels $11.90
pair, clear plastic
Pintores, par, claro plastico

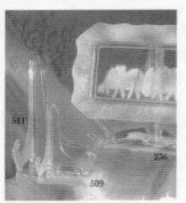

Finishing Touches

669

845   **Aurora Table Lamp** $39.90
crystal/plum (8½" high)
Handmade.
*Lampara de Mesa, cristal/azul
rejiso*

692   **Patio Lite** $12.90
crystal/white (7½" high)
Luz de Patio, blanco
Shimmering Lites not included.

091   **2 pc. Starburst Votives** $9.90
blue topaz
*2 piezas Votivos Starburst
topacio azul*

845

669   **Ponderosa Pine** $9.90
Clearfire Candle
Ponderosa Pine Vela Clearfire

4520   **Shimmering Lites** $12.90
black cherry (2 – 8 oz. Bags)
Luz Tremalante, cereza oscura

4530   **Shimmering Lites** $12.90
vanilla (2 – 8 oz. Bags)
Luz Tremalante, vainilla

4500   **Shimmering Lites** $12.90
peach (2 – 8 oz. Bags)
Luz Tremalante, durazno

4510   **Shimmering Lites** $12.90
cinnamon apple (2 – 8 oz. Bags)
*Luz Tremalante, canela
manzana*

*Each Bag of Shimmering Lites
includes 4 wicks.*

692

091

4500
4530
4510
4520

671   **Heart Vase Clearfire Candle** $14.90
cinnamon apple (5" high)
Vaso Forma Corazon Clearfire
This newly patented idea from
Candle-lite burns much slower than
regular candle wax and will provide
many hours of enjoyment. (5" high)

671

15

Classic Accents

575 Sandwich Votive Tree $12.90
black (11" high)
Arbol Votivo Sandwich, noir
(Votive Holders available on
page 23 and 26.)

539 Heart Votive Tree $9.90
black (8½" high)
Arbol Votivo Corazon, noir
Includes three crystal votive cups.

595 Angel Ring $44.90
pewter (4½" dia.)
Anillo de Angle, peltre
Genuine pewter cast exclusively
for Tiara. (Candle not included.)

557 Octagon Jar Basket $11.90
black (10" high)
Costa Tarro Octagono, noir
The perfect holder for our 24 oz.
and 12 oz. Octagons.
(Candle not included.)

612 Pillar Stand $12.90
black (9½" high)
Sostenedor de Velon, noir
Holds a 9" or 6" Pillar.
(Candle not included.)

057 14" Hurricane Shade $14.90
crystal (5" dia. base)
Pantalla de Cristal para Vela 14"

551 Hurricane Cradle $12.90
brass (12½" l, 3½" w)
Soporte de Huracan, bronce
Perfect support for #057,
14" Hurricane Shade.

6682 3" Rose Candle Ring $9.90
mauve
*Anillo de Vela Rosas de 3"
malva*

16

Captivating Crystal

These complementary pieces reflect the inherent beauty of glass, capturing the brilliant reflections of light. Accent your candle collection with any of these pieces.

069	7¼" Daisy Vase crystal *Vase Grande Margarita,* *cristal*	$19.90
049	5½" Daisy Vase crystal *Vase Pequeño Margarita,* *cristal*	$14.90
553	Marbles crystal (4 – 100 pc. packs) *Canicas, cristal*	$9.90

212	Prism Votive Holders pair, crystal (2" high) *Votivos Prisma, cristal*	$8.90
256	Stackable 3 pc. Votives crystal (2½" high) *3 pzas. Votivos Montonables* *cristal*	$11.90
211	Celestial Candle Holders pair, crystal (5½" dia.) *Candeleros Celestial, cristal*	$8.90

219	Whitehall Candle Holders pair, crystal (1⅛" high) *Candeleros Whitehall, cristal*	$8.90
208	Reflections Candle Holders pair, crystal (2½" high) *Candeleros Reflexión, cristal*	$8.90
224	4 pc. Sandwich Coasters crystal (4½" dia.) *St. Salvamanteles 4 pzas.* *cristal*	$14.90

17

Sandwich Peach

Our Silhouettes Stemware is perfect for your
formal dining occasions.

740   2 pc. Wine $24.90
     peach/crystal (8 oz.)
     Vino 2 piezas
     durazno/cristal

741   2 pc. Goblet $24.90
     peach/crystal (12 oz.)
     Copa 2 piezas
     durazno/cristal

742   2 pc. Flute $24.90
     peach/crystal (5 ¾ oz.)
     Champán 2 piezas
     durazno/cristal

Enter a world of romance and nostalgia with
Tiara's Sandwich Peach Collection. Its antique design
will add warmth and beauty to any table setting.

Classic Tones

968   24 pc. Sandwich Collection $94.90
peach
Colección de 24 piezas, durazno
Includes: 4 Tumblers,
4 Dinner Plates, 4 Salad Plates, 4 Cups, 4 Saucers,
2 Vegetable Bowls, and a Salt & Pepper Set.
(Regularly $120.50.) *Save $25.60!*

Hostesses: This cannot be taken as a 1/2-price item!

934 *Sd. Salad Plate $18.90
peach (8" dia.)
*Plato para Ensalada, durazno

945 *Sd. Coffee Cup $14.90
peach (9 oz.)
*Taza de Cafe, durazno

946 *Sd. Saucer $15.90
peach (6⅜" dia.)
*Platillo, durazno

947 *Sd. Dinner Plate $22.90
peach (10" dia.)
*Plato de Cena, durazno

948 *Sd. Tumbler $19.90
peach (10 oz.)
*Vaso, durazno

961 Sd. 16 pc. Starter Set $62.90
peach (Includes: 934, 945, 946,
and 947.) Save $7.70!
Vajilla de 16 piezas, durazno

929 *Sd. Soup Bowl $19.90
peach (22 oz.)
Cuenco para sopa, durazno

959 Sd. Salt & Pepper $14.90
peach (4½" high)
Salero y Pimientero, durazno

*Packaged in four-piece sets.
*Empaquetado en juegos de 4 piezas.

929

959

Peach Accents

954

948

945

946

947

20

Complementary Selections

Complete your table setting by choosing
your favorites from these additional
peach items! These additions are
sure to bring warmth and beauty
to any table setting!

928   Sandwich Two-Tier $19.90
     Tidbit Tray, peach (9½" high)
     *Bandeja de 2 pizos para Bocaditos
     durazno*

950   Sd. 2 pc. Vegetable $14.90
     Bowls, peach (8" dia.)
     *Cuencos para Verduras 2 piezas
     durazno*

927   Sandwich 4 pc. Table Wine $19.90
     peach (8½ oz.)
     *Vasos de Vino para Mesa Sandwich
     4 piezas, durazno*

953   Sandwich 64 oz. Pitcher $19.90
     peach
     Jarra, durazno

956   Sandwich Crimped Salad Bowl $12.90
     peach (10" dia.)
     Cuenco de Ensalada Borde Rizado, durazno

Elegant Accessories

*Serving guests from elegant Sandwich accessories
will turn entertaining into a special occasion. Choose from a
wide array of accessories and serve your guests in style.*

398 6 pc. Floral Medley $13.90
12 oz. Beverage
*Juego de Vasos para Refrescos
6 piezas, 12 onzas*

974 Flowers and Lace $9.90
4 pc. 12 oz. Beverage
*Vasos para Refrescos, 4 piezas
12 onzas*

978 Sandwich Wall Clock $54.90
peach (12" dia. Battery not included.)
Reloj, durazno

987 Sandwich Small Canister $14.90
peach (5¼" high, 26 oz. capacity)
Recipiente Pequeno, durazno

988 Sandwich Medium Canister $16.90
peach (7¼" high, 38 oz. capacity)
Recipiente Mediano, durazno

989 Sandwich Large Canister $18.90
peach (8¾" high, 52 oz. capacity)
Recipiente Grande, durazno

996 Sandwich 5 pc. Canister Set $45.90
peach (Consists of one each: Small,
Medium, and Large.) *Save $4.80!
Juego de 5 Recipientes, durazno*

Soft Patterns

900 Sd. Puff Box $12.90
peach
*Sd. Envase de Albajas
durazno*
This set includes two puff
box bottoms with one lid.
These stackable puff
boxes are perfect for
powder, jewelry or
trinket items.

970   Sd. 12" Three-Part $12.90
Relish Tray
peach
Bandeja de 3 compartimientos
durazno

971   Sd. 12" Egg Tray $12.90
peach
Bandeja para Huevos, durazno

972   Sd. 12" Platter $12.90
peach
Platón, durazno

689   Sd. 3 pc. Buffet Set $34.90
peach
Juego de Aperitivos 3 piezas
durazno
Includes: Platter, Three-Part
Relish, and Egg Tray.
Save 3.80!

958

951

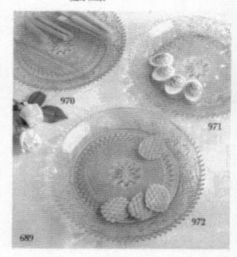

970

971

972

689

954

908

956

910   Sandwich Glo Lamp $10.90
peach (5½" high)
Lámpara Glo Lamp Sandwich
durazno

910

908   Sd. 4 pc. Sherbet $18.90
peach (3½" high)
Juego de Helado, 4 piezas
durazno

951   Sd. 8 pc. Snack Set $29.90
peach
Juego de 8 piezas para
Merienda, durazno
Includes: 4 Oval Trays with
special ring design to hold the
4 Juice Glasses included in the
set.

954   Sd. 2 pc. Oval Trays $9.90
peach (8½" x 6¾")
Bandejas Ovaladas, 2 piezas
durazno

956   Sd. 2 pc. Crimped $9.90
Votives, peach (3 ½" high,
candles included.)
Candelero de Votivo con Borde
Rizado, 2 piezas, durazno

958   Sd. 4 pc. Juice $14.90
Glasses, peach (7 oz.)
Vasos para Jugo, 4 piezas
durazno

96

8.90

5.90

23

Experience the captivation of the Sandwich spruce pattern. Its warm, rich tones have quickly become a favorite among Sandwich collectors.

Silhouettes

Complement your Spruce collection with Tiara's elegant stemware.

244 2 pc. Wine $24.90
     spruce/crystal (8 oz.)
     Vino 2 piezas, abeto/cristal

245 2 pc. Flute $24.90
     spruce/crystal (5¼ oz.)
     Champán 2 piezas, abeto/cristal

246 2 pc. Goblet $24.90
     spruce/crystal (12 oz.)
     Copa 2 piezas, abeto/cristal

Sandwich Spruce

For over 160 years, the lacy design of Sandwich glassware has been a traditional favorite among dinnerware enthusiasts.

468 **24 pc. Sandwich** **$94.90**
Collection, spruce
Colección de 24 piezas abeto
Includes: 4 Tumblers,
4 Dinner Plates,
4 Salad Plates, 4 Cups, 4
Saucers, 2 Vegetable Bowls,
and Salt & Pepper Set.
(Regularly $120.50.)
Save $25.60!

*Hostesses: This cannot be
taken as a 1/2-price item!*

596 **Honey Dish** **$14.90**
spruce (6" high)
*Recipiente de Miel/Tapa
abeto*

596

Spruce Accents

484	*Sd. Tumbler	$19.90	spruce (10 oz.) *Vaso, abeto*
487	*Sd. Coffee Cup	$14.90	spruce (9 oz.) *Taza de Café, abeto*
488	*Sd. Salad Plate	$18.90	spruce (8" dia.) *Plato para Ensalada, abeto*
493	*Sd. Dinner Plate	$22.90	spruce (10" dia.) *Plato de Cena, abeto*
820	*Sd. Soup Bowl	$19.90	spruce (6¼" dia.) *Cuenco para Sopa, abeto*
390	16 pc. Sd. Starter Set	$62.90	spruce (Includes: 488, 493, 445, and 487.) *Save $7.70!* *Vajilla Inicial 16 pzas. Sandwich abeto*

436 Sd. Salt & Pepper $14.90
spruce (4½" high)
Salero y Pimientero, abeto

447 Sd. 2 pc. Crimped Votives $9.90
spruce (3½" high)
Candles included.
Votivos Sd. 2 pzas., abeto

524 *Corn-on-the-Cob $19.90
Holders, spruce (8½" long)
Sostenedores Mazorca de Maíz, abeto

445 *Sd. Saucer $13.90
spruce (6½" dia.)
Platillo, abeto

*Packaged in four-piece sets.
*Empaquetado en juegos de 4 piezas.

26

Elegant Simplicity

*Sandwich dinnerware is perfect for the most elegant
to simplest of affairs. Guests will love the beauty of the
pattern. You'll love the versatility.*

483 Sd. 64 oz. Pitcher $19.90
     spruce
     Jarra, abeto

484 *Sd. Tumbler $19.90
     spruce
     Vaso, abeto, 4 piezas

486 Sd. Wall Clock $54.90
     spruce
     (12" dia. Battery not included.)
     Reloj, abeto

489 Sd. 2 pc. Vegetable $14.90
     Bowls, spruce (8" dia.)
     *Cuencos para Verduras, abeto
     2 piezas*

476 Sd. 3 pc. Buffet Set $54.90
     spruce
     Juego de Aperitivo 3 piezas, abeto
     Includes: Platter, Three–Part
     Relish, and Egg Tray.
     Save $3.80

485 Sd. Two–Tier Tidbit $19.90
     Tray, spruce (9½" high)
     *Bandeja de 2 pisos para Bocaditos
     abeto*

490 Sd. 12" Platter $12.90
     spruce
     Platón, abeto

491 Sd. 12" Egg Tray $12.90
     spruce
     Bandeja para Huevos, abeto

492 Sd. 12" Three–Part $12.90
     Relish Tray, spruce
     *Bandeja de 3 Compartimientos
     abeto*

     *Packaged in four-piece sets.
     Empaquetado en juegos de 4 piezas.

27

Complement your Spruce
collection with Tiara's timeless
ensembles! Complete your
table setting with the new
Spruce Water Goblets!

448 Sd. 2 pc. Oval Trays $9.90
     spruce (8½" x 6¾")
     Bandejas Ovaladas, 2 piezas,
     abeto

549 Sd. 4 pc. Sherbets $18.90
     spruce (3½" high)
     Juego de Helado, 4 piezas, abeto

417 Sandwich 4 pc. Goblets $19.90
     spruce (8 oz.)
     Sandwich Copa, abeto

Timeless Ensembles

28

Distinguished Charm

The refined beauty of the Sandwich pattern will never
go out of style. Its distinguished charm demands repeating. Look
for Sandwich items reintroduced from a bygone era.

457   Sd. Crimped Salad Bowl $12.90
spruce (10" dia.)
*Cuenco de Ensalada Borde Rizado
abeto*

480   Sd. Medium Canister $16.90
spruce
(7 ½" high, 38 oz. capacity)
Recipiente Mediano, abeto

457   Sd. 3 pc. Medium $45.90
Canister Set, spruce
Save $4.80!
*Sd. 3 pzas. Recipientes Grande
abeto*
(Consists of 3- #480.)

588   Sd. Footed Compote $14.90
spruce
Sd. Compota de Pie, abeto

464   Sd. 8 pc. Snack Set $29.90
spruce
*Juego para Merienda 8 piezas
abeto*
Includes: 4 Oval Trays with
special ring design to hold the 4
Juice Glasses included in the set.

465   Sd. 4 pc. Juice Glasses $14.90
spruce (7 oz.)
Vaso para Jugo, 4 piezas, abeto

Ponderosa Pine

140 24 pc. Ponderosa Pine $94.90
Collection, crystal
Colección de 24 piezas, cristal
Includes: 4 Ice Teas, 4 Dinner Plates,
4 Salad Plates, 4 Juice Glasses,
4 Mugs, 2 Vegetable Bowls,
and Salt & Pepper Set.
(Regularly $122.30.) *Save $27.40!*
*Hostesses: This cannot be taken as
a 1/2-price item!*

165 *Ponderosa Pine Individual $18.90
Salad Bowl, crystal (5" dia.)
*Cuencos Individuales para Ensalada
cristal*

174 *Ponderosa Pine $19.90
Handled Beverage
crystal (13 oz.)
*Vaso con Asa para Refrescos
cristal*

*Packaged in four-piece sets.
*Empaquetado en juego de 4 piezas.

*Experience the wonder of the
pure and natural life with Tiara's
Ponderosa Pine Collection.*

161 *Ponderosa Pine Mug $15.90
   crystal (9 oz.)
   *Vaso con Asa para Refresco
   cristal

162 *Ponderosa Pine Juice $15.90
   crystal (9 oz.)
   *Vaso para Jugo, cristal

167 Ponderosa Pine $12.90
   Salt & Pepper
   crystal (4½" high)
   Salero y Pimientero, cristal

Dinnerware Basics

154 *Ponderosa Pine $18.90
   Soup Bowl, crystal (22 oz.)
   *Cuenco para Sopa, cristal

160 *Ponderosa Pine 10" $22.90
   Dinner Plate, crystal
   *Plato de Cena, cristal

163 *Ponderosa Pine Goblet $19.90
   crystal (12 oz.)
   *Copa, cristal

166 *Ponderosa Pine $17.90
   8" Salad Plate, crystal
   *Plato para Ensalada, cristal

172 *Ponderosa Pine Ice Tea $19.90
   crystal (18 oz.)
   *Vaso para Té Helado, cristal

*Packaged in four-piece sets.
*Empaquetado en juego de 4 piezas.

406 16 pc. Ponderosa Pine $68.90
   Starter Set, crystal
   Juego Ponderosa Pine Inicial
   16 pzas., cristal
   Includes: 160, 161, 163, and 166.
   (Regularly $76.60.) Save $7.70!

176   Ponderosa Pine 2 pc. $16.90
     Chip-N-Dip
     crystal
     Cuenco y Fuente para Patatas
     Fritas y Salsas, 2 piezas, cristal
     Includes: 12¾" Serving Tray and
     5" diameter Bowl.

253   Ponderosa Pine $19.90
     Two-Tier Tidbit Tray
     crystal (9½" high)
     Fuente Dos Pisos P. Pine, cristal

168   Ponderosa Pine $11.90
     Serving Plate
     crystal (12¾" dia.)
     Plato de Servicio, cristal

169   Pondrosa Pine $11.90
     Three-Part Relish Tray
     crystal (12¾" dia.)
     Bandeja de 3 Compartimientos
     cristal

170   Ponderosa Pine $11.90
     Egg Tray
     crystal (12¾" dia.)
     Bandeja para Huevos, cristal

Nature's Reflections

519   Ponderosa Pine 3 pc. Buffet Set $31.90
     crystal
     Juego de 3 piezas para Aperitivos, cristal
     Includes: Platter, Egg Tray, and Three-Part
     Relish. *Save $3.80!*

159   Ponderosa Pine Pitcher $19.90
     crystal (74 oz.)
     Jarra, cristal

164   Ponderosa Pine Salad Bowl $16.90
     crystal (9½" dia.)
     Cuenco para Ensalada, cristal

173   Ponderosa Pine 2 pc. $16.90
     Vegetable Bowls, crystal (7½" dia.)
     Cuencos para Verduras, cristal, 2 pzas.

709 Laurice Vase $59.90
24% lead crystal (7½" high)
Vase Laurice
24% cristal plomado
Showcase this brilliant masterpiece by Fostoria in any room
setting.

718 Laurice Votive $19.90
Holder
24% lead crystal
(3½" dia., 3½" high)
Laurice Envase Votivo
24% cristal plomado

191 Whitehall Lamp $49.90
crystal (22" high)
Lámpara Whitehall, cristal

701 Swan Bowl $46.90
24% lead crystal
Cuenco Cisne
24% cristal plomad
True classics, treasured
keepsakes by Fostoria.

055 Sandwich $12.90
Picture Frame
crystal (6" x 7½")
Marco para Foto Sandwich
cristal
This item can be positioned
as shown or vertically to
hold a 3½" x 5" photo.

220 Sandwich 6 pc. $19.90
Oval Snack Trays, crystal
(8½" x 6½")
6 pz. Bandejas Ovaladas de
Aperetivos Sandwich, cristal
A delightful way to serve
cake, nuts, and punch at
your festivities!

250 Sandwich 14 pc. $59.90
Punch Set, crystal
14 pzas. Juego Ponche
Sandwich cristal
Includes: 9 qt. Bowl, 12
Cups, and a clear Acrylic
Ladle.

252 Sandwich 12 pc. $24.90
Extra Punch Cups, crystal
12 pzas. Taza de Ponche
Sandwich Extra, cristal

137 Cake Knife $24.90
lead crystal (13" long)
Cuchillo para Tortas
cristal plomado

138 Cake Server $24.90
lead crystal (11" long)
Servidor de Torta, cristal
plomado

090   **Silhouette Pitcher** $39.90
crystal (60 oz.)
Silhouette Jarra, cristal

071   **Brio Margarita Set** $46.90
crystal
Juego Margarita Brio, cristal
Handmade in Turkey. Brio by Colony
includes an 85 oz. pitcher and 4 pc. 12 oz.
goblets.

079   **Silhouette 4 pc. Tumblers** $24.90
crystal (12 oz.)
Silhouette 4 piezas Vasos, cristal

081   **Silhouette Candle Lamp** $29.90
crystal (10" high)
Silhouette Lampara de Vela, cristal
The soft glow of candle light will
beautify your table setting. Each
candle lamp comes with a 6" peach
taper. Change the candle and decorate
the lamp to fit the changing seasons!

092   **Silhouette Candle Lamp** $54.90
pair
Silhouette Lampara de Vela, par
Save on the pair. A pair of these would
glow beautifully on a mantel top.

Exceptional
Clarity

Sparkling Facets

206   Pitcher $14.90
      crystal (32 oz.)
      Jarra, cristal

207   *Double Old Fashion $19.90
      crystal (11 oz.)
      Vaso al Estilo Antigua, cristal

209   *Beverage/Highball $19.90
      crystal (15 oz.)
      *Vaso para Refrescos/Copas
      cristal*

213   *Wine/Juice $24.90
      crystal (7 oz.)
      Copa de Vino/Jugo, cristal

217   *Goblet $27.90
      crystal (9 oz.)
      Copa, cristal

392   Suzanne Vase $14.90
      black (7½" high)
      Jarron para Flores, noir

001   *Powder Horn Mug $28.90
      crystal etched (9 oz., 8" high)
      *Vaso con asa forma cuerno
      cristal/grabado*
      A great gift for all the men in
      your life!

030   *Hunter Horn Mug $25.90
      crystal (12 oz.)
      *Vaso con Asa Forma Trompeta
      de Caza, cristal*

085   Colonial Candy Box $11.90
      & Cover, crystal (5¼" high)
      Caja para Dulces/Tapa, cristal
      This unique design, reminiscent
      of Colonial America, is a salute
      to the forefathers of our great
      country.

      *Packaged in four-piece sets.
      *Empaquetado en juegos de
      4 piezas.

017 Venetian Candle Holder $24.90
pair, crystal (7⅜" high)
Candeleros Veneciano, cristal

018 Venetian Candle Lamp $28.90
crystal (14½" high)
*Lampara Veneciano para Velas
cristal*
Includes: crystal base, shade,
adaptor, and taper candle.

019 Suzanne Vase $12.90
crystal (7½" high)
Jarron para Flores, cristal

057 14" Hurricane Shade $14.90
crystal (5" dia. base)
Pantalla de cristal para vela, 16"

572 Globe and Adaptor $18.90
crystal
Globo y Adaptador, cristal
Turn your favorite candlestick
into a candle lamp by adding our
glass adaptor and elegant venetian globe. (Candle holder and
candle are not included.)

020 Madonna $59.90
crystal/etched (10" high)
Madonna, cristal grabada
A timeless masterpiece, handcrafted exclusively for Tiara.

236 Lord's Supper Tray $17.90
crystal/etched (7" x 11")
*Santa Cena del Señor
cristal/grabado*

*Designed for Tiara, our cross necklace is
produced at Dalzell-Viking. Each cross
measures 1½" x 1¼" and comes with a
40" satin cord and an elegant white box
ready for gift giving.*

146 Cross Necklace $19.90
crystal/etched, black cord
Collar Con Cruz, cristal/grabado
Adjust the satin cord to any
desired length!

232 2 pc. Chalice Set $16.90
crystal/etched (7" high)
*Chalice 2 piezas
cristal/grabado*
These beautiful chalices will hold a
favorite beverage or votive candle.

Springtime Look

Create an atmosphere of warmth and springtime with Tiara's new Sunswept collection. Each item is handcrafted at L.E. Smith and is sure to brighten any setting.

363 Sunswept Basket $29.90
pink (7½" high)
Cesta Barida de Sol, rosado

368 Sunswept Lamp $34.90
pink (7½" high)
Lámpara Barida de Sol, rosado

365 Sunswept Glo Ball $27.90
pink/crystal (5½" high)
Resplandor Redonda Barida de Sol, rosado/grabado

301 Radiance Basket $56.90
yellow (8½" high)
Cesta Radiance, amarillo

These items will add warmth and sunshine to any setting! Brighten up your decor with this unique color of glass!

37

Handled With Care

Step into those carefree days of make
believe once again and experience the
magic of Mother Goose and her
nursery rhyme friends.

462 3 pc. Child's Service Set $17.90
blue
Servico de Niños 3 pzas. azul
Includes: 8 oz. Mug, 6" Bowl,
and 8½" Plate.

924 3 pc. Child's Service Set $17.90
peach
Servico de Niños 3 pzas. durazno
Includes: 8 oz. Mug, 6" Bowl,
and 8½" Plate.

Handmade at Dalzell-Viking, the praying
girl and praying boy are wonderful gifts that
will be treasured for a lifetime.

943 Sd. Picture Frame $14.90
decorated blue
(Holds 3½" x 5" photo.)
Marco para Foto, decorado azul
A beautiful blue lustre has been
added to this crystal frame to
give it a special touch.

380 Praying Girl $19.90
pink (6" high) Handmade.
Niña Arrodillada, rosado

467 Praying Boy $19.90
blue (6" high) Handmade.
Niño Arrodillado, azul

38

026 Suzanne Vase $9.90
     aquamarine (5½" high)
     Jarron, aquamarina

148 Whiskers $18.90
     crystal/etched (4½" high)
     El Perrito, cristal/grabado
     Whiskers, the dog, is an adorable addition
     to your desktop, shelf or table. Handcrafted
     in solid crystal with etched surface for
     detail, he's the quietest pet you'll ever
     adopt! Produced by Dalzell-Viking.

150 Priscilla $18.90
     crystal/etched (5" high)
     El Gatito, cristal/grabado
     Priscilla, the kitten, is handcrafted in solid
     crystal with an etched surface for detail.
     Produced for Tiara by Dalzell-Viking, she's
     a perfect companion to your decor.

Delicately crafted accents
make special gifts that
anyone will treasure!
Soft color combined with
elegant lines create these
unique gifts that are
suitable for any occasion!

066 Bunny $12.90
     decorated pink
     Conejito, decorado rosado

068 Bunny $12.90
     decorated blue
     Conejito, decorado azul

024 Cat $12.90
     decorated pink
     Gato, decorado rosa

553 Sandwich Picture Frame $14.90
     decorated pink
     Holds 3½" x 5" photo.
     Marco para Foto, decorado rosado

353 Heart Paperweight $18.90
     pink/etched (3½" wide)
     Handmade.
     Pisapapeles forma Corazon, rosa/grabado

Hostess Plan

BOOKING CREDIT $$!!

Bookings with $150.00 in net sales, held within 30 days, will earn you extra *Free Shopping Dollars!*

Bookings		Credit
1st	=	$10.00
2nd	=	$40.00 more!!
3rd	=	$25.00 more!!

Every booking after the 2nd adds another $25.00 to the total shopping credit. (Example: 3rd booking = $25.00, 4th booking = $25.00 etc.)

**Bookings must be held within 30 days with net sales of $150.00 or more per booking. Hostesses may "re-book" and hold within 60 days to meet booking requirements.

$75.00 FREE SHOPPING

When your net sales are $300.00 or more! (Subject to applicable Hostess Order Fees, see "Order Handling Fees" shown above.)

Plus:

• Earn **$50.00** for two bookings!

• Receive **Gifts** from our Hostess Treasures Program starting at $250.00 in net sales! $5.00 fee on each gift selected.

Schedule your own Giftarama Today! (*See your Tiara Associate for full details.)

RECEIVE ANY SINGLE ITEM IN OUR CATALOG FOR 1/2 PRICE

(Starter Sets, Buffet Sets and Collections cannot be taken as a 1/2-price item.) When your net sales are $300.00 or more and your giftarama is paid in full when it is submitted to the Home Office, you can choose any single item in our catalog for 1/2-price.

ORDER HANDLING FEE

An order handling fee of $3.00 is to be paid by the Hostess on merchandise ordered with Free Shopping Dollars. Regardless of the total amount of Free Shopping Dollars earned, the fee is only $3.00 per qualified giftarama of $150.00 in net sales.

MERCHANDISE SHIPPING FEES

Shipping fees equal to 10% of the total order amount are to be paid by ordering guests as shown on the guest selection card.
Example: Items ordered total $25.00:
$25.00 x 10% = $2.50 shipping and handling.

BY HOSTING AN AVERAGE GIFTARAMA YOU'LL RECEIVE

$250.00 Net Sales	- $60.00	Free Shopping
	$40.00	*Gift Value* - Hostess Treasures $250 Level
2 Bookings	- $50.00	Free Shopping
	$150.00	TOTAL FREE GIFTS and SHOPPING!

TIARA'S HOSTESS CREDIT		WHEN TWO BOOKINGS ARE HELD**	
When Net Sales Are:	You'll Receive:	$50.00 Bookings	Bookings Bonus +Shopping Credit
$150.00 - 199.99	$25.00	+ 2 Bookings	$75.00 Total
200.00 - 249.99	50.00	+ 2 Bookings	100.00 Total
250.00 - 299.99	60.00	+ 2 Bookings	110.00 Total
300.00 - 349.99	75.00	+ 2 Bookings	125.00 Total
350.00 - 399.99	85.00	+ 2 Bookings	135.00 Total
400.00 - 449.99	100.00	+ 2 Bookings	150.00 Total
450.00 - 499.99	110.00	+ 2 Bookings	160.00 Total
500.00 - 549.99	125.00	+ 2 Bookings	175.00 Total
550.00 - 599.99	135.00	+ 2 Bookings	185.00 Total
600.00 - 649.99	150.00	+ 2 Bookings	200.00 Total
650.00 - 699.99	160.00	+ 2 Bookings	210.00 Total
700.00 - 749.99	175.00	+ 2 Bookings	225.00 Total
750.00 - 799.99	185.00	+ 2 Bookings	235.00 Total
800.00 - 849.99	200.00	+ 2 Bookings	250.00 Total
850.00 - 899.99	210.00	+ 2 Bookings	260.00 Total
900.00 - 949.99	225.00	+ 2 Bookings	275.00 Total
950.00 - 999.99	235.00	+ 2 Bookings	285.00 Total
1000.00 -	250.00	+ 2 Bookings	300.00 Total

40

Preferred Hostess Plan

418   Sandwich Basket, spruce
Cesta Sandwich, abeto

When your total net sales from three or more Giftaramas held during the fiscal year reach $600 or more, you're eligible to receive this beautiful handmade basket.

Sign up now as a Preferred Hostess and earn your first Collector Series basket. This first time series of three beautiful handmade baskets will be a must to achieve. Your Associate will award you your first basket when you reach $600 in paid-in-full net sales accumulated during the fiscal year. (July '97 – June '98.) Your Associate will award you with the second (#275 – Vintage Blue) and third basket (#802 – Sienna) for every $600 in paid-in-full net sales accumulated during the fiscal year.

Regional Sales Offices

Southeastern Sales Office:
Sybil Campbell
2144 Rocky Ridge Ranch Road
Hoover, AL 35216
(205-985-9874)

Southeast Texas Sales Office:
Rosalinda & Jorge Salinas
222 Lomas St.
Rio Grande City, TX 78582
(210-487-0393)
(713-692-5567, Houston)

Rio Grande Valley Sales Office:
Romanita & Pablo Villarreal
Rt. 21, Box 1871
Mission, TX 78572
(956-584-8668)

Southwestern Sales Office:
Tommie Hinski
709 Keith
Pasadena, TX 77504
(713-943-0868)

Mid-Western Sales Office:
Robert Obney
W-8589-A Territorial Rd.
Whitewater, WI 53190
(608-883-2929)

Northwestern Sales Office:
Hal Scott
6978 Pampas Way
Fair Oaks, CA 95628
(916-966-6508)

International Sales Office:
James F. Beitler
P.O. Box 2278, Kingshill
St. Croix, VI 00851-2278
(809-773-5453)

Executive Offices

Tiara Exclusives
717 "E" Street
Dunkirk, IN 47336
(765-768-7821)

Jerry Vanden Eynden
President

Carol Capps
Field Sales Vice President

Ralph Waddell
Senior Vice President

Jeff Hatch
Sales Promotion Coordinator

Props used in the photography of this catalogue
are not available through Tiara Exclusives.
Design: Lancaster Colony Design Group
Photography: Paul Poplis Photography and Eclipse Studios

Catalog effective through July 1998

Tiara Product Information Manual Contents

This text document contains information about the dates that Tiara glass designs were produced and the origins of the molds, and which companies made the various pieces.

-

TIARA EXCLUSIVES

PRODUCT

INFORMATION

MANUAL

Revision 1/95   #20109

INDEX

"The future belongs to those who believe in the beauty of their dreams."
                                                    -Eleanor Roosevelt

Tiara Exclusives is proud to present the beauty of your dreams. As an Associate, Hostess, or Customer, you've been given the opportunity to surround yourself and others with tasteful, functional glassware. Tiara is not an alternative to shopping in retail stores, it is a preference shared by those with a distinct appreciation for elegance and high quality.

Tiara's Product Information Manual was designed with the collector in mind. Where did this pattern originate, how is this color produced, how can it be used to complement your home, or that of a friend? This up-to-date factual information will help you answer these questions and more!

By exploring these pages, you can enter the world of fine glassware and gain an appreciation of design created by fine craftsmanship.

Join us now as we delve deeply into the reality of the Tiara dream. Then share your knowledge with others. Let them experience the appeal of fine gifts in glassware by Tiara Exclusives.

THE CREATION OF GLASS

Over 4,000 years ago, perhaps on the sands of Egypt, Syria or Babylonia the creation of glass began. Since then mankind has added, little by little, to the glassmaker's art. The skill of the glassmaker has been a source of beauty, treasured by all.

It is natural that you, a Tiara Associate, should want to know something about the way glass is created. Making glassware by hand is the oldest industry in America, started in the Jamestown Colony in 1608. Many of the techniques and tools of the early days are used in the manufacture of Tiara items. Each item is exclusive with Tiara and will not be found in any other line.

Glass is truly the product of earth and fire! Made of silica, soda ash, lime and feldspar, small amounts of various other chemicals such as copper, selenium, manganese and cadmium are added to make a "batch". After careful mixing of the selected ingredients, a quantity of broken glass - called cullet - is often added to the "batch" to speed up the melting process.

MOLD EQUIPMENT

At the Indiana Glass Mold Shop, the primary concern is keeping mold equipment in a good state of repair. However, new molds are also produced here.

A design for a new mold is first worked out on paper, with the necessary consideration given to requested specifications, design factors and machine capabilities. A wood pattern is then generally made to show the entire mold as it will finally be produced.

The final molds are made of cast iron, consisting of a bottom plate, a body mold, [one piece block mold or joint mold] a ring and a plunger.

A complete set of molds can range in cost from $9,000 to $50,000 depending on whether they are hand or machine molds and the size and complexity of design for the item to be produced.

Machine molds range from 12 to 40 molds per set and it is estimated that we have approximately 2,500 complete sets.

Hand molds generally have two molds per set. We have approximately 1,500 sets of hand molds.

With the use of color variations, grouping variations, etc., it is possible to produce thousands of different items.

Due to extreme heat, pressure, and corrosiveness of materials used in making glassware, it is necessary to clean the contact surface of the molds each time they are used. Various polishing stones and air grinders are used to thoroughly clean and polish the molds.

The joints of the molds are continually being worn away and must be welded and carefully rematched by hand.

Indiana Glass Company employs a highly skilled group of individuals in the Mold Department who are dedicated to the excellence of the finished product demanded by the discriminating customer.

2

THE PRODUCTION OF GLASS

HAND

Hand blown and hand pressed glassware has been produced in this country for almost two hundred years.

Two types of tanks are generally used in the hand made production of glassware - day tanks and continuous tanks.

The tank into which the glassworker shovels the "batch", has been pre-fired to an intense heat of about 2700° F. In about 18 hours, the glass is ready to be gathered and blown.

Day tanks hold only about 5 tons of molten glass. They are filled with batch material and melted for 16 hours, then worked for only 8 hours each day.

Individual "shops" consisting of anywhere from 6 to 18 individuals are arranged for the production of a handmade or mouth blown item.

A man called a gatherer standing on a platform, holds a long rod called a gathering rod. This rod is placed into the tank and rotated in one continuous motion. This causes the glass to gather on the end of the rod. The rod carrying the glass is then transferred from the tank to the cast iron mold. The presser, or the man standing in front of the mold with shears, cuts the correct amount of glassware from the rod. The amount of glass cut normally varies no more than ½ of one ounce.

The presser then slides the mold under the plunger and pulls the lever which moves the plunger into the mold. After a predetermined amount of time the plunger is released from the mold. The mold is removed from beneath the plunger, opened and the piece of glassware is removed. The take-out person places the ware in a device called a "snap". The ware is then transferred to a "glory hole". The amount of fire contained in the glory hole imparts a beautiful lustre to the glassware and at the same time makes the glass pliable enough to be finished. The final shaping of the article is done by the finisher.

Immediately after the ware is finished, it is taken to the lehr. After passing through the lehr, it is carefully scrutinized by an inspector and packed for our customers.

MACHINE MADE

In the machine manufacture of glass, lime, soda ash and sand are mixed with broken glass and fed into the end of a furnace.

A gas flame coming from the side above the melted glass keeps the material in the tank between 2700° and 2900° F.

In the furnace gas flames from side ports go across the surface of the glass and into a heat chamber or regenerator on the opposite side. Every 20 minutes the direction of firing is reversed to take advantage of the heat that accumulates in the regenerators on each side.

3

THE PRODUCTION OF GLASS

MACHINE MADE Continued

The melted glass then passes through the tank throat into a refining
chamber where impurities are further melted out.   Several long fore-
hearths or feeders lead from the refiner where the temperature of the
glass is reduced to approximately 2000° F. The glass at this point is
pushed through an orifice and cut off by shears into uniform gobs.
These gobs are pressed by a plunger into the shape of the article being
manufactured.

The ware is then cooled by air to the point where it can be transferred
into the glazing operations.

Glazers serve a dual purpose. Firstly, they enable the fire polishing
of the top edges and side walls of the glassware. Secondly, the glazers
are a means of delivering the ware to the front end of the annealing
ovens.

Inspectors at the other end of the annealing ovens are examining each
piece and sorting carefully, removing the bad ware.

At first an inspector may keep 20% and discard 80% of the ware produced.
Over a period of hours, however, adjustments are made so that
approximately 85% of the ware is of excellent quality.

4

THE COLORS OF GLASS

AMBER

Tiara's golden amber differs from the common ambers found throughout the industry in that its hue is much closer to that of natural golden amber. Amber in its natural form is the fossilized sap of trees. It is mostly found in the Mediterranean area where it is used as a semiprecious stone. Tiara's golden amber has this same clarity of hue and depth of brilliance which makes it an ideal medium when used with the warm wood tones and linen textures associated with Colonial America.

AQUAMARINE

Introduced in 1991 aquamarine was a color developed by Indiana Glass. The transparent blue-green hue of this color is light and cheery. Chosen for selected gift items in the Tiara line, it is a nice complement to the current color trends.

AMETHYST

Similar in color to the jewel it was named after, amethyst glass is a dark, romantic shade of purple that can look almost black in denser areas of a given item. This color is of a handmade variety and was produced for Tiara by Fenton Art Glass, and prior to 1986, by the Hand Shop at Indiana Glass Company.

AZURE BLUE

This bright blue reminds us of the sky on a clear sunny day. Introduced in 1991 it has maintained a following of collectors and is a good decorating choice for a bedroom or bath. This color is only offered in handmade items. Azure blue is produced for Tiara by Dalzell Viking.

BLACK

A captivating accent to supplement any color grouping, rich black glass is unassuming yet decorative. Chemically, black glass is almost identical to the lustrous volcanic glass found in mountainous regions throughout the world. Delicate to the touch and in composure, black glassware should be given the care of fine crystal.

CHANTILLY GREEN

Springtime freshness radiates from Tiara's chantilly green. To brighten a room, or the heart of a loved one, the transparency of this color adds the cool touch of a spring breeze to any home. A form of chrome is used to produce this enlightening shade.

CRYSTAL

A clear colorless crystal is the greatest achievement of the glassmakers craft. The earliest glasses were opaque. It took hundreds of years of experience to develop crystal as we know it today. The colorless transparency is no accident and it can only be obtained by careful selection of materials and constant vigilance in melting and refinement. It is very similar to rock crystal which is a natural form of amorphous silica. This has been used for centuries, particularly by the Chinese, as a semiprecious stone in the making of jewelry and fine figurines.

CRYSTAL, ETCHED

The process for frosting glass dates back to the 1800's when it was discovered in France. Some glassmakers, looking for a fast way to cool their glass, dug a pit in the ground, buried their glass and when it was dug up the next day, the glass was frosted, although not evenly like that of Tiara. When the soil was analyzed, it was discovered that the soil had a high acid content.

Satin glass has been popular for many years and was prized in ancient times. "Tiara has made frosted glass available to the American household for everyday service. Cold drinks and punches never seem as cold as when they are served in frosted ware, and the subtlety of the etching complements any colorful decorative style." [Art Harshman — Tiara Topics - September, 1977] [Discontinued, December 1989.]

DUSTY ROSE

An attractively shaped piece of handmade glassware seems to become even more beautiful when this subtle yet rich shade of darkened mauve is used to form the finished masterpiece. Introduced to the Tiara collection in 1986, it has gained a dedicated following of collectors, decorators and gift-buyers. You need it in your home, but you'll want to share it because of its special beauty.

FIERY RUBY

Ruby is defined as "a red variety of corundum, used as a gem".

Our fiery ruby is a perfect example of how the sparkle and beauty of a gem can be reflected in glassware by skilled craftsmen. It is a striking color that develops when the piece is reheated. Selenium in combination with cadmium sulfide is the coloring agent for Tiara's fiery ruby.

As an accent ruby has the elegant properties that finish a decor. Subdued, yet transparent, it catches a glimmer of light only to return it more vibrantly to the glass lover's eye.

Tiara Exclusives is proud to offer this beautiful color to their customers with all the charm and grandeur associated with fine glassware.

6

GREEN

Popular at Christmas, Tiara's green is similar to the emerald green produced in Indiana Glass Hand Shops several years ago. Available in selected giftware during the holiday season, the current green items are produced by hand for Tiara at Fenton Art Glass.

ICE BLUE

The cool, breezy shade of blue offered by Tiara Exclusives is a gift favorite. Sparkling with the freshness of spring flowers, it accents many darker shades to bring a special light-hearted touch to any setting.

Our ice blue is similar to a very transparent light blue that was introduced around 1940 to simulate a chunk of ice and its color reflections. Copper is used to create just the right shade for the Tiara collectable items.

IMPERIAL BLUE

A strikingly deep, rich color, Tiara's imperial blue is a favorite among favorites. The tone is clear, but not over-powering. A statement in interior decorating and giftware made with grandeur.

LEAD CRYSTAL

Additives such as red lead or litharge are substituted for lime in glassware. These materials produce a softer glass with added brilliance and a clear true ring. Lead crystal is a preference in many homes because of the clarity and elegance it adds naturally to any setting. Tiara salutes Fostoria Glass Company, responsible for the introduction of our own luxurious lead crystal patterns offered, and Lancaster Glass Company for the production of our lead crystal patterns. [See "Facets"]

Since 1993, 24% Lead Crystal has been imported from Germany. Lancaster Glass, producer of Lead Crystal products for Tiara, gradually phased out lead production over a period of years following Lancaster Colony Corporations purchase of Fostoria. This phase out was due to environmental restrictions and concerns.

OCEAN SPRAY

A blend of blues and greens, shaded very carefully for a perfectly eye-catching hue of teal, is the rich accent you've been looking for. Teal colors have been a popular addition to homes for decades. Tiara's ocean spray is a reflection of the continuing demand for unique color and flair for style. [Discontinued in 1988.]

7

PEACH

Decorators prefer light, breezy colors in houseware designs which are relaxing and cheerful. Color trends for the 1990's include floral and fruit-like muted shades which are stimulating to the senses and provide a comfortable atmosphere.

Tiara's peach color is a soft shade that blends well with rich wood furniture and an array of floral designs. Unlike darker color selections, it has the capability to enlighten and enhance every line of design in a chosen glassware item due to its reflective nature. [Introduced in July of 1989.]

PINK

Pink is a light, refreshing color that carries with it a devoted following of collectors that date back to the Depression.

Tiara's pink is a clear, true definition of this pleasant color. Selenium is the base metal element often used in obtaining the shades of pink that are prominent in the glassware today. From small children to grandparents, this color remains a treasured favorite for those who buy or receive it in the form of beautiful glassware.

PLATINUM

A soft grey/blue color that blends perfectly with today's contemporary styling. The quiet shading of platinum catches every glimmer of light and softly reflects the designs in the glassware.

Nickel and cobalt are added to the batch mixture to produce this shaded blue.

Enchantingly yours from Tiara Exclusives!

PLUM

Produced for Tiara by L.E.Smith, plum is a rich dark shade of amethyst, appearing only in handmade products. Introduced by Tiara in 1994, the incredible depth and beauty of this color promises to attract a host of new Tiara collectors.

PREMIER BLUE

Darker tones of blue complement floral and wood tones with a softness that commands attention. Tiara's premier blue is a decorator favorite for every room in the home.

A blend of copper, nickel, cobalt and chrome create this marvelous color, and it is offered with vivid respect to the popular country tones you want in your home.

8

PROVINCIAL BLUE

This color reflects both the beauty of opalescent glass and the charm of a warm shade of blue called provincial. From country decorating to gift-giving, the striking appearance of provincial blue is destined to be a favorite choice of those with impeccable taste for charming style. [Tiara's introduction, 1988. Discontinued: December 1991.]

ROSE PINK

A soft pastel shade of pink [with a somewhat purple cast], rose pink was introduced in the Hostess Treasures section of the catalog in 1991. A very delicate color, rose pink is subject to fluctuation in hue and can vary from lighter to darker on any given day of production. Produced for Tiara by Fenton Art Glass, each item in rose pink is carefully hand crafted.

SAGE MIST

Desert tones of peach and green were quite popular in 1989-1990. Tiara introduced the sage mist in 1990 to meet these decorating trends. The opaque quality of this pastel green lent itself to a variety of Southwestern styles and patterns. Sage mist was produced by Fenton Art Glass. All pieces were handmade. This color was discontinued in December of 1991.

SEA MIST

Soft and dark, the tranquil green color of the ocean is a trendy shade with lots of decorating flair. Popular in housewares departments across the country, Tiara's sea mist can easily fit into any room in your home. Produced for Tiara by Fenton Art Glass. Introduced in 1992.

SPRUCE

A blend of hunter green and teal, spruce was introduced in December of 1993. The color blends beautifully with burgundy, mauve, peach and off-white. Its introduction was an exciting step for Sandwich, once again allowing the customers a choice of colors in our traditional dinnerware line. This dark blue-green tone is achieved by adding carefully measured amounts of chrome, copper & cobalt to the existing crystal formula.

TEA ROSE

Picture if you will a soft pink dessert, rich with flavor and secret ingredients, topped with an elegant swirl of pure whipped cream. Then experience Tiara's tea rose! Subtle shades of pink are tipped in white by the hands of a skilled glassmaker. Tea rose is an opalescent color which allows a vivid image to be captured in glass for the discriminating buyer who wants more than just a piece of glass. [Introduced in 1987. Discontinued December, 1989.]

9

TEAL MIST

The opalescent qualities of teal mist allow each item to be tipped with a soft white glow around the edges when they are reheated. This transparent shade of light green, tipped with white, was added to the Tiara line in 1991. Opalescence varies with each piece produced, because they are made entirely by hand. Produced for Tiara by Fenton Art Glass.

VINTAGE BLUE

This antique shade of blue could have come straight out of Great Grandma's attic. With a passion for enhancing floral patterns and brightening dark wood tones, vintage blue is produced for Tiara by L.E. Smith. Introduced in 1992.

WISTERIA

Rich romantic shades of color seem to shamelessly copy the fragrant wisteria that blooms each year in New England. Complementing it's surroundings with tastefully elegant flair, Tiara has captured this wonderful hue forever in handmade splendor, especially for you. [Tiara's introduction, July 1989. Discontinued: Dec. 1991]

WHITE LACE CRYSTAL

Also referred to as "opalescent", this is not a color, but a property of glass which involves color. White lace crystal is produced by combining special heat-sensitive ingredients to a common glass mixture. After the glass article is formed, it is reheated in a furnace which causes certain areas of the exposed surface to turn a milky white. This "opalescent" property in glassware can be traced back to the late 1800's.

Tiara's white lace crystal magnifies the beauty of "opalescence" in attractive giftware and decorator accents for you. [Introduced: 1987. Discontinued: Dec. 1991.]

YELLOW MIST

Yellow mist was developed in the early 1970's and is quite unlike any other yellow glassware available today. The transparent color will allow light to shine through it as it reflects light rays. Cerium-titanium is the metal for the color yellow.

Popular in both serving and decorative pieces, this color of glassware is destined to be cherished by collectors in future generations.

DINNERWARE SELECTIONS

CHILDREN'S COLLECTION

Enter the make-believe world of special friends and special parties. A magic moment sparks the imagination, and with childish bubbling laughter, you are off to a beautiful land of friends and fun. Scaled in size for small hands with big ideas, gifts from the Tiara Children's Collection are destined to be heirloom treasures for generations to come.

The Margery Daw Plate and Nursery Rhyme Cup were originally introduced by Indiana Glass Company in 1918. The cereal bowl was designed for Tiara Exclusives in 1977. This 3-piece set has been offered by Tiara in amber, blue, pink, apricot, and peach. The plate was offered for a limited time in lime.

A Child's Beverage Set was offered exclusively by Tiara. The tumblers were designed and introduced in 1978, and have been produced in amber, pink and blue. The pitcher was designed for the Tiara collection and introduced in 1985, and has been produced in pink [through 1988] and blue [through 1990].

A cherished gift collection, bound to carry for a lifetime the memories of childhood when eating and drinking were a proud effort! Start a tradition in your family with a child's gift set from Tiara today!

		Mold Information	Introduction
#372	3 pc. Child's Beverage Set, pink	Machine	1985 [Disc. '90]
#465	3 pc. Child's Beverage Set, blue	Machine	1985 [Disc. '88]
#384	3 pc. Child's Service Set, pink	Machine	1984 [Disc. '89]
#952	3 pc. Child's Service Set, apricot	Machine	1991 [Disc. '91]

Currently Available:
#462	3 pc. Child's Service Set, blue	Machine	1985
#924	3 pc. Child's Service Set, peach	Machine	1997

Produced for Tiara by Dalzell-Viking, the Kneeling Boy and Girl have been offered by Tiara, originally during the Christmas season in crystal etched, and then in traditional pink and blue starting in 1993.

		Mold Information	Introduction
#076	Kneeling Boy, crystal etched	Handmade	1992
#090	Kneeling Girl, crystal etched	Handmade	1992

Currently Available [renamed]
#380	Praying Girl, pink	Handmade	1993
#467	Praying Boy, blue	Handmade	1993

11

CROWN DINNERWARE

With styling fit for a king, this lovely dinnerware adds a "crowning touch" to the Tiara Exclusives' line.

Drinkware from this pattern has been traced back to the early 1900's. An Indiana Glass catalog predating 1910, pictures two of the stemware pieces offered in the Tiara Crown Dinnerware line. Additional items in the pattern have been traced to a U.S. Glass Factory in Tiffin, Ohio. Their pattern was called Kings Crown or Thumbprint. Produced in the early 1950's by Indiana Glass Company, several colors and painted variations of the Crown Dinnerware can be found.

Now produced exclusively for Tiara, the Crown Dinnerware in imperial blue is a strikingly rich collection of formal dinnerware for your home. Tiara's Crown Dinnerware has become a favorite in Tiara households from coast to coast. [Tiara's introduction, 1986.]

		Mold Information	Introduction
#780	Crown Dinner Plates	Machine	1986 [Disc. '95]
#781	Crown Salad Plates	Machine	1986 [Disc. '95]
#782	Crown Cups	Machine	1986 [Disc. '95]
#783	Crown Saucers	Machine	1986 [Disc. '95]
#784	Crown Goblets	Machine	1986 [Disc. '94]
#785	Crown Cocktail	Machine	1986 [Disc. '94]
#786	Crown Platter	Machine	1986 [Disc. '94]
#787	Crown Console Bowl	Machine	1986 [Disc. '95]

Additions:

#788	Crown Beverage	New Molds/Machine	1988 [Disc. '94]
#789	Crown Dessert	New Molds/Machine	1988 [Disc. '95]
#791	Crown Cake Plate	Handmade [Original Mold	1989 [Disc. '91]
#804	Crown Tidbit Tray	From Salad Plate	1990 [Disc. '94]
#805	Crown Photo Plate	From Salad Plate	1990 [Disc. '94]
#442	Crown Sugar/Creamer	New Molds/Handmade	1991 [Disc. '94]
#777	Crown Pitcher	New Molds/Machine	1992 [Disc. '95]
#829	Crown Candy Box & Cover	Handmade [Original Mold]	1992 [Disc. '93]

Complements:

#653	Crown Pillar Candle	Designed for Tiara	1988
#796	Dewdrop Candy Box & Cvr.	Handmade [Original Mold]	1988 [Disc. '91]
#830	Royal Butter Dish & Cvr.	Handmade [Original Mold] [Imperial/Cape Cod]	1992 [Disc. '94]
#831	* Tulip Basket	Unknown/Handmade	1992 [Disc. '94]

* Hostess Treasures item — see also: Tulip Basket

#838	Suzanne Salt & Pepper	Designed by Fostoria	1992 [Disc. '95]
#840	Veronique Egg Tray	Machine Made — IGC Mold	1992 [Disc. '95]
#841	Veronique Wall Clock	Machine Made — IGC Mold	1992

PONDEROSA PINE

What must have been in Art Harshman's mind when he designed Ponderosa Pine for Tiara Exclusives? Was he thinking of a small log cabin, nestled on the side of a mountain with a cool pine breeze blowing through an open window? When you admire the Ponderosa Pine, you're sure this must have been his inspiration. This casual design is clear and true, reminiscent of the massive forests that adorn beautiful countrysides. Tiara is constantly designing new, functional additions to this favorite grouping. A tastefully arranged bouquet of fresh-cut flowers and greenery are the perfect and final complement you can give to a service of Ponderosa Pine.

Introduced in 1981 the Ponderosa Pine Pattern has known great popularity. It is available only through Tiara Associates, designed especially for Tiara Customers, and produced with care by Indiana Glass Company!

The following items have been introduced in crystal:

		Mold Information	Introduction
#154	P.P. Soup Bowls	New Molds	1991
#159	P.P. Pitcher	New Molds	1987
#160	P.P. Dinner Plate	New Molds	1981
#161	P.P. Mug	New Molds	1981
#162	P.P. Juice	New Molds	1981
#163	P.P. Goblet	New Molds	1981
#164	P.P. Salad Bowl	New Molds	1982
#165	P.P. Ind. Salad Bowl	New Molds	1982
#166	P.P. Salad Plates	New Molds	1982
#167	P.P. Salt & Pepper	New Molds	1983
#168	P.P. Serving Plate	New Molds	1984
#169	P.P. 3-Part Relish	New Molds	1984
#170	P.P. Egg Tray	New Molds	1984
#171	P.P. Carafe	Handmade/New Molds	1984 [Disc. '90]
#172	P.P. Ice Tea	New Molds	1985
#173	P.P. Vegetable Bowls	New Molds	1986
#174	P.P. Handled Mug	New Molds	1985
#176	P.P. Chip-N-Dip	Same as #168 & #165	1989
#185	P.P. Tidbit Tray	Same as #166	1990

Chantilly Green		Mold Information	Introduction
[Customer Special Only]			
#569	8 pc. Handled Beverage	Same as #174	1986 [Disc. '87]
#564	3 pc. Buffet Set	Same as #168; #169, 170	1986 [Disc. '87]

Christmas Issue—Holiday Season Only
Crystal Etched

		Mold Information	Introduction
#242	P.P. Vegetable Bowl	Same as #173	1994
#143	P.P. Ind. Salad Bowls	Same as #165	1994
#147	P.P. Juice	Same as #162	1994
#190	P.P. Large Bowl	Same as #164	1994
#354	P.P. Goblet	Same as #163	1994

13

SANDWICH GLASS

Tiara's Sandwich pattern began as the focal point of the entire line. It was originally introduced in our 1970 catalog in ruby. A limited selection of items were available at the time. Golden amber was then chosen because of its beauty when blended with the earth tones and natural wood finishes of today's home decorating.

Sandwich Glass originated from the Boston and Sandwich Glass Company in Sandwich, Massachusetts. Deming Jarvis had his intricate, lacy designs hand-cut into iron molds, and by utilizing his original hand-pressing process, began manufacturing the first hand-pressed glass ever made in 1825.

Nearly 150 years later, Tiara Exclusives, with molds designed by Indiana Glass Company in the 1920's, introduced its line of sparkling Sandwich. Among that group of 1920's molds were many popular items including: the Tumbler, Goblet, Vegetable Bowl, Snack Set, and the basic Starter Set which included Dinner Plates, Salad Plates, Saucers, and Cups.

To keep pace with the ever-changing ideas in the kitchen and home decorating functions, Tiara designed new pieces in the later '70's to complement the line. Those wares included: the Sandwich Basket, Ashtray, Salt and Pepper, Dinner Bell, Candle Holders, and Pitcher.

The 1980's saw this elegant pattern expanded to include the Mini Vase, Sugar and Creamer, Individual Salad Bowls, Votives, Butter and Cover, and of course, the multi-functional Canisters in three useful sizes.

For your information the evolution of this entire line has been listed as it was introduced and discontinued in various colors and styles.

Ruby		Mold Information	Introduction
#200	Sandwich Goblets	Handmade	1970 [Disc. '70]
#201	Sandwich Place Setting [Plate, Salad Plate, Cup, Saucer]	Handmade	1970 [Disc. '70]
#202	Sandwich 16 pc. [Starter Set]	Handmade	1970 [Disc. '70]
#203	Sandwich Party Server	Handmade	1970 [Disc. '70]
#204	Sandwich Sugar/Creamer	Handmade	1970 [Disc. '70]
#205	Sandwich Pitcher	Handmade	1970 [Disc. '70]
#206	Sandwich Candy Box & Cover	Handmade	1970 [Disc. '70]
#207	Sandwich Wine Set [Decanter Stopper, Tray, Goblets (6)]	Handmade	1970 [Disc. '70]
#240	Sandwich Glo Lamp, Decorated Ruby	Machine	1976 [Disc. '83]

Amber		Mold Information	Introduction
#208	Sandwich 8 Oz. Goblets	Machine	1971 [Disc. '89]
#209	Sandwich Place Setting	Machine	1971 [Disc. '77]
#210	Sandwich 16 pc. Starter Set	Machine	1971 [Disc. '77]
#211	Sandwich Party Server	Handmade	1971 [Disc. '71]
#212	Sandwich Sugar/Creamer Set	Handmade	1971 [Disc. '80]
#213	Sandwich Pitcher	Handmade	1971 [Disc. '83]
#214	Sandwich Candy Box & Cover	Handmade	1971 [Disc. '71]
#215	Sandwich Wine Set	Hand & Machine	1971 [Disc. '74]
#216	Sandwich Candle Stick [3½]	Handmade	1971 [Disc. '82]
#217	Sandwich Console Bowl	Handmade	1971 [Disc. '75]
#218	Sandwich Console Set [Bowl & 2 Candle Holders] [Available as Individual pieces.]	Handmade	1971 [Disc. '74]

14

Amber Cont.

		Mold Information	Introduction
#219	Sandwich 13" Platter	Handmade	1971 [Disc. '77]
#220	Sandwich Domed Butter Dish & Cover	Hand & Machine	1971 [Disc. '86]
#221	Sandwich Basket	Handmade	1971 [Disc. '89]
#222	Sandwich Ashtray	Handmade	1972 [Disc. '72]
#223	Sandwich Berry Bowl [8" dia.] [Not available individually after '72]		1972 [Disc. '72]
#224	Sandwich Nappy (4") [Not available individually after '72]	Machine	1972 [Disc. '72]
#226	Sandwich 8 pc. Snack Set (4 Oval Trays, 4 Punch Cups)	Machine	1972 [Disc. '89]
#037	Cruet & Stopper	Handmade	1973 [Disc. '73]
#200	Sandwich 10 oz. Tumblers	Machine	1974 [Disc. '89]
#201	Sandwich 3 oz. Juice	Handmade	1974 [Disc. '76]
#202	Sandwich 6" Deep Nappy	Handmade	1974 [Disc. '83]
#203	Sandwich 11 pc. Wine Set [Tray 8 New Goblets, Decanter, Stopper]	Hand & Machine	1974 [Disc. '82]
#204	Sandwich 8 pc. Wine Goblet	Machine	1974 [Disc. '81]
#227	Sandwich Salt & Pepper Set	Hand & Machine	1973 [Disc. '89]
#228	Sandwich Berry Set [#223 & 2 sets of #224]	Machine	1973 [Disc. '83]
#229	Sandwich Puff Box & Cover	Machine	1974 [Disc. '84]
#230	Sandwich Tiered Ensemble (3 puff box bottoms, 1 lid)	Machine	1974 [Disc. '74]
#231	Sandwich 4 pc. Bridge Set	Machine	1974 [Disc. '82]
#233	Sandwich Footed Sherbet Set	Machine	1974 [Disc. '77]
#235	Sandwich 16" Platter	Handmade	1975 [Disc. '80]
#237	Sandwich Old Lamp	Machine	1975 [Disc. '89]
#238	Sandwich Celery Tray	Handmade	1975 [Disc. '81]
#239	Sandwich 7" Bread & Butter Plate	Machine	1975 [Disc. '77]
#205	Sandwich Mini Basket	Handmade	1976 [Disc. '84]
#206	Sandwich Footed Cake Plate	Hand & Machine	1976 [Disc. '80]
#207	Sandwich Crimped Vase	Handmade	1976 [Disc. '82]
#241	Sandwich Hexagonal Bowl	Machine	1976 [Disc. '77]
#242	Sandwich Candy Box & Cover [7½" high.]	Handmade	1976 [Disc. '78]
#243	Sandwich Center Bowl	Handmade	1976 [Disc. '83]

Bicentennial Blue

The following items were produced in 1976 for a limited Collector's Series in the Sandwich Pattern.

Hostesses Only: #247 9 pc. Wine Set

Customer Specials:
#244 Assortment A:
Four Sherbets; Four Goblets; One Celery Tray and One-16 pc. Starter Set.

#245 Assortment B:
One Domed Butter & Cover; One Salt & Pepper; One Pitcher; One Console Bowl and One Sugar/Creamer Set.
#246 Assortment C:
Four 10 oz. Tumblers; Four 3 oz. Juice Glasses; One Berry Bowl; Four Dessert Bowls and One 8 pc. Snack Set.

This color was produced only once, and is considered extremely valuable in collectors circles.

Amber Cont.		Mold Information	Introduction
#222	Sandwich 16" Wall Clock	Handmade	1977 [Disc. '78]
#223	Sandwich Wall Sconce	Machine	1977 [Disc. '83]
#256	Sandwich Bell	Machine	1977 [Disc. '83]
#201	Sandwich Platter	Machine	1978 [Disc. '89]
#217	Sandwich Napkin Holder	Handmade	1978 [Disc. '84]
#214	Sandwich 14 pc. Punch Set [Bowl, Ladle, 12 Punch Cups]	Machine	1978 [Disc. '82]
#218	Sandwich Egg Tray	Machine	1978 [Disc. '89]
#224	Sandwich 3-Part Relish Tray	Machine	1978 [Disc. '89]
#225	Sandwich 6 oz. Punch Cup [1 dozen]	Machine	1978 [Disc. '78]
#255	Sandwich 9 oz. Coffee Cup	Machine	1978 [Disc. '78]
#257	Sandwich Saucer	Machine	1978 [Disc. '78]
#258	Sandwich Tall Candle Holder [8½" high.]	Handmade	1978 [Disc. '86]
#261	Sandwich 4 pc. Place Setting	Machine	1978 [Disc. '81]
#262	Sandwich 16 pc. Starter Set	Machine	1978 [Disc. '89]

Crystal

The following items were produced in 1978 in crystal, and introduced as a limited Collector's Series.

Customer Special:		Mold Information	Introduction
#263	Sd. 17 pc. Crystal Serving Set [One-8 pc. Snack Set; Four Sherbets; One Berry Bowl and Four Dessert Bowls]	Machine	1978 One Production

Hostess Special:			
#264	Sd. 16 pc. Crystal Starter Set	Machine	1978 One Production
#265	Sd. 17 pc. Crystal Wine Set	Hand & Machine	1978 One Production
#266	Sd. 5 pc. Cry. Beverage Set [Pitcher and four Goblets]	Hand & Machine	1978 One Production

Amber Cont.		Mold Information	Introduction
#209	Sandwich 12" Wall Clock	Machine	1979 [Disc. '89]
#219	Sandwich Coasters	Machine	1979 [Disc. '82]
#211	Sandwich Crimped Salad Bowl	Machine	1980 [Disc. '89]
#230	Sandwich 8 oz. Juice Tumbler	Handmade	1980 [Disc. '81]
#239	Sandwich Salad Bowl	Machine	1980 [Disc. '82]
#244	Sandwich Two-Tier Tidbit	Machine	1980 [Disc. '83]
#245	Sandwich Footed Candle Holders	Machine	1980 [Disc. '83]
#246	Sandwich Footed Sherbet Set, 4 pc.	Machine	1980 [Disc. '82]
#247	Sandwich 5-part Relish Tray	Machine	1980 [Disc. '82]
#248	Sandwich 4 pc. Dinner Plates	Machine	1980 [Disc. '82]

Regal Blue [Customer Specials]		Mold Information	Introduction
#492	Sandwich Old Lamp	Machine	1981 One Production
#493	Sandwich Ftd. Compote [Hostess Gift]	Machine	1981 One Production
#486	Sandwich Two-Tier Tidbit	Machine	1981 One Production
#549	Sandwich Puff Box & Cover	Machine	1981 One Production

16

Amber Cont.	Mold Information	Introduction
#253 Sandwich Mint Vase	Machine	1981 [Disc. '86]
#254 Sandwich Footed Sugar & Creamer	Handmade	1981 [Disc. '86]
#260 Sandwich 5" Salad Bowl	Machine	1981 [Disc. '89]
#278 Sandwich Footed Compote	Machine	1981 [Disc. '83]
#279 Sandwich Classic Lamp	Handmade	1981 [Disc. '82]
[from Wine Decanter]		
#280 Sandwich 4-part Relish Tray	Machine	1981 [Disc. '82]
#281 Sandwich 7½" Canister	Machine	1981 [Disc. '91]
#282 Sandwich Footed Mug	Machine	1981 [Disc. '83]
#283 Sandwich Table Wine	Machine	1981 [Disc. '83]
#284 Sandwich 3-Tier Candy Box & Cover	Machine	1981 [Disc. '82]

Chantilly Green	Mold Information	Introduction
#339 Sandwich Wall Clock	Machine	1982 [Disc. '86]
[Hostess Gift] [Line Item 1985]		
#340 Sandwich Platter	Machine	1982 [Disc. '86]
#341 Sandwich Egg Tray	Machine	1982 [Disc. '86]
#342 Sandwich 3-Part Relish Tray	Machine	1982 [Disc. '86]
#343 Sandwich Basket	Handmade	1982 [Disc. '86]
#344 Sandwich 9 pc. Wine Set	Hand & Machine	1982 [Disc. '86]
#345 Sandwich Tall Candle Holders	Handmade	1982 [Disc. '86]
#346 Sandwich 8 pc. Snack Set	Machine	1982 [Disc. '82]
#347 Sandwich 8¾ Canister	Machine	1982 [Disc. '86]
#348 Sandwich 7¼ Canister	Machine	1982 [Disc. '86]
#349 Sandwich 5¾ Canister	Machine	1982 [Disc. '86]
#350 Sandwich Compote [Hostess Gift]	Machine	1982 One Production
#438 Sandwich 16" Platter	Handmade	1982 One Production
[Hostess Gift]		

Amber Cont.	Mold Information	Introduction
#210 Sandwich Jewel Box & Cover	Handmade	1982 [Disc. '83]
#215 Sandwich Tall Handled Basket	Handmade	1982 [Disc. '83]
#222 Sandwich Ashtray	Machine	1982 [Disc. '86]
#233 Sandwich 5¾" Canister	Machine	1982 [Disc. '91]
#234 Sandwich 8¾" Canister	Machine	1982 [Disc. '89]
#236 Sandwich Domed Candle Holder	Machine	1982 [Disc. '84]
#241 Sandwich 9 pc. Wine Set	Hand & Machine	1982 [Disc. '91]

Chantilly Green Cont.	Mold Information	Introduction
#343 Sandwich Mini Basket	Handmade	1982 [Disc. '83]
[Hostess Gift]		

Pine Green	Mold Information	Introduction
#422 Pair of Sandwich Glo Lamps	Machine	1983 One Production
[Customer Special]		

Regal Blue	Mold Information	Introduction
#458 Sandwich Mini Vase	Machine	1983 One Production
[Hostess Gift]		

17

Chantilly Green Cont.	Mold Information	Introduction
#304 Sandwich 2 pc. Vegetable Bowls	Machine	1982 [Disc. '86]
#305 Sandwich 10 oz. Tumblers	Machine	1982 [Disc. '86]
#306 Sandwich 8" Salad Bowls	Machine	1983 [Disc. '86]
#308 Sandwich Goblets	Machine	1983 [Disc. '86]
#309 Sandwich Footed Mug	Machine	1983 [Disc. '83]
#310 Sandwich Table Wine	Machine	1983 [Disc. '83]
#351 Sandwich 16 pc. Starter Set	Machine	1983 [Disc. '86]
#352 Sandwich Pitcher	Handmade	1983 [Disc. '83]
#353 Sandwich 6 pc. Wine Goblets	Machine	1983 [Disc. '83]
#557 Sandwich 8 pc. Snack Set [Same as #346]	Machine	1983 [Disc. '86]

Amber Cont.	Mold Information	Introduction
#212 Sandwich Vegetable Bowls	Machine	1983 [Disc. '89]
#242 Sandwich Mini Decanter w/stopper	Handmade	1983 [Disc. '85]
#252 Sandwich 2 pc. Oval Trays	Machine	1983 [Disc. '89]
#273 Sandwich Gravy Boat	Handmade	1983 [Disc. '84]

Chantilly Green Cont.	Mold Information	Introduction
#300 Sandwich Salt & Pepper	Machine	1984 [Disc. '86]
#307 Sandwich Domed Butter Dish & Cover	Hand & Machine	1984 [Disc. '86]
#355 Sandwich Footed Cake Plate	Hand & Machine	1984 [Disc. '84]
#362 Sandwich 4 pc. Dinner Plates	Machine	1984 [Disc. '86]

Amber Cont.	Mold Information	Introduction
#248 Sandwich 4 pc. Dinner Plates [Reintroduced]	Machine	1984 [Disc. '89]
#251 Sandwich Footed Cake Plate (Used Wine Tray & small Candle Holder to make this.)	Hand & Machine	1984 [Disc. '84]

Pink	Mold Information	Introduction
#256 Sandwich Dinner Bell [Booking Gift]	Machine	1984 One Production

Ruby	Mold Information	Introduction
#141 Sandwich Tall Handled Basket	Handmade	1984 [Disc. '86]
#142 Sandwich Jewel Box & Cover	Handmade	1984 [Disc. '85]

Black	Mold Information	Introduction
#816 Sandwich Wall Clock [Customer Special]	Machine	1985 One Production

Crystal	Mold Information	Introduction
#730 Sandwich 16 pc. Snack Set [Hostess Gift]	Machine	1985 One Production *see 1993
#731 Sandwich 3 pc. Platters [Customer Special]	Machine	1985 One Production
#732 Sandwich 5 pc. Place Setting [10 oz. Tumbler; Dinner Plate; Cup; Saucer; Salad Plate] [Hostess Gift]	Machine	1985 One Production

Chantilly Green Cont.	Mold Information	Introduction
#301 Sandwich Footed Creamer & Sugar	Handmade	1985 [Disc. '86]
#313 Sandwich Mini Vase	Machine	1985 [Disc. '86]
#316 Sandwich Crimped Salad Bowl	Machine	1985 [Disc. '86]
#326 Sandwich Ash Tray	Machine	1985 [Disc. '91]
#364 Sandwich Glo Lamp	Machine	1985 [Disc. '91]
#368 Sandwich 14 pc. Punch Set	Machine	1985 Customer Special

Amber Cont.	Mold Information	Introduction
#243 Sandwich Pitcher	Machine	1986 [Disc. '89]
#246 Sandwich Votives	Machine	1986 [Disc. '91]
#269 Sandwich Sugar/Creamer w/lid	Handmade	1986 [Disc. '89]
#270 Sandwich 2 pc. Champagne/Sherbet	Handmade	1986 [Disc. '89]
#607 *Sandwich 12" Wall Sconce	Machine	1986 [Disc. '89]
*Consisted of Platter & Crimped Votive [Hostess Gift]		

Chantilly Green Cont.	Mold Information	Introduction
#317 Sandwich Votives	Machine	1986 [Disc. '91]
#352 Sandwich Pitcher	Machine	1986 [Disc. '86]
#937 *Sandwich 12" Wall Sconce	Machine	1986 [Disc. '87]
*Consisted of Platter & Crimped Votive [Hostess Gift]		

Hazel Brown	Mold Information	Introduction
Sandwich Glo Lamp [Customer Special] [Part of #413 - 3 pc. Glo Lamp Spec: pink; regal blue; hazel brown]	Machine	1986 One Production

Platinum	Mold Information	Introduction
#775 Sandwich Jewel Box & Cover	Handmade	1986 [Disc. '90]

Amber Cont.	Mold Information	Introduction
#245 Sandwich Butter Dish & Cover	Hand & Machine	1987 [Disc. '89]
#202 Sandwich Mini Vase [Same as #253]	Machine	1987 [Disc. '89]

Black	Mold Information	Introduction
[Customer Specials]		
#819 Sandwich Small Canister	Machine	1987 One Production
#820 Sandwich Medium Canister	Machine	1987 One Production
#821 Sandwich Large Canister	Machine	1987 One Production

Amber Cont.	Mold Information	Introduction
#219 Sandwich Candle Lamp	Machine	1988 [Disc. '91]
#713 *Sandwich Tidbit Tray	Machine	1988 [Disc. '91]
*Made from 12" Platters [Customer Special]		

Chantilly Green Cont.	Mold Information	Introduction
#939 *Sandwich Tidbit Tray	Machine	1988 [Disc. '89]
*Made from 12" Platters [Customer Special]		

19

Peach		Mold Information	Introduction
#689	Sandwich 3 pc. Buffet Set	Machine	1989
#935	12 pc. Modified Starter Set	Machine	1990
	[Dinner Plates, Cups, Saucers]		
#936	Sandwich Crimped Salad Bowl	Machine	1990
#944	Sandwich Individual Salad Bowls	Machine	1990
#945	Sandwich Coffee Cup	Machine	1990
#946	Sandwich Saucer	Machine	1990
#947	Sandwich Dinner Plates	Machine	1990
#948	Sandwich 10 oz. Tumbler	Machine	1990
#950	Sandwich Vegetable Bowls	Machine	1990
#951	Sandwich 8 pc. Snack Set	Machine	1990
	(Uncrimped Votives Instead of		
	Punch Cups]		
#954	Sandwich 2 pc. Oval Trays	Machine	1990
#955	Sandwich 2 pc. Wall Sconce	Machine	1990
	[Hostess Treasures]		
#956	Sandwich 2 pc. Crimped Votives	Machine	1990
#958	Sandwich 4 pc. Juice Glass	Machine	1990
	[made from un-crimped votive]		
#961	Sandwich 16 pc. Starter Set	Machine	1990
	[Dinner Plates, Cups, Saucers,		
	Salad Bowls]		
#966	Sandwich Sugar/Cream w/lid	Handmade	1990
#970	Sandwich 3 part Relish	Machine	1990
#971	Sandwich Egg Tray	Machine	1990
#972	Sandwich Platter	Machine	1990
#976	Sandwich Basket	Handmade	1990
#978	Sandwich Wall Clock	Machine	1989
#931	Sandwich Butter & Cover	Handmade	1991 [Disc. '94]
#932	Sandwich Napkin Holder	Handmade	1991
#933	Sandwich Pitcher	Machine	1990
#934	Sandwich Salad Plates	Machine	1991
#959	Sandwich Salt & Pepper	Machine	1991
#987	Sandwich Small Canister	Machine	1991
#988	Sandwich Medium Canister	Machine	1991
#989	Sandwich Large Canister	Machine	1991
#908	Sandwich 4 pc. Sherbet	Machine	1992
#897	Sandwich Candle Holder	Handmade	1992 [Disc. '94]
	[Customer Specials]		
#927	*Sandwich Table Wine	Machine	1990
#930	*Sandwich Footed Mug	Machine	1991
#913	Sandwich Oval Photo Plate	Machine	1991
	[Limited Availability]		
#923	Sandwich Round Photo Plate	Machine	1991
	[Limited Availability]		
#998	*Sandwich Glo Lamp, pr. —also #910	Machine	1991
	*Added to Regular Line in 1993		
#920	Sandwich Goblets	Machine	1992 [Disc. '93]
#928	Sandwich Two-Tier Tidbit Tray	Machine	1993
#937	Sandwich Tall Candle Holder	Handmade	1993

Crystal		Mold Information	Introduction
#055	Sandwich Picture Frame (New Molds)	Machine	1993
#220	Sandwich 6 pc. Oval Trays	Machine	1993
#250	Sandwich 14 pc. Punch Set	Machine	1993
#252	Sandwich 12 pc. Punch Cups	Machine	1993

Decorated		Mold Information	Introduction
#333	Sandwich Picture Frame	Same as #055	July '94
	Decorated Pink		
#343	Sandwich Picture Frame	Same as #055	July '94
	Decorated Blue		
	[Limited Availability]		

20

Spruce		Mold Information	Introduction
#483	Sandwich Pitcher	Machine	1993
#484	Sandwich 10 oz. Tumblers	Machine	1993
#486	Sandwich Wall Clock	Machine	1993
#487	Sandwich Coffee Cups	Machine	1993
#488	Sandwich 8" Salad Plates	Machine	1993
#489	Sandwich Vegetable Bowls	Machine	1993
#490	Sandwich Platter	Machine	1993
#491	Sandwich Egg Tray	Machine	1993
#492	Sandwich Relish	Machine	1993
#476	3 pc. Buffet Set	Machine	1993
#493	Sandwich Dinner Plates	Machine	1994
#456	Sandwich Basket	Handmade	July '94
#463	Sandwich Napkin Holder	Handmade	July '94
#473	Sandwich Sugar & Creamer	Handmade	July '94
#485	Sandwich Two-Tier Tidbit	Same as #488 & #493	July '94
#436	Sandwich Salt & Pepper	Machine	1995
#437	Sandwich Crimped Bowl	Machine	1995
#445	Sandwich 4 pc. Saucers	Machine	1995
#447	Sandwich 2 pc. Crimped Votives	Machine	1995
#448	Sandwich 2 pc. Oval Trays	Machine	1995
#449	Sandwich Wall Sconces	Machine	1995
#464	Sandwich 8 pc. Snack Set	Machine	1995
#465	Sandwich 4 pc. Juice	Machine	1995
#471	Sandwich Tall Candle Holder	Handmade	1995
#820	Sandwich Soup Bowls	Machine	1995

21

ACCESSORIES

A TOUCH OF COUNTRY

Step into the world of "country". Smell the fresh bread baking in a fireside oven. As you walk outside to the well for a bucket of crisp clear water, a horse-drawn carriage ambles lazily down the lane.

Gazing into the barnyard, you see the cows grazing precariously close to your newly planted flower bed. Enjoy the relaxing atmosphere of a country home. Then, experience "A Touch of Country" from Tiara Exclusives.

"A Touch of Country" was designed exclusively for Tiara in 1987. Six rich colors provide a scenic, original design for decorative, personal-use housewares.

		Introduction
#507	Candle Lamp	1988 [Disc. 1989]
#508	4 pc. Beverage, 14 oz.	1988 [Disc. 1989]
#510	3 pc. Storage Set	1988 [Disc. 1990]
#512	4 pc. Beverage, 12 oz.	1988 [Disc. 1989]

FLOWERS AND LACE

A unique combination of delicate peach flowers on a carefully etched background gives Tiara's Flowers and Lace a flair for dressing up your favorite countertop or dinner service. Designed exclusively for Tiara, this pattern, released in January, 1990, is perfect for complementing our new Sandwich Dinnerware in peach.

Selections include:

		Introduction
#973	3 pc. Storage Jar Set	1990 [Disc. '94]
#974	4 pc. 12 oz. Beverage	1990
#975	7 pc. Juice Set	1990

The 4 pc. 12 oz. Beverage Set and 7 pc. Juice Set were available for a limited time in 1990 as a Customer Special in blue.

FLORAL MEDLEY DESIGNS

This exclusive silk-screened decoration requires pain staking and precise decorating methods that most Companies wouldn't dream of! Produced exclusively for Tiara by Bartlett-Collins, this is surely the most beautiful every-day drinkware you'll own. Designed exclusively for Tiara.

		Introduction
#398	6 pc. 12 oz. Beverage	1992
#378	3 pc. Storage Jar Set	1993 [Disc. '95]

BEVERAGE AND PARTY SERVICE

CELEBRATION

A wedding, a holiday, or an informal family gathering, all are perfect
for the Celebration Service. Breezy leaves lie undisturbed in harmonious
crystal, waiting to serve your every need.

Each piece was carefully sized for multiple usage. Complementary to any
theme, the Punch Set is a perfect wedding gift. Glass Coasters are the
protection every fine piece of wood furniture needs.

From Serving Plates and Bowls to the perfectly sized Cake Plate, this
distinguished pattern was designed in 1984 by Tiara Exclusives for your
"celebration" in style.

		Introduction
#103	4 pc. Snack Plates	1986 [Disc. '88]
#104	Tray	1984 [Disc. '89]
#109	4 pc. Coasters	1985 [Disc. '88]
#110	2 pc. Serving Bowls	1986 [Disc. '89]
#111	Party Bowl	1986 [Disc. '89]
#113	14 pc. Punch Set	1986 [Disc. '92]
#104	Tray [reintroduced]	Jan '92 [Disc. '92]

EXCLUSIVELY YOURS

It is believed that lead was first added to glass to aid in the melting
process of the batch materials.

Tiara believes that lead was added to glass for an elegant touch, a
splendid resonant ring, and gleaming brilliance. In 1984 Tiara
Exclusives introduced the Exclusively Yours pattern. Crafted and
designed for Tiara by Fostoria, a respected and renowned name in lead
crystal, the drinkware became a preferred selection for Tiara Customers.

Exclusively Yours was an excellent gift choice, but few who experience
the beauty of fine lead crystal can part with it. You deserve the best,
and with Tiara, it's Exclusively Yours!

		Introduction
#070	Double Old Fashion	1984 [Disc. '91]
#071	Beverage/Highball	1984 [Disc. '91]
#072	Goblet	1984 [Disc. '91]
#073	Wine Juice	1984 [Disc. '91]
#074	Ice Tea	1984 [Disc. '91]
#056	Pitcher	1986 [Disc. '91]

Exclusively Yours was replaced by "Facets" in January of 1992.

FACETS IN CRYSTAL

We got the lead out! Our new crystal drinkware selections look familiar, but the prices will amaze you. Formerly called Exclusively Yours, our Facets in crystal is produced for Tiara by Indiana Glass Company, without the lead!

	Introduction
#206 Pitcher [32 oz.]	1992
#207 4 pc. Double Old Fashion [11 oz.]	1992
#209 4 pc. Beverage/Highball [13 oz.]	1992
#213 4 pc. Wine/Juice (7 oz.)	1992
#214 4 pc. Ice Tea [12 oz.]	1992 [Disc. '94]
#217 4 pc. Goblet [9 oz.]	1992

QUEEN ANNE

European lead crystal in all its charm and grandeur has a delicate touch, impressive shape, and a style befitting the homes of America.

Tiara introduced the Queen Anne Collection in 1987. Imported from Romania this contemporary grouping of stemware and a gently styled decanter are the finishing touch you've been looking for. Reminiscent of old world Queen Anne Windows, the pattern is carefully handcut by skilled craftsmen and then polished by hand to add the lustre only lead crystal can offer.

	Mold Information	Introduction
#870 2 pc. Ice Tea	Mouthblown	1987 [Disc. '89]
#871 2 pc. Goblet	Mouthblown	1987 [Disc. '89]
#872 2 pc. Wine	Mouthblown	1987 [Disc. '89]
#873 2 pc. Flute	Mouthblown	1987 [Disc. '89]
#874 Decanter [Disc. '91].	Mouthblown	1987 [Disc. '91]

MEADOW FANTASIES

Introduced as a customer special in 1987, the Meadow Fantasies Collection of imported, mouthblown, handcut crystal offered a new direction for Tiara Customers. The pattern was available exclusively through Tiara, and the light country blossoms, resembling thistles in bloom, enjoyed great popularity. [Imported European crystal]

	Introduction
#740 Bowl	1986 [Disc. 1990]
#741 Vase	1986 [Disc. 1989]
#742 Pitcher	1986 [Disc. 1989]
#743 Cake Plate & Cover [Hostess Treasures]	1988 [Disc. 1989]
#744 Rose Bowl	1988 [Disc. 1991]
#745 Bud Vase	1988 [Disc. 1990]

24

GENTLEMEN'S CHOICE

13 oz. Mugs – Designed exclusively for Tiara over a period of two years, a complete set of detailed wildlife scenes were introduced. Avid sportsmen and deserving gentlemen have delighted in receiving one or all sets of our 13 oz. Handled Mugs.

The mugs are produced by Indiana Glass Company, (by machine) and the artwork was first applied by a silk screen process until 1992, when decals replaced the challenging silk screen methods.

Crystal:

		Introduction
#029	Pheasant Hunt Mugs, crystal	1989
#108	Deer Mugs, crystal	1991 [Disc. '95]
#226	Bear Mugs, crystal	1993
#249	Fishing Mugs, crystal	1992 [Disc. '95]

Black:

#391	Deer Mugs, black	1993 [Disc. '94]
#400	Pheasant Hunt Mugs, black	1993 [Disc. '95]

HUNTER HORN MUGS

Designed especially for Tiara Exclusives. Sleek lines and gentle shaping create a relaxed environment for your favorite beverages.

Carefully crafted, thickly styled, the Hunter Horn Mugs fit easily into the hand for cool refreshing soft drinks or hot spicy ciders. They have remained a favorite gift for fathers and grandfathers alike who enjoy the simplicity of this unique set.

		Introduction
#030	Hunter Horn Mugs, crystal	1980
#550	Hunter Horn Mugs, black	1982 [Disc. '83]

MINI MUGS

Designed in 1964 by Indiana Glass Company. Just the right size for little people with big ideas, these adorable little mugs make refreshments even more important for the small, thirsty people you know.

		Introduction
#006	Mini Mugs	1974 [Disc. '88]

PATIO TANKARDS

Satiny smooth etching on clear crystal is a delight in beverage service. The tankard molds were acquired by Indiana Glass in 1969. Tiara introduced this set in 1978 which, until 1987, included a pitcher. The tankards were also offered in pink etched in 1983.

		Introduction
#046	Patio Tankards	1978 [Disc. '88]

POWDER HORN TUMBLERS

The origin of the Powder Horn Tumblers dates back to 1959. Initially offered by Indiana Glass Company, these eye-catching tumblers were also produced in black and milk glass.

		Introduction
#040	Powder Horn Tumblers	1977 [Disc. '89]

Silhouette Stemware

Our new Silhouette Stemware is finished exclusively for Tiara by Susquehanna Glass. Each piece can be an exceptional compliment to the popular Sandwich Dinnerware in peach.

The European design of our Silhouettes Stemware adds a new dimension to our product line. The production process for this type of stemware requires precise timing and exceptional skill. Understanding the steps involved helps us appreciate the true value of this particular product line.

The blank pieces of stemware are produced by Durand in France. The dual colors are achieved from two separate tanks of glass; one peach and one crystal. As the stem is formed from the peach tank, the top or "bowl" area is blown to exact shape and size from a crystal tank. The two pieces are quickly united and fused with intense fire to form a single elegant piece of stemware, which is then carefully polished for a brilliant, clear finish. The product is then forwarded to Susquehanna Glass in the United States for the final and equally challenging process of cutting our pattern into each piece. Afterward it is closely inspected, packed and shipped to Tiara Exclusives, ready for its final destination, the Tiara customer.

Further research of our selected pattern provided an interesting history. It was used on stemware marketed to upscale department stores in the 1930's, 40's and 50's, and it was called, believe it or not, the Tiara Pattern!

An excellent gift choice, Silhouettes Stemware is durable and dishwasher safe. You will appreciate both the high quality and the graceful European styling whenever a formal dinnerware setting is desired. [100% lead-free.]

January 1995 introductions include:

		Mold Information
#740	8 oz. Wine, pair	Blown/handcut
#741	12 oz. Goblet, pair	Blown/handcut
#742	5 3/4 oz. Flute, pair	Blown/handcut

26

DECORATOR GROUPINGS

ANNA HUTTE

In 1993, Tiara Exclusives is proud to offer 24% lead crystal products, imported from Germany. Products of this type from Germany are known for their excellent quality and elegant design. Each item is offered exclusively by Tiara in the United States! Handcrafted by masters of the glass-making art, the offerings are competitively priced and absolutely beautiful!

Our introduction included four collections. Each of these designs were created by Franz Pfund, Senior Chief Designer of Anna Hutte who reportedly "presently is the most capable artist for designing shapes and designs for crystal products."

These handmade lead crystal items differ in composition from our standard "soda lime" glass. High quality quartz sand, potash and soda, in addition to other chemical mixtures are melted at approximately 3000 F. in special fireproof tanks.

To maintain the lustre and brilliance, simply hand wash in warm water with a mild detergent. Never use the dishwasher! The color decorations are applied by hand and baked in a special kiln at approximately 1000 F. for permanence. The unique handles on the baskets are applied with a special adhesive under ultraviolet beams. The following items are available, packed in a Tiara box, individually labeled: Tiara by Anna Hutte:

La Fleur (Pronounced: La Flur)

Elegant 24% lead crystal with etched daisies. Choose from:

		Mold Information	Introduction
#290	Footed Compote [8½" high.]	Handmade	1993 [Disc. '95]
	Hostess Treasures $500 Level		
#291	Candy Box & Cover [6½" high.]		
	Hostess Treasures $250 Level	Handmade	1993 [Disc. '95]
#292	Basket [8" high.]	Handmade	1993 [Disc. '95]
#315	La Fleur Cake Plate & Cover	Handmade	1993 [Disc. '95]
	Hostess Treasures $750 Level		
	or as alternative to $75.00 in		
	Free Shopping for 3 bookings.		
	The glass dome is from Indiana Glass.		
#331	Rectangular Tray		
	Hostess Treasures $500 Level	Handmade	1994 [Disc. '95]

Mercedes (Pronounced: Mer-say-dees)

Elegant 24% lead crystal with ruby decoration. Choose From:

		Mold Information	Introduction
#285	Vase [7½" high.]	Handmade	1993 [Disc. '95]
#286	Candy Box & Cover [7½" high.]	Handmade	1993 [Disc. '95]
#287	Console Bowl [4½" high.]	Handmade	1993 [Disc. '94]
#293	Prestige Ball [5" high.]	Handmade	1993 [Disc. '95]
#294	Prestige Heart Gift Box & Cover		
	[1½" high, 3" diameter.]	Handmade	1993 [Disc. '95]
#310	Prestige Vase [3½" high.]	Handmade	1993 [Disc. '95]

ANNA HUTTE Cont.

Rendezvous   (Pronounced: Ron-day-voo)

Elegant 24% lead crystal items with 24k gold decoration are a wonderful
gift idea for weddings and anniversaries. Choose from:

		Mold Information	Introduction
#280	Vase [6" high.]	Handmade	1993 (Disc. '94]
#282	Candy Box & Cover		
	[1993 Preferred Hostess Gift]	Handmade	1993 [Disc. '93]
#283	Basket [6½" high.]	Handmade	1993 [Disc. '95]
#284	2 pc. Candle Sticks (5" high.)	Handmade	1993 [Disc. '95]
#309	Rendezvous Bowl	Handmade	1994 [Disc. '94]

AURORA

The Aurora collection is handmade exclusively in plum for Tiara by L.E.
Smith. [Introduced 1995.]

#845 Table Lamp [8 1/2" high.]
This Lamp includes a handmade crystal base which can also be used with
a 2.5x6 pillar candle, and a handmade plum shade. The set includes a
crystal votive cup and a 10 hour unscented votive.

#847 Vase [12-14" high.]
This vase can range in height from 12 - 14" due to the completely
handmade process used to achieve the shape.

Molten glass is first mouthblown into a cast iron mold then held upside
down and swung by using an aqu old process of affixing a snap to the
base during the cooling stage. Heights will vary from one finisher to
the next, like a snowflake, no two are alike.

#848 Basket [7 3/4" high.]
Two pots of glass must be melted simultaneously to produce this
particular basket. First, plum glass is gathered and pressed into shape
for the "bowl" area. This piece is then reheated and passed to a
finisher who crimps the piece by hand. In the meantime crystal is
gathered and rolled into a long tube - shape and pressed onto one side
of the basket following the crimping process and then attached and cut
off by the finisher on the opposite side of the basket. Using a wooden
tool, he carefully rounds and shapes the handle as it cools. As with all
handmade baskets, crimping and handle thickness and shape will vary.

#859 Orchid Oval Tray [8½" x 14".]
There's been some discussion as to whether or not this is actually an
orchid, but that is what the original designer called this tray! This
item is hand-pressed in plum exclusively for Tiara. This tray was
designed in the late 1980's by L.E. Smith as part of a 4 pc. collection.

#874 Hurricane Lamp [12½" high.]
This piece is an elegant and versatile item that will dress up any room
in your home. The base is handmade in plum exclusively for Tiara. We
added a blown crystal shade and an 8" formal dinner candle from Candle-
lite to complete the look. The 12" Globe can be removed and used with
candle rings or statues, making it a versatile and valuable part of this
3 pc. Hurricane Lamp.

Cape Cod was originally introduced in 1932. Imperial Glass Corporation of Bellaire, Ohio was the first Company to successfully press the first piece in this distinguished pattern.

Imperial was well known for their expertise in producing decorative ware, lamp shades and serving ware, to include "Nuart" & "Nucut" Candlewick and Cape Cod.

Cape Cod was marketed extensively through the 1930's and 40's. Collectors now anxiously search for this pattern in flea markets and antique stores because of its historical value.

We have located references regarding the production of Cape Cod in Ritz Blue and Antique Blue. We are reasonably certain our new Vintage Blue from L.E. Smith will not interfere with the collectability of this pattern, since none of the items recorded in these colors are now offered by Tiara.

The mold equipment is original! The items offered are from vintage 1947 molds. Enjoy this limited collection of authentic handmade Cape Cod from mold equipment owned by Indiana Glass Company! Produced for Tiara by L.E. Smith.

	Mold Information	Introduction
#795 Petite Basket	Handmade	1993 [Disc. '95]
#796 Cape Cod Footed Bud Vase	Handmade	1993 [Disc. '95]
#797 Cape Cod Two-part Relish	Handmade	1993 [Disc. '95]

COLONY GARDENS COLLECTION

Our Colony Gardens selection of items are produced from Fostoria mold equipment called "Colony" pattern. This particular pattern was introduced in 1938 by Fostoria and included beverageware, serving pieces and many decorative items. Also known as the 2412 line, this pattern enjoyed a long, and successful existence in the Fostoria line. Many of the molds are no longer workable, but we are happy to provide you with selected favorites, produced from original molds. All items listed are handmade.

		Introduction
#859	Square Flower Bowl, wisteria [Imperial mold] [see also: Daisy Pattern]	1991 [Disc. '91]
#865	Basket, wisteria	1989 [Disc. '91]
#860	Bowl, wisteria	1991 [Disc. '91]
#862	Powder Box & Cover, wisteria	1989 [Disc. '91]
#861	Footed Tray, wisteria	1989 [Disc. '91]
#864	Bowl & Plate, wisteria [Hostess Treasures] Previously called Lotus Lily Bowl & Plate, this item was also offered in past colors of ruby, premier blue and chantilly green.	1990 [Disc. '93]
#863	Colonial Bell, wisteria Previously available in premier blue as a contest prize, [1986]. Imperial mold.	1990 [Disc. '91]
#407	Basket, teal mist	1991 [Disc. '93]
#408	Bowl, teal mist [Hostess Treasures]	1991 [Disc. '92]
#409	Footed Tray, teal mist	1991 [Disc. '93]
#410	Colonial Bell, teal mist	1991 [Disc. '93]

The following items were offered in October of 1991 as contest prizes. They have never been a part of the regular line. [Disc. '92.]

#411	Colony Gardens Flared Dessert Bowl, teal mist
#412	Colony Gardens Cupped Console Bowl, teal mist
#413	Colony Gardens Platter, teal mist

DAISY PATTERN

In the early 1920's - 30's, cut glass was very popular. It sparkled with a beauty only the wealthy could afford. Soon manufacturers were looking for ways to take advantage of the popularity of such items. Molds like the Daisy pattern were designed with intricate detail and deep prisms to make each item sparkle like cut glassware. The molds made it possible to provide a less expensive alternative to authentic cut glass, which could be marketed to a much wider range of customers and incomes.

The resurgence of antique styling, and the endless search for the beautiful items like Grandma had, make Tiara's Daisy pattern a favorite choice. Each piece is handcrafted from original Imperial mold equipment. Once a part of the line Imperial called Collector's Crystal, Tiara has maintained the value of those earlier pieces by offering the Daisy Collection in sea mist.

		Mold Information	Introduction
#563	Bowl [7" dia.]	Handmade	July 1992 [Disc. '94]
#565	Crimped Sherbet [3½" high.]	Handmade	July 1992 [Disc. '93]
#566	Square Flower Bowl [9½" dia.] This Bowl was previously offered in wisteria & dusty rose.	Handmade	July 1992 [Disc. '94]
#567	Oval Relish [8" long.] This Oval Relish was previously offered in dusty rose.	Handmade	July 1992 [Disc. '94]
#564	Footed Compote [Hostess Treasure]	Handmade	July 1992 [Disc. '93]

DESERT BLOSSOMS

We took the everlasting charm of a calla lilly design and added the undeniable beauty of a color called sage mist. The Desert Blossoms Collection blends well with any Southwestern decor. Previously know as the "Leaf" Bowl and Candle Holders, the bowl and candle holders have been offered in sunset, burnt honey and black. The mold for the bowl is used to make the basket. The candle holder also serves as a soap dish with an equipment change. All items in sage mist were handmade for Tiara by Fenton Art Glass. [IGC mold #1009. Date of original molds estimated to be 1930-1945.]

		Introduction
#556	Two-lite Candle Holder	1991 [Disc. '91]
#558	Basket	1990 [Disc. '91]
#559	Candle Holder	1990 [Disc. '91]
#560	Vase	1990 [Disc. '91]
#561	Soap Dish	1990 [Disc. '91]
#562	Bowl [Hostess Treasure]	1990 [Disc. '91]

DOGWOOD COLLECTION

In the late 1930's, a myriad of new glassware designs emerged from the Indiana Glass Hand Shop. Many of these noteworthy patterns are known for their collectable value. Exact dates of introduction on the #: Dogwood Pattern from Indiana Glass are not available, but the items can be traced back to this pre-war period. The bell was produced for Tiara by Dalzell Viking. No mold history is available.

Tiara's 1991 Fall introduction included selected treasures, handcrafted in crystal, and carefully etched to perfection. Produced from original molds, this collection is a fitting remembrance of the legendary Dogwood blossoms that appear each year in all their splendor.

		Mold Information	Introduction
#109	Mini Basket [6" high.]	Handmade	1991 [Disc. '94]
#114	Bon-Bon Dish [2¾" high, 5" dia.]	Handmade	1991 [Disc. '94]
#116	Three-part Candy Dish & Cover [4½" high, 6" dia.]	Handmade	1991 [Disc. '94]
#120	Bookend [6½" high.]	Handmade	1991 [Disc. '91]
#131	Handcrafted Floral Bell [6½" high.]	Handmade	1992 [Disc. '94]

EMPRESS PATTERN

Purchased by Indiana Glass Company in 1953 from McKee Glass Company, this set of molds carries a unique design which was called the "Louvre" pattern. Previously produced by the Indiana Glass Hand Shop in coral, and Fenton Art Glass in dusty rose, it took on a striking new appearance in azure blue.

Produced by Dalzell-Viking for Tiara, each piece is crafted by hand with painstaking accuracy.

		Mold Information	Introduction
#602	Jewel Box & Cover [5½" X 3½"]	Handmade	1991
#603	Basket [7½" high.] Hostess Treasures	Handmade	1991 [Disc. '94]
#604	Tray [7½ X 11½"]	Handmade	1991
#605	Oval Bowl [13" long X 4½" high.]	Handmade	1991

All four items were also offered in pink as contest prizes for Associates in 1992.

#606	Candle Stick [8½" high.]	Handmade	1992 [Disc. '92]

IMPRESSIONS

The Impressions grouping includes an assortment of handmade items with a touch of nostalgia for your home.

The Laurel Basket and Marmalade Jar were originally produced by Indiana Glass Company beginning as early as 1945. All items listed were produced for Tiara by Fenton Art Glass.

		Introduction
#123	Laurel Vase, tea rose [IGC #1010 Pattern]	1989 [Disc. '89]
#124	Windmill Basket, tea rose [Hostess Treasures - Imperial Mold]	1988 [Disc. '89]
#125	Laurel Basket, tea rose [IGC #1010 Pattern]	1987 [Disc. '89]
#126	3-Toed Bowl, tea rose [Imperial Mold]	1987 [Disc. '89]
#127	Laurel Marmalade Jar & Cover, tea rose [IGC #1010 Pattern]	1987 [Disc. '89]
#128	Fan Vase, tea rose [Imperial Mold]	1987 [Disc. '89]
#129	Laurel Console Bowl, tea rose [IGC #1010 Pattern]	1988 [Disc. '89]
#613	Swan, white lace crystal [Imperial Mold]	1988 [Disc. '91]
#615	Laurel Basket, white lace crystal [IGC #1010 Pattern]	1990 [Disc. '91]
#616	Laurel Marmalade Jar, white lace crystal [IGC #1010 Pattern]	1990 [Disc. '90]
#617	3-Toed Bowl [Imperial Mold]	1990 [Disc. '91]
#618	Laurel Console Bowl, white lace crystal [Hostess Treasures] [IGC #1010 Pattern]	1990 [Disc. '91]
#619	Windmill Basket [Imperial Mold] [Hostess Treasures] white lace crystal	1990 [Disc. '91]
#088	Laurel Cake Plate [IGC #1010 Pattern] [Hostess Treasures] white lace crystal	1990 [Disc. '91]
#086	Laurel Console Bowl, white lace crystal [IGC #1010 Pattern]	1990 [Disc. '91]

MARQUIS COLLECTION

Handmade by skilled craftsmen, our Marquis Collection is a combination of decorative favorites in a dark, blue-green shade of glass called teal. Produced exclusively for Tiara by L.E. Smith, all molds are the property of Indiana Glass Company. Items in this grouping are as follows:

		Introduction
#123	Candle Holders, teal [4" high.] teal	1993 [Disc. '94]
#871	Pineapple Candle Holders, ruby	Available July - Dec. '93, '94
#420	Pineapple Candle Holders, teal	1993 [Disc. '93]
#427	Center Bowl, teal	1993 [Disc. '94]
#432	Mini Basket, teal [5½" high.] Offered in ruby as a Hostess Special Purchase in December 1993.	1993 [Disc. '94]
#434	Bowl & Plate, teal Previously available in ruby, chantilly green and premier blue.	1993 [Disc. '94]
#444	Basket, teal [8" high.]	1993 [Disc. '94]
#422	Vase, teal [7¼" high.] Offered in black in 1989.	1993 [Disc. '94]

ROSALEE

An absolutely delightful pattern, molds for this collection were purchased by Indiana Glass many years ago. The beauty of our Rosalee items lies in the fact that real roses wither away, but glass ones can be treasured for a lifetime.

#721 Crimped Bud Vase [6" high.]
From our Imperial mold collection, this vase was available in a variety of colors during tenure at Imperial Glass, but the 1994 edition from Tiara is its first appearance in dusty rose! [Handmade.]

#722 Crimped Basket [8" high.]
We've been unable to determine the origin of this mold. It resembles an Imperial mold, but we have no history of it in our Imperial records. Regardless of its history, its absolutely stunning in dusty rose. [Handmade.]

#723 Double Crimped Bowl [7½" diameter.]
Made from the same mold as our Basket [722] this bowl is finished with an elegant double crimped edge. It makes a wonderful centerpiece, and a perfect gift for our Preferred Hostesses. [Handmade.]

SPRING SONG

The pieces in this collection were introduced by L.E. Smith in 1983. Several valves can be used to create designs in the oval or round area in the center of each item.

The "scroll and fret" design was patterned after commemorative plates produced by L.E. Smith for the Franklin Mint.

This series has been available in pink, but never with the particular valve design offered by Tiara. Each piece is handcrafted at L.E. Smith, exclusively in pink, for Tiara Exclusives.

The pink color and delicate pattern, we think you'll agree, are pleasing accessories for decorating, and make splendid gifts.

		Mold Information	Introduction
#343	Spring Song Basket	Handmade	1993 [Disc. '95]
#344	Spring Song Oval Trinket Box	Handmade	1993 [Disc. '95]
#345	Spring Song Tri-Candle	Handmade	1993 [Disc. '95]
#349	Spring Song Ball [Limited Offering]	Handmade	1994

SPRING SONG ACCENTS

		Mold Information	Introduction
#339	Swan	Handmade	1994
#353	Heart Paperweight	Handmade	1994

SWAN SERENADE

Introduced by L. E. Smith in 1989, the Swan Bowl and Candle Holders have only been offered in crystal/etched.

Handmade by L.E. Smith, the design is both captivating and elegant. Although additional items in this pattern are offered by L.E. Smith, we chose to limit our introduction to these especially beautiful and functional items. Available through the Hostess Treasures Program.

They are produced exclusively for Tiara in pink/etched.

		Mold Information	Introduction
#346	Swan Serenade Candle Holder	Handmade	Dec. '93
	Hostess Treasures $500 Level		
#347	Swan Serenade Bowl	Handmade	Dec. '93
	Hostess Treasures $250 Level		
#338	Swan Oval Tray		
	Hostess Treasures $250 Level	Handmade	1994

SUZANNE

Designed for Tiara Exclusives by Fostoria Glass Company, the Suzanne Collection is just another example of the beautiful highlights that fine lead crystal can offer. Complementing glassware or china, the Suzanne styling has a smooth, sleek line that sparkles with true brilliance. Popular as giftware for anniversaries, weddings, etc., the Suzanne Collection has become a favorite of the discriminating buyer.

The molds for our Suzanne items were moved from Lancaster Glass to Indiana Glass in 1990/91. This was due to the discontinuance of lead crystal production.

		Introduction	
#075	Suzanne Vase, lead crystal	1986	[Disc. '91]
#076	Suzanne Vase, lead crystal	1984	[Disc. '89]
#080	Suzanne Candy Box and Cover, lead cry	1985	[Disc. '88]
#084	Suzanne Salt and Pepper, lead crystal	1985	[Disc. '91]
#026	Suzanne Vase, aquamarine [5½" high.]	1991	
#027	Suzanne Candy Box & Cover, aquamarine	1991	[Disc. '94]
#019	Suzanne Vase, crystal [7¾" high.]	1990	
#392	Suzanne Base, black [7¾" high.]	1993	

The Suzanne Salt & Pepper was reintroduced in imperial blue in 1992. See "Crown Dinner Accessories."

VANESSA

Owned by L.E. Smith, this set of molds has [as of 1994] only been offered in crystal. Produced exclusively for Tiara in plum, the "Vanessa" line blends beautifully with the dark florals and brocades which have recently enjoyed popularity.

		Mold Information	Introduction
#881	Double Crimped Basket [6½" high.]	Handmade	1994
#882	Double Crimped Bowl [7¾" dia.]	Handmade	1994
#883	Banana Basket [6¼" high.]	Handmade	1994
#884	Covered Candy Dish [6¼" dia.]	Handmade	1994

VENETIAN

Designed for Tiara by Fostoria Glass Company in 1984, this elegant pattern has a lustre and brilliance that adds a touch of grace to any setting. Our "Tiara by Fostoria", Venetian Candle Holders and Lamps are tastefully designed and sized proportionately to soften a room with romantic candlelight. Precision cutting, authentic lead crystal, fine craftsmanship are from Tiara exclusively for you!

		Introduction
#046	Venetian Candle Lamp	1986 [Disc. '90]
#078	Venetian Candle Holder, [5½" high.]	1984 [Disc. '87]
#079	Venetian Candle Holder, [3" high.]	1984 [Disc. '90]

These molds were also moved from Lancaster Glass to Indiana Glass in 1990. Produced in crystal and offered at a much more economical price than their lead counterparts.

		Introduction
#017	Venetian Candle Holder, pair, crystal [7¾" high.]	1990
#018	Venetian Candle Lamp, crystal	1990
#393	Venetian Candle Holders, pair, black [5½" high.]	1993 [Disc. '95]
#032	Venetian Candle Holders, paid, crystal etched [7¾" high.]	1993

VICTORIAN ENSEMBLE

Deep rich color and a wonderful collection of shapes and styles have made the Victorian Ensemble a popular tradition in decorating. The dusty rose color synonymous with this grouping is produced for Tiara by Fenton Art Glass. [Handmade] Items produced in other colors are listed here because they were originally a part of the Victorian Ensemble.

Fenton Production		Introduction
#278	Eve Vase [see #735], cobalt	
	Offered as a contest prize in March [One Production]	1992
#279	Eve Console Bowl [see #736], cobalt	
	[Contest Hostess Gift]	1992 [Disc. '93]
#727	Baroness Candle Lamp [Imperial Mold]	1990 [Disc. '93]
	[Hostess Treasures]	
#735	Eve Vase [Fostoria "Baroque" Mold]	1990 [Disc. '93]
#736	Eve Console Bowl [Fostoria "Baroque" Mold]	1990 [Disc. '91]
#747	Lady Rebecca [Imperial "Dresden" Mold]	1989 [Disc. '92]
	Previously available as a contest prize in chantilly green	
#748	Baroness Basket [No mold history available]	1989
	Also offered in sea mist in 1993.	
#753	Oval Relish [Imperial "Collectors Crystal" Mold]	1992 [Disc. '94]
#754	Floral Medley Tray [No mold history available]	1988 [Disc. '88]
#754	Baroness Candle Holder 5" [Imperial Mold]	1991 [Disc. '93]
#755	Boudoir Vase [Imperial "Threaded" Pattern]	1988 [Disc. '94]
	Also offered in peach in 1993.	
#756	Eve Mint Dish [Fostoria "Baroque" Pattern]	1988 [Disc. '90]
#760	Eve Center Bowl [Fostoria "Baroque" Mold]	1989 [Disc. '89]
#761	Square Flower Bowl	1992 [Disc. '93]
	[Imperial "Collector's Crystal" Mold] [Previously offered in Colony Gardens collection in wisteria.]	
#762	Baroness Bowl	1991 [Disc. '92]
#763	Eve Three-Part Candy Box & Cover	1988 [Disc. '91]
#764	Imperial Ashtray ["Pillow Box" Mold]	1988 [Disc. '94]
#765	Fan Box & Cover [Imperial Mold]	1989
	[Previously available in chantilly green]	
#768	Boudoir Rose Bowl [Imperial "Threaded" Pattern]	1989 [Disc. '89]
#751	Victorian Water Bottle [Hostess Treasures $250]	1992 [Disc. '94]
#728	Three-Toed Mini Basket, dusty rose [7" high.]	1993
	Previously offered in provincial blue, tea rose & peach in basket form. This item has also been offered in white lace crystal, and sea mist as a Bon Bon Dish. (Imperial Mold)	

Dalzell-Viking Production-pink		Introduction
#396	Floral Medley Tray [12¼" x 8¾" dia.] Handmade	1992 [Disc. '94]
#398	Floral Medley Tray [10¼" x 7¾" dia.] Handmade [Same as #754]	1992 [Disc. '94]

35

WATER LILY ACCENTS

Offered by Tiara for those glass lovers who have a passion for beautifully handcrafted glass with an undeniably feminine touch, we are proud to present Water Lily Accents. Clear true designs are softly captured in romantic splendor by the glassmaker's hands. Hold a piece of opalescent Water Lily up to a light and experience the fire forever sealed inside each entrancing item. The pattern, designed by Anthony Rosena for Fenton Art Glass in the early 1970's, is produced opalescence by Fenton, exclusively for Tiara.

		Introduction
#146	Water Lily Christmas Candle Holder, ruby [July-December Only]	1990
#147	Water Lily Christmas Basket, ruby [July-December Only]	1990
#401	Water Lily Candle Holders, teal mist	1991
	[Customer Special—one month only-November]	
#417	Water Lily Basket, teal mist	1991
	[Customer Special—one month only—October]	
#591	Water Lily Christmas Basket, green [July-December Only]	1990
#592	Water Lily Christmas Candle Holder [July-December Only]	1990
#608	Water Lily Fruit Bowl, white lace crystal	1987 [Disc. '89]
#609	Water Lily Console Bowl, white lace crystal	1987 [Disc. '89]
#610	Water Lily Bud Vase, white lace crystal	1987 [Disc. '89]
#611	Water Lily Candle Sticks, white lace crystal	1987 [Disc. '89]
#612	Water Lily Basket, white lace crystal	1987 [Disc. '89]
#613	Swan [Imperial Mold] white lace crystal	1987
	[Moved to Impressions collection]	1990
#692	Water Lily Fruit Bowl, provincial blue	1990 [Disc. '91]
#693	Water Lily Bud Vase, provincial blue	1990 [Disc. '91]
#694	Water Lily Candle Holders, provincial blue	1990 [Disc. '91]
#695	Water Lily Basket, provincial blue	1990 [Disc. '91]
#757	Water Lily Mini Basket, dusty rose	1988 [Disc. '91]
	[Hostess Treasures]	

The following Water Lily items were offered as contest prizes only.

		Introduction
#585	Water Lily 3-Toed Bowl, provincial blue	1991 only
#586	Water Lily Jardiniere, provincial blue	1991 only
#587	Water Lily Covered Candy Dish, provincial blue	1991 only

Black	Mold Information	Introduction
#813 Water Lily Bud Vase	Handmade	1993 [Disc. '95]
#814 Water Lily Basket	Handmade	1993 [Disc. '95]
#817 Water Lily Ftd. Candy Box & Cover	Handmade	1993 [Disc. '95]
[Hostess Treasures $250]		

WINDMILL BOWL

Handmade for Tiara by Fenton Art Glass, this mold has been used for Baskets, in white lace crystal (1990) Hostess Treasures, ruby (Recruiting Promotion 1993) and peach, 1994 Customer Special. Offered originally as a contest prize in 1991, the Windmill Bowl, which is made from the same mold, has been available in our Hostess Treasures $250 Level since 1992. Mold origin: Imperial Glass Co.

	Introduction
#733 Windmill Basket, dusty rose	1992 [Disc. '95]

WINDMILL PITCHER

Fashioned from an Imperial mold, this captivating item is handmade for Tiara by Fenton Art Glass. Date of original manufacture undetermined.

Hostess Treasures Item, $500

	Introduction
#734 Windmill Pitcher, dusty rose [7" high.]	1994

HOLIDAY SUPPLIES

LEAD CRYSTAL BELLS

Tiara was proud to offer a seasonal collection of specially designed bells in our catalog. In years past, availability was limited to purchases from one or two monthly flyers immediately prior to the holidays. 1988/89 brought the Christmas and Valentine's Bells into the regular line, offering them as a thoughtful gift for many occasions, instead of limiting them to holidays and collectors.

Selections included:

1988 Christmas Bell
Artists worked diligently to prepare the beautiful design on our 1988 Christmas Bell called "Winter by the Covered Bridge". The blending of white, etch and gold gives the design a strikingly lifelike appearance on our fine lead crystal bell.

1989 Christmas Bell
The decoration was designed exclusively for Tiara by Lancaster Colony Design Group. Produced by Lancaster Glass, our sister Company, the charm and variety of Tiara's Bell Collection is continued with our 1989 design. Bells are always a nice choice for those "hard-to-buy-for" people on your Christmas Shopping List!

1989 "From the Heart" Bell
Designed exclusively for Tiara by Lancaster Colony Design Group, this message lets the receiver interpret its true meaning. The floral wreath in rich colors adds sincerity to the phrase, and was fashioned in lead crystal with a gold handle.

1990 Christmas Bell
Fashioned in lead crystal for Tiara, by sister Company Lancaster Glass, this elegant bell is a charming addition to the Tiara Christmas Bell collection. Designed especially for Tiara, the wreath and bow pattern is a welcome sign for friends and guests during the jolly Christmas season. Pewter Handle. (6½" high)

#066 Valentine's Bell, lead crystal
Designed exclusively for Tiara, this delicate, lacy design is signed simply, "With Love". A perfect gift idea for many occasions, this item was produced for Tiara in lead crystal by Lancaster Glass.

CHRISTMAS GIFT COLLECTION

Awaken on Christmas morning to the crispness of winter. Gazing out the window, you can see the old church that has witnessed Christmas celebrations for generations. Adorned with red bows and fresh snow glistening on the age old steeple, you feel the warmth of the season well up inside. Truly you are home for the holidays! Tiara's new Christmas design captures the memories, or the dreams of a perfect family Christmas on a glassware selection you'll need for your home.

		Introduction
#334	Christmas Bell [6½" high.]	1992 [Disc. '93]
#624	Christmas 4 pc. 12 oz. Beverage	1992 [Disc. '93]

CHRISTMAS MEMORIES

Designed exclusively for Tiara in 1993, The Christmas Memories Collection is unique in the fact that four different locations were used to complete the set.

This traditional Christmas design seems to echo our yearning for a simpler time and the spirit of Christmas long ago.

#006 Bell. This item was produced by Tiara by Dalzell-Viking. Handmade and decorated with a hand-applied decal. [Introduced July 1993. Christmas Season Only.]

#121 Suncatcher. Produced by Behrenberg on hand-cut glass, exclusively for Tiara, the suncatcher is a new slant to Christmas decor. [6" x 6"] [Introduced July 1993. Christmas Season Only.]

#340	6 pc. 12 oz. Beverage.	Silk-screened exclusively for Tiara
#341	2 pc. 27 oz. Storage Jar Set.	by Bartlett-Collins. Introduced
#342	6 pc. Votive Cups.	1993, Christmas Season only.

| #012 | "Family" Platter | Produced for Tiara by Indiana Glass |
| #022 | "Scrooge & Tiny Tim" Platter | Company. Introduced November 1993, Christmas Season Only. |

CHRISTMAS REMEMBRANCE

The beginning of our own collectable Nativity Set was a proud accomplishment for 1988. Our Nativity collection started with a wooden stable and handpainted figurines of Mary, Joseph, and Baby Jesus. In 1989 Tiara Exclusives added the 3 pc. Shepherd Set. A beautiful remembrance of the first Christmas, this set was truly a Tiara Exclusive. Discontinued: 1989.

CHRISTMAS TREE

This adorable Christmas Tree in azure blue is the perfect keepsake for your family Christmas. Handmade by Dalzell-Viking - it's guaranteed to bring joy every year when you unwrap the decorations for the holiday season. [6" high.]

		Introduction
#625	Tree, azure blue	July 1992
#103	Tree, crystal w/silver tree top	1992
	(Used as a contest prize in 1992)	

38

NATIVITY SCENE

Designed in 1993 exclusively for Tiara, this crystal etched statue is handmade by Dalzell-Viking. A necessary component of your holiday decor, the Nativity Scene is suitable for year round remembrance of the Holy Family.

	Introduction
#007 Nativity Scene, crystal/etched [5¾" high.]	July 1993

SANTA'S WORKSHOP

Year after year, Santa makes his rounds, pausing on rooftops, then returning to the mysterious workshop at the North Pole. Our selection of Christmas items are the perfect stock for Santa's bundle of gifts and merriment!

This festive grouping of decorative items takes the guesswork out of Christmas Shopping!

1989:	Introduction
#431 4 pc. 14 oz. Beverage	1989 [Disc. '89]
#436 4 pc. 12 oz. Beverage	1989 [Disc. '89]
#447 Candle Lamp	1989 [Disc. '89]

WOODEN MUSIC BOX

Introduced in July of 1988, this completely handcrafted Wooden Music Box came complete with Christmas carollers and a church. Its song "Joy to the World" is an old-time Christmas favorite. This item was imported exclusively for Tiara. [Discontinued December, 1988]

39

ADORE BUD VASE

This mouthblown vase was introduced in 1986. The unique shaping of this
item lends itself to rich black glass. Handpainted versions of the
Adore Bud Vase have been offered as follows:

		Introduction
#820	Adore Bud Vase, handpainted mauve/rose floral [Hostess Treasures]	1990 [Disc. '91]
#806	Adore Bud Vase, handpainted peach/green floral [Hostess Treasures]	1990 [Disc. '91]

ATHENA VASE

Handmade in crystal by Dalzell-Viking, our Athena Vase is produced from
Imperial mold equipment. At approximately 10" high, the heavy styling
allows for large and impressive floral displays. Original date of
manufacture undetermined.

		Introduction
#133	Athena Vase, crystal (10" high.)	1994 [Disc. '95]

BRANCH VASE

The delicate design of this mouthblown item lends a striking accent to
any room. Standing 18½" high, this bold black vase is the perfect
vessel for your favorite arrangement. Designed by Tiara Exclusives in
1985, it has also been produced in amber and chantilly green.

Handpainted versions of this vase have been offered as follows:

		Introduction
#819	Branch Vase, handpainted mauve/rose floral [Hostess Treasures]	1990 [Disc. '91]
#825	Branch Vase, handpainted lily Hostess Treasures]	1990 [Disc. '94]
#828	Branch Vase, handpainted white floral [Hostess Treasures]	1988 [Disc. '89]

EDEN VASE

Preferred Hostesses in 1978 could earn this lovely vase in our
traditional amber glass. Offered in our regular line in 1990, it
appears equally appealing in peach. [Mouthblown, 10" high.]

		Introduction
#922	Vase, peach	1991 [Disc. '93]

HUMMINGBIRD VASE

Found in the 1988 Booking Program, the Hummingbird Vase was once called
the "Hum" Vase, and was featured in an oriental collection from Imperial
Glass. It was, at that time, produced in an opaque jade color. Tiara
offered this intricate design in a rich teal color called ocean spray,
perfect for accenting your decor.

		Introduction
#751	Vase, ocean spray	1986 [Disc. '89]

40

MARQUIS VASE

Designed and produced by Indiana Glass Company in the late 1930's, this vase was part of a large collection of items called the #303 Pattern. Introduced by Tiara in July, 1989, its age-old style seems to take an innovative new look in elegant black glass. [See also Marquis Collection.]

		Introduction
#809	Vase, black	1989 [Disc. '93]

PARADISE VASE

Previously offered by Tiara in 1983, the Paradise Vase looked nice in crystal. Peach, however, seems quite becoming also. Available in the 1990 Fall Hostess Treasures Program, this item is made from molds dating back to 1910. [Mouthblown, 12½" high.]

PEACOCK VASE

While the exact age of the mold has not been determined, the intricate design and deep cut pattern of the beautiful peacock is rarely seen in modern mold making. From Indiana Glass Company in the early 1900's to Tiara's introduction in 1982, this magnificent 15" vase has maintained its stunning beauty.

Previously offered by Tiara in chantilly green and horizon blue, 1988 saw the Peacock Vase in sparkling ocean spray for Tiara's Booking Program. [Discontinued December, 1988]

		Mold Information	Introduction
#730	Peacock Vase, dusty rose Hostess Treasures $750 Level	Mouthblown	Dec. '93

PRIMROSE VASE

This tall captivating mouthblown vase has been available from Tiara since 1986. Offered in a variety of colors, it has remained a popular selection. The mold origin is unknown. [17½" high]

		Introduction
#424	Primrose Vase, amethyst	1991
#444	Primrose Vase, platinum [Customer Special July Only]	1985 [Disc. '85]
#500	Primrose Vase, periwinkle, with handpainted flowers [Hostess Treasures]	1988 [Disc. '88]
#746	Primrose Vase, dusty rose	1989 [Disc. '91]
#911	Primrose Vase, imperial blue [Booking Program]	1986 [Disc. '87]

QUEEN'S VASE

Back by popular demand, our lovely Queen's Vase is a classic decorative item, mouthblown and hand-finished exclusively for Tiara.

		Introduction
#055	Queen's Vase, green	1975 [Disc. '77]
#293	Queen's Vase, cobalt	1984 [Disc. '86]
#143	Queen's Vase, ruby [9¾" high.]	1991 [Disc. '91]

ROSE PILLOW VASE

The versatile Rose Pillow Vase was made in coral and was also available in platinum. This handpressed gem was originally called a #143 Footed Cigarette when it was first designed in 1930 by U.S. Glass.

		Introduction
#375	Rose Pillow Vase, coral	1983 [Disc. '90]
#776	Rose Pillow Vase, platinum	1983 [Disc. '90]

ROSE VASE

Introduced into our Hostess Treasures Program in 1991, this statuesque vase was offered in rose pink. In our new sea mist color, this mouthblown masterpiece is a nice floor-type addition to your home. [13" high.] Introduction Date: July 1992 Discontinued Date: 1993

VICTORIA VASE

Tall and captivating, this lovely vase rises over 16" high to hold your favorite silk or dried flower displays with elegance.

Introduced as a Hostess Treasures item in July, 1988, it was later included in Tiara's regular.

		Introduction
#849	Victoria Vase, premier blue	1989 [Disc. '93]

WALL VASE

Handcrafted from original Imperial mold equipment this unusual Wall Vase adds a new dimension to wall decor. Add a handful of silk flowers or use it near your phone with a spray of tissue paper and a supply of pens and small note sheets! Date of original manufacture undetermined.

		Introduction
#909	Wall Vase, peach [6" high.]	1994

42

GIFT SPECIALTIES

ACCESSORIES

Our relationship with Fostoria dates back to the early 1980's when Tiara began to introduce an exclusive line of drinkware (now called Facets) and items which included Venetian Candle Holders and Suzanne Giftware.

We are now proud to add Fostoria Lead Crystal accessories to our current collection of authentic lead crystal items.

	Mold Information	Introduction
#137 Cake Knife [13" long.]	Machine Made	Dec. 1993
#138 Cake Server [11" long.]	Machine Made	Dec. 1993
#261 Letter Opener [9¼" long.]	Machine Made	Dec. 1993

CLASSIC BASKET

Handmade in vintage blue and carefully crimped by skilled craftsmen, this beautiful mid-size basket comes from our collection of Imperial mold equipment. Produced exclusively for Tiara by L.E. Smith - it's a must have gift! [7½" high.] Hostess Treasures $250 Level Gift. Offered in pink in March of 1994 as a Contest Prize.

COLONIAL CANDY BOX

Molds for the Colonial Candy Box were purchased from Federal Glass Company in 1964. This item was introduced by Tiara in 1983. Past colors include Blue Etched, Ice Blue, Chantilly Green, Amber, Coral, Amethyst, Ruby Decorated and Black. Currently available in Crystal, the Colonial Candy Box is a great decorating accessory or gift idea for proud Americans. [5¾" high.]

CONCORDIA CANDY DISH & COVER

This adorable handmade Candy Dish & Cover in dusty rose is produced from Fostoria molds, and comes from a line called the Vintage pattern. at a ½" diameter, its' just perfect for cosmetic puffs at your dressing table, or mints in the den. Date of original Manufacture undetermined.

	Introduction
Hostess Treasures Item, $250	1994 [Disc. '95]
#737 Candy Box & Cover, dusty rose	

CONSTELLATION COOKIE JAR AND COVER

The 9" Constellation Cookie Jar and Cover was introduced by Tiara in 1972. Past colors of sunset, teal, yellow mist, and burnt honey join the most recent white lace crystal.

Originally designed by Indiana Glass in 1950, several items from the Constellation pattern have been offered during Tiara's history. [Disc. 1989]

CONQUISTADOR BOWL

Designed and produced by Indiana Glass Company in the late '30's this beautiful 3-toed design has a flair for decorating with style. Use as a center bowl with flowers, or fresh fruits for an eye-catching display of color. [Indiana Glass Pattern #1004] Tiara's introduction date: July, 1989   Discontinued Date: 1991

43

CROWN FOOTED CHALICE & COVER

The $500 Level of our Hostess Treasures Program featured this footed candy box in ruby, in 1991. Also produced in 1984 by Tiara in chantilly green and cobalt blue, this mold equipment is from Fostoria. [Previously known as Hapsburg Chalice & Cover.] Base and cover are both handmade. [12" high.]

DEWDROP BASKET

From the same mold family as the Dewdrop Candy Box & Cover, this 1930's vintage pattern is a wonderful accent piece, especially complimentary to our Crown Dinnerware line. This basket was added to our Hostess Treasures Collection in July 1988. [Was also produced in fiery ruby.]

		Introduction
#143	Dewdrop Basket, fiery ruby	1985 [Disc. '87]
#678	Dewdrop Basket, provincial blue	1990 [Disc. '91]
#797	Dewdrop Basket, imperial blue [Hostess Treasures]	1988 [Disc. '90]

DEWDROP CANDY BOX

Accent a room with a handcrafted masterpiece called the Dewdrop Candy Box and Cover. Designed in the 1930's, the Dewdrop pattern remains a favorite in Tiara circles at an enchanting value. Originally manufactured by Indiana Glass Company, the handmade splendor and uniqueness was produced for Tiara Exclusives by Fenton Art Glass in rich imperial blue. Past colors by Tiara include fiery ruby and chantilly green. [Discontinued: 1990] See also: Crown Complements

ELEPHANT

Indiana Glass Company designed the unique Pachyderm in 1981 for the National Federation of Republican Women. Manufactured for Tiara Exclusives in pink etched, blue etched, chantilly green etched, and crystal etched glass, the Elephant will stand quietly holding candies and mints, or hide away secretly until a gift occasion brings him out of the closet!

		Introduction
#839	Elephant, imperial blue [4½" high.]	June 1992

GENTRY CANDLE LAMP

Introduced in the Fall of 1991, the twisted design of this authentic black glass candle holder reflects quite nicely on its new purpose as a candle lamp. We added a crystal globe and a white tapered candle to finish the fine look. [13½" high] [Discontinued: 1991]

HANDLED OVAL CANDY DISH

From the Imperial Glass Company line of Collector's Crystal comes our #807, striking black Oval Candy Dish. Patterns of this type were originally designed to resemble cut glass, and are great for producing sparkle on any table! [8¾" long] Discontinued 1993.

HONEY DISH AND COVER

The Honey Dish and Cover is a long-time favorite with Tiara Hostesses and Customers. It holds a full comb of honey or can be filled with your favorite candies, nuts, soaps, and even jewelry. The 6" high container has been produced in a variety of colors. Past Tiara listings include: aquamarine, amber, milk glass, crystal, crystal etched, horizon blue, horizon blue etched, ice blue, ice blue etched, pink, pink etched, regal blue etched, chantilly green, chantilly green etched, amethyst, imperial blue and black.

The Honey Dish and Cover can be traced back as far as 1911 through Indiana Glass Company records.

Introduction
#919 Honey Dish, peach   1993 [Disc. '95]
#036 Honey Dish, aquamarine/etched   1994 Only
     [Limited Edition, Founder's Day]

LOVEBIRDS CANDY DISH & COVER

In our wide and varied collection of unique items, the Lovebirds Candy Box & Cover has found residence. Handmade for Tiara by Dalzell-Viking. This mold is part of the Dalzell-Viking Collection, and originally came from the now defunct Westmoreland Glass Company. Original design date is estimated to be the 1930's.

Introduction
#450 Lovebirds Candy Dish, azure blue   1993 [Disc. '94]
     [5¾" high.]

MIRANDA BASKET

This elegant basket in black is a decorator's delight. As a centerpiece to stylish black and white decor or an accent piece for more traditional color schemes, this handmade basket is just what you've been looking for! Mold origin is undetermined.

Introduction
#832 Basket, black   1992
     [11¼" high.]

MONARCH

The Monarch Pattern was designed in the early 1900's by Indiana Glass Company. Its sharp, distinctive pattern was produced to represent the effect of highly expensive cut-glass, which was so prominent at the time. In 1988 Tiara reintroduced the Beverage Set in the Hostess Treasures Program, and the Bowl in the Booking Program. The Bowl was discontinued in December, 1988, and the 5 pc. Beverage Set was discontinued in December, 1989.

OIL LAMP

#099 Hearthside Oil Lamp, spruce [9 3/4" high.]
The base of this lamp is handmade from an old Imperial mold. The sheer crystal globe and gold-tone fittings finish the piece nicely. Whether your taste is romance or nostalgia this Lamp is a beautiful addition to your decor. [Lamp oil not included.] Handmade base. Introduced: 1995 as a $750 Level Hostess Treasures Gift. Available January-June only.

45

PINEAPPLE BASKET

Handmade for Tiara by L.E. Smith in authentic ruby glass, this striking piece is produced by age-old methods from a mold owned by L.E. Smith. Origin unknown. This item was also offered by Tiara for a limited time in crystal. [1992]

#870 Pineapple Basket, ruby

Introduction
1993

ROYAL CANDY BOX AND COVER

Mold equipment purchased in 1962 by Indiana Glass Company from Hazel Atlas, led to the 1986 introduction of Tiara's Royal Candy Box and Cover in black glass. Originally called the Radiant Candy Box, this attractive piece is machine pressed. [Discontinued: 1990]

SPOON HOLDER

Handmade in spruce by Fenton Art Glass, this item is produced from original Imperial mold equipment. Not unlike the one grandma kept on her dining room table for teaspoons, it can hold a short stemmed bouquet of flowers or packages of artificial sweetener as well! Original date of manufacture undetermined.

#460 Spoon Holder, spruce [3½" dia.]

Introduction
1994

STRAWBERRY JAR AND COVER

This design has been traced back to the early 1900's, and was originally produced by Indiana Glass Company. Introduced by Tiara in 1972, previous colors by Tiara include: lime, chantilly green etched, sunset, coral, horizon blue and fiery ruby. [Discontinued December, 1988]

SUZANNE CANDY BOX & COVER

Designed in 1985, exclusively for Tiara by Fostoria, the Suzanne Candy Box was originally produced in 24% lead crystal. In 1991, we brought this striking glassware design back in a cheerful aquamarine color! [5½" high.]

TULIP BASKET

This beautiful large basket with a tulip pattern was introduced in rose pink as a recruiting award in April of 1991. It was then listed in the Hostess Treasures Collection in January 1992, and was featured with the Crown Dinnerware line in imperial blue in 1992. Now available to hostesses in the new sea mist color - it's a perfectly stunning idea for your home. [11½" high.] Introduction Date: July 1992

AMERICAN FIGURE SERIES

Tiara Exclusives celebrates 500 years of America's history with a series of handpainted statues designed and produced exclusively for you. You'll enjoy!

1492 - 1592 Period of Discovery Figure - Christopher Columbus
1592 - 1692 Period of Settlement Figures - Governor William Bradford & Squanto
1692 - 1792 Period of Independence Figure - Thomas Jefferson
1792 - 1892 Period of Westward Expansion Figure - Gold Miner
1892 - 1992 Period of Industrialization Figure - Henry Ford

Each figure includes a brief history of noteworthy facts regarding our proud American heritage.

CAMEO BASKET

First designed by Indiana Glass in 1965, the lovely Cameo pattern was introduced by Tiara in 1978.

Used in special Tiara promotions in the past and offered in teal, horizon blue, and blue etched, the basket was last produced in Tiara's authentic black glass. The original 1970 Tiara catalog featured this item in horizon blue. [Discontinued in December, 1988.]

CAPTAIN'S DECANTER

Uniquely crafted and mouthblown, the Captain's Decanter with stopper is a Tiara design from 1985. Standing 9" high with a diameter of 9¾", this chantilly green decanter is a true conversation piece. It was once used in a Tiara promotion in vibrant cobalt blue.

Styled after decanters of an earlier time when ships rolled and tossed on the high seas, the wide base and 113 oz. capacity is a step into the extraordinary, exclusively from Tiara. Discontinued 1993.

COMMEMORATIVE TRAYS

#204 Star Spangled Banner, crystal etched   [Introduced: January 1992.]
     Previously offered by Fostoria Glass Company in crystal, this
     beautiful handmade tray is a lasting remembrance of Frances Scott
     Key, who wrote our National Anthem. [8" X 10½"] [Disc. 1992.]

#203 Mount Rushmore, crystal etched   [Introduced: January 1992.]
     A tribute to the "Shrine of Democracy" our Mount Rushmore handmade
     tray also originated at Fostoria Glass Company and features four of
     our most memorable Presidents: Washington, Jefferson, Roosevelt and
     Lincoln. Destined to be a collector's item! [8" X 10½"] [Disc.
     1992.]

COUNTESS DRESSER SET

The Countess Dresser Set is assembled and produced for Tiara by Fenton Art Glass. The handmade/mouthblown components of this beautiful dusty rose/crystal etched set, make it an extremely valuable collection.

The mouthblown Perfume Bottle with hand ground stopper, the handpressed Ring Tray, Trinket Box with Cover and Oval Tray, add up to a suggested retail of $94.90!

	Mold Information	Introduction
#305 Countess Dresser Set Hostess Treasures [$750 Level]	Handmade	Dec. '93 [Disc. '95]

CRITTERS

Back by popular demand, in a new color, our adorable little Glass Critters are a multipurpose nick-knack you'll adore. Use them as a paperweight, bookends, or shelf-sitters! [Approx. 4" high.]

Azure Blue		Mold Information	Introduction
#620	Frog	Handmade	1992 [Disc. '92]
#621	Mouse	Handmade	1993 [Disc. '93]
#622	Bear	Handmade	1992 [Disc. '94]
#623	Owl	Handmade	1992 [Disc. '93]
Pink			
#375	Bear	Handmade	1593 [Disc. '94]
#376	Mouse	Handmade	1993 [Disc. '93]

These items were previously offered by Tiara in 1985 in crystal etched.

CROWN CANDLE

Using the Crown pattern as a guideline, our sister company, Candle-lite, designed a special extrusion, shaping this candle to perfectly complement the Crown Dinnerware line. Scented with a refreshing wildflower aroma, it promises to warm your home in glowing fragrance. Produced exclusively for Tiara by Candle-lite in 1988.

DAISY DIANE CONSOLE BOWL

Mold equipment on this pattern dates back to the 1920's. Tiara introduced this lovely bowl in 1984. It has been offered in chantilly green and cobalt. Used as a centerpiece for a buffet or table, the pattern was a perfect example of functional beauty in glassware. [Discontinued in July, 1988.]

EAGLE ASHTRAY

Originally designed by Indiana Glass Company in 1971, this ashtray was produced in the Hand Shop of Indiana Glass through the early 1980's and is now made by Dalzell-Viking. The spinning process used in making this item creates shape and thickness variations which make each piece unique. Past Colors include: amber, amethyst, azure blue [1993], crystal, lime, lead crystal, smoke, and yellow mist

At 10½" diameter, it has a conversational appeal, and is almost too pretty to use.

#635 Eagle Ashtray, azure blue

Introduction
July 1993

EGG & COVER

Like an old friend, the Egg & Cover is back for a visit! Originally designed exclusively for Tiara, this handmade Egg & Cover was first offered in our 1973 catalog in horizon blue and lime green. Some years later, a yellow version was offered as a contest prize. Now back in azure blue, it fits nicely with our Empress Collection of unique handmade glassware. [6¾" high.]

#574 Egg & Cover

Mold Information
Handmade

Introduction
1993 [Disc. '94]

FLAMINGO BOWL

We've been unable to locate mold history on this undeniably different bowl. The pattern of birds in the bottom serve to support the bowl as feet. Handmade for Tiara Exclusives by Dalzell-Viking, this item is produced from a mold owned by Indiana Glass Company.

#572 Flamingo Bowl, azure blue

Introduction
1993 [Disc. '93]

FLORAL MEDLEY TRAYS

Back by popular demand in a pleasing shade of pastel pink, these handcrafted trays are functional serving items for breads and pastries. Produced for Tiara by Dalzell-Viking from the original molds, the smaller tray was also available for a limited time in dusty rose. [1988] [See Victorian Ensemble.]

	Introduction
#387 Floral Medley Tray, pink (10¾" X 7¾")	1991 [Disc. '94]
#398 Floral Medley Tray, pink (12¼" X 8¾")	1994 [Disc. '94]

FRUIT BASKET

Originally called the 301 Pattern, this design dates back to the Depression. Introduced by Tiara in 1986, it has been produced in imperial blue, only. Available exclusively in our 1988 Hostess Treasures Program, this item was discontinued in July, 1988.

GENERATIONS

Generations: Even the name sounds like something that will last! For the first time ever - Tiara is offering a 6" X 6" candle, with 3 center wicks and a total of approximately 5½ lbs. of beautifully scented wax for your needs.

Generations of time will pass before this tremendous candle finishes its vigil under your careful guidance. Burning time for this candle is approximately 476 hours.

When the lights go out, and the batteries run down, wouldn't it be nice to have Tiara's 6" X 6" Generations three wick pillar handy to light up a room? Produced as follows, exclusively for Tiara by Candle-lite.

	Introduction
Generations Pillar, peach [peach scent]	1990 [Disc. '94]
Generations Pillar, blue [wildflower scent]	1990 [Disc. '94]
Generations Pillar, white [pine scent]	1990 [Disc. '95]
Generations Pillar, red [hollyberry scent]	1992

LEAF CANDLE LAMP

An unusual container that can accent any room when arranged by an imaginative hostess, this Candle Lamp was designed in 1983 by Tiara. The soft, pink etched leaf design is also perfect for serving frosty desserts topped with whipped cream! [Also produced in crystal etched glass.]

	Introduction
#452 Candle Lamp	1983 [Disc. '94]

LEAF BOWL AND CANDLE HOLDERS

Introduced by Tiara in 1974, this elegant combination has known great popularity as a unique centerpiece grouping. Produced in such colors as sunset, burnt honey, and black, it was a favorite for Tiara customers in our 1988 Hostess Treasures Brochure. [Discontinued December, 1989.] [See Desert Blossoms.]

LORD'S SUPPER TRAY

Earliest histories of this unique item can be traced back to the late 1880's when the Lord's Supper Tray was produced by Model Flint Glass Works of Albany, Indiana. This factory was closed around 1902, and a number of the existing molds were purchased by Indiana Glass Company a short time thereafter. Early production by Indiana Glass often carried gold or platinum decoration around the edges or on the back of the tray.

Tiara introduced this item in 1972. It has been produced in several colors including: sunset, pink, ice-blue, platinum, teal, burnt honey, crystal, apricot, peach and decorated.

Along with its many practical uses as a serving piece or bread tray, it is also a unique gift from the past that will blend with any decor and make an unusual accent piece, especially when placed on a stand beside the shimmering glow of candlelight. An ideal gift for clergymen, it is also available to churches for fund-raising.

Currently available in 1995 in aquamarine.

MUSHROOM LAMP

Introduced in 1985, the 4½" high, machine pressed Mushroom Lamp was available in pink and blue from Tiara Exclusives. This was originally a set of molds purchased from Federal Glass Company. The new design was cut into the molds by Indiana Glass Mold Makers in 1985. [Disc. 1991]

PEACOCK BOOKEND

Traced back as far as the 1920's, we have not located the original introduction date of this unique and beautiful handmade bookend. Designed for Indiana Glass Company, it is truly an exclusive way to support your favorite books! [5¾" high.]

		Introduction
#571	Bookend, azure blue	1993 [Disc. '94]

PONDEROSA PINE PILLAR CANDLE

Styled to match our beautiful Ponderosa Pine Dinnerware, this candle is produced exclusively for Tiara by our sister company, Candle-lite. Its white color and pine scent make it a versatile addition to any home. Introduction date: January, 1989. #630 Ponderosa Pine Pillar in red with Hollyberry scent was introduced in 1990.

PRISCILLA & WHISKERS

Produced for Tiara in solid crystal with overall etched surface, Priscilla and Whiskers are handmade from molds owned by Dalzell Viking.

		Introduction
#148	Whiskers [dog], crystal etched	1994
#150	Priscilla [cat], crystal etched	1994

REAL "ESTATE" IDEAS

1988 was the beginning of a new line of specialty gift items for Tiara. Featuring a specially selected grouping of American homes, our collection of handpainted houses, crafted in gypsum, includes a history and title for each of the following:

		Introduction	
#778	Keener Log Cabin	Jan. '88	[Disc. '88]
#779	Dwight Barnard House	Jul. '88	[Disc. '91]
#769	Mission Dolores	Jan. '89	[Disc. '91]
#794	Absinthe House	Jul. '89	[Disc. '91]
#801	Penfield Reef Lighthouse	Jan. '90	[Disc. '91]
#803	Bartholomew G. Courthouse	Jan. '91	[Disc. '92]

SMOKER SET

A handsome table or desk accessory, assembled by Indiana Glass Company in 1971, the Smoker Set had been produced for Tiara in black, horizon blue, crystal etched, and now platinum. [Discontinued in 1988, the set included: Urn, Lighter/Urn and four Ashtrays.]

SWEET PEAR PICKLE DISH

Originally called #601 Avocado pattern, Tiara's handcrafted Sweet Pear 8" Pickle dish is a hit with hostesses.

This item previously produced by Tiara in burnt honey and emerald green, was last available in yellow mist. Adapted by Tiara in 1982, the #601 Avocado pattern was designed by Indiana Glass Company in 1929. Various items in this pattern have been offered by Tiara since its introduction. [Discontinued in December, 1988]

PREFERRED HOSTESS GIFTS

Year	Gift	Color
1977	Strawberry Jar and Cover	Lime
1978	Fruit Vase	Amber
1979	12" Vase	Crystal Etched
1980	Strawberry Jar and Cover	Sunset
1981	Sandwich Butter Dish	Teal
1982	Sandwich Mini-Basket	Yellow Mist
1983	Strawberry Jar & Cover	Coral
1984	Leonardo Footed Urn & Cover	24% Lead Crystal
1985	Hapsburg Chalice and Cover	Emerald Green
1986	Harvest Footed Fruit Bowl	Premier Blue
1987	Lace Basket	Lymon Etched
1988	Desiree Vase	Lymon Etched
1989	Desiree Bud Vase	Lymon Etched
1990	Handpainted Tiger Lily Vase	Black
1991	Sandwich Mini Basket	Peach
1992	Water Lily Jardiniere	Teal Mist
1993	Rendezvous Candy Box & Cover	Lead Crystal/gold
1994	Melissa Tall Covered Candy Dish	Pink
1995	Rosalee Double Crimped Bowl	Dusty Rose

Tiara's Preferred Hostess Plan is an unmatched opportunity in the world of Direct Selling. Not only are Tiara Preferred Hostesses treated to special mailings and contests, they are also privy to some very appealing gifts.

INDIANA GLASS AND TIARA

The term "glass" is used to denote a variety of substances made from differing materials. Glass is both hard and brittle, and is usually either transparent or translucent.

Glassmaking in the United States is traced back to the early 1800's when an enterprising Boston Merchant began the Sandwich Glass Company in Sandwich, Massachusetts.

The first glassware was produced at the Sandwich Glass Company and included items such as jars, bottles and tableware.

The Beatty-Brady Glass Company was founded by George Beatty and James C. Brady in 1895, who originally purchased from U.S. Glass Company the idle A.J. Beatty and Sons Factory in Steubenville, Ohio.

In 1896 they purchased a newly built Pennsylvania Railroad carshop building in Dunkirk, Indiana.

In 1899 The Beatty-Brady Glass Company joined the National Glass Company and the plant was operated as the Beatty-Brady Glass Works.

In 1904, Indiana Glass Company leased the plant from National under a directive handed down from the Board of Directors.

National Glass was released from their receivership in 1908 and the assets of Dunkirk were purchased by Indiana Glass Company.

Indiana Glass Company was incorporated in 1909 to make hand-made and machine made tableware.

Industrial pressed glass, primarily auto headlight lenses, was produced in the 1920's and 1930's.

Financial difficulties resulted in major stockholders taking over active management in 1953.

Indiana Glass Company merged with Lancaster Lens Company of Lancaster, Ohio in 1955, which resulted in the formation of Lancaster Glass Corporation.

Additional management changes were made, and in 1962 Indiana Glass Company became part of Lancaster Colony Corporation.

In 1970 a subsidiary of Indiana Glass, Tiara Exclusives was formed. Tiara's product is a selection of decorative and tableware items produced for the exclusive sale to customers through Independent Associates.

Tiara Exclusives has been fortunate enough to purchase many pieces of equipment over the years from other plants that have been forced to shut their doors. From these purchases many excellent molds have been found to create exciting "new" pieces to add to our line.

The most notable in our current line would be the molds purchased from Federal Glass Company and Imperial Glass Company.

FEDERAL GLASS COMPANY

Federal Glass Company was founded in 1900 at Columbus, Ohio by Robert J. and George Beatty.

They began producing pressed tableware in 1906. Both hand and machine pressed ware were manufactured until 1946 when the hand shops were closed down and the plant became fully automated. Federal continued to produce a full line of tableware and beverage ware until it closed in February of 1980.

Tiara has faithfully reproduced items #10085 [crystal] and #10432 [black] Colonial Candy Box and Cover from these Federal molds. This piece was also made for Tiara promotions in blue etched, ice blue, chantilly green, amber, coral, amethyst and decorated ruby colors.

FOSTORIA GLASS

With Lancaster Colony Corporation's 1985 purchase of Fostoria Glass Company, not only was a whole new line of lead crystal accessible to Tiara Exclusives [as described elsewhere in this manual] but also made available were several older molds that could be used in producing exciting "new" items.

Tiara is delighted to present many beautiful wares from our Fostoria mold collection exclusively for you.

The life-like satiny figure of the crystal etched Madonna, the exquisitely crafted and hand-blown platinum Water Bottle, the versatile premier blue La Shea Water Bottle, the Hapsburg Footed Chalice and Cover, the Windsor Crown Chalice, Coronation Lamp and Vase, Victoria Vase and Eve Candy Box and Cover are all wonderful additions made possible by these rescued molds!

Tiara's paperweight collection adds that Fostoria touch to many desk tops throughout the land.

IMPERIAL GLASS COMPANY

In 1901 a new glass company was incorporated in Bellaire, Ohio. It was know as Imperial Glass Company.

Production began in 1904 with the primary product being pressed tableware. In 1958 after years of peaks and valleys successwise, Imperial purchased most of the mold equipment from the newly defunct A.H. Heisey Glass House in Newark, Ohio. Two years later a large purchase of mold equipment was made from Cambridge Glass Company which had closed its doors in 1958.

Lenox, Inc. purchased the plant in 1972 and operated the plant under the name New Imperial Corporation until the operation was sold to Consolidated Stores of Columbus, Ohio and Lancaster Colony Corporation on November 20, 1984.

Imperial molds used in the Tiara line include the stunning platinum Victoria Vase, the bold, black Milady Vase, Adore Bud Vase, the dainty Bouquet Mini Basket in provincial blue, the Impressions 3-Toed Bowl, the Imperial Ashtray in dusty rose, the Pie Wagon and Cover in crystal and the Dove Candy Box and Cover in crystal.

GLASS GLOSSARY

ANNEAL: Removes objectionable stresses in glassware by controlling the cooling speed.

BASE: The bottom of an item.

BATCH: The raw materials properly mixed, to be melted and changed into molten glass.

BLOCK MOLD: A one piece mold.

CHILLMARK: A wrinkled surface condition on glassware.

CHIP: An imperfection in glass due to breakage of a small fragment out of an otherwise regular surface.

CONTINUOUS TANK: A glass furnace in which the level of molten glass remains constant because the feeding of batch continuously replaces the glass taken out.

CULLET: 1. Waste of broken glass, usually suitable as an addition to raw batch.

2. Foreign cullet: cullet from an outside source.

3. Domestic cullet: (factory cullet) which will later be cut off and discarded or remelted.

DAY TANK: A periodic melting unit, usually designed to be emptied by each day of hand-gathering.

ETCH: Marking or decorating the surface of a glass item by using hydrofluoric acid or other agent.

ETCHED: Treated by etching.

FINISHER: The workman who does the final work, such as polishing or placing the handle or foot on a piece of ware.

FIRE-POLISH: To make glass smooth, rounded or glossy by heating in a fire.

FORMING: The shaping of hot glass.

GATHER: To get glass from a pot tank on a pipe or punty.

GLORY HOLE: An opening to the hot interior of a furnace used to reheat the glass in hand working.

GOB: A portion of molten glass gathered on a punty or pipe.

LEHR: A long, tunnel-shaped oven used for annealing glass items by controlling the cooling speed.

OVERPRESS: An imperfection in glass, excess glass projections resulting from an imperfect closing of mold joints.

PASTE MOLD: A mold lined with adherent carbon, used wet for blown ware.

PRESSED GLASS: Glassware formed by pressure between a mold and a plunger.

PUNTY: A device to which ware is attached for holding during fire polishing or finishing.

SEAM: A mark on a glass surface resulting from a joint of matching mold parts.

SEED: An extremely small "bubble" in glassware.

SHEAR MARK: A scar appearing in glassware caused by the cooling action of the cutting shear.

SNAP: A device for gripping a piece of formed glass for fire polishing and finishing.

TANK: A melting unit in which the container from the molten glass is constructed from refractory blocks.

DEMONSTRATION TECHNIQUES

As you become comfortable in front of the giftarama guests, you will want to add information that builds value to our product and offers various uses for the items. Many good points can be gained by learning to "listen" to the guests as they express ideas during the demonstration and shopping period.

The following are a few popular selling points and ideas:

1. Suggest stemware and crystal items for bridal showers or start your own bridal registry for the completion of her beverage service. Dinnerware patterns are also a perfect idea for bridal collections.

2. Remind the guests of the versatility of the dinnerware patterns which can be dressed up with beautiful lace and candlelight or dressed down for casual use with place mats. Either way, they are as practical and durable enough for young families to enjoy for years to come!

3. We are in the "gift giving" business so be sure to mention holidays and occasions requiring a gift in months to come.

4. Several of our items are made to be used together, such as: console or centerpiece bowls and candle holders. Always display or mention a complete grouping of items that complement each other.

5. The Child's Bowl is great for encouraging small children to finish their breakfast by telling them "Mother goose is waiting for you at the bottom of the bowl". This could cause disaster however, if your intellectual youngster turns it over to see if you're fibbing!

6. The Venetian Candle Lamp is a perfect bridal shower gift. The bride can turn the candle holder upside down to carry her wedding bouquet and then assemble the lamp at the reception. It will always carry special memories for her to treasure.

7. The Sandwich Small Canister was surely intended as an attractive cuspidor for pipe tobacco.

8. We are sometimes in need of a gift on short notice and Tiara has several "perfect" stick-in-the-closet" gifts for just such occasions. Suggestions are: Hunter Horn Mugs, Honey Dish, Paperweights, Ponderosa Pine Salad Sets, and Beverage Ware.

9. As you become familiar with Tiara's prices, you will become aware of similar items on the retail market. When you can compare our product to a retail item that costs more but has no guarantee or exclusivity, bring it to your guest's attention at the giftarama.

10. For ideas that work in your part of the country, ask successful Associates what they sell the most of and how they demonstrate it. Popularity will vary in different regions of the country on each pattern and respective items in the line.

11. As a final suggestion to increase sales at your giftarama, remember, "The eye always buys more than the ear". In other words:
   A. Keep your products and tote bags clean.
   B. Arrange an effective display by using fabrics that represent the holidays and harmonize both with the products and the current season.
   C. Follow the Tiara training and demonstrate each item individually from the totebags. You will bring attention to it and help its beauty and usefulness stand alone.
   D. Keep any extra, inexpensive items you carry to remind your guests of up-coming holidays simple. That is, use only a "few" plastic colored eggs in basket or on the egg tray to remind people of Easter or place a lovely red Valentine's Day Card on your table in January!

HOLIDAY DISPLAY SCHEDULE

Working far enough in advance to allow delivery is important, therefore, we suggest the following display schedule for the best success:

Valentine's Day	January giftaramas
Easter	February & March giftaramas
Mother's Day	April giftaramas
Father's Day and June Weddings	May giftaramas
Independence Day and yard parties	June giftaramas
Tiara Founder's Day	July with customer specials
Labor Day and Christmas	August with new products
Halloween and Christmas	September giftaramas
Thanksgiving and Christmas	October giftaramas
Christmas [last minute shopping]	November giftaramas
Good time to stock up on "gift closet" items	December giftaramas with delivery after the New Year

Always mention birthdays, weddings, anniversaries, birth, retirement gifts and get-well gifts. Also, young people enjoy Tiara for graduation and "Hope Chest" gifts.

WHAT IS A FLAW IN GLASS?

Is a small bubble in a fine piece of stemware a flaw? How about a cord, or a mold mark? The answer is definitely no, but it's sometimes difficult to convince a customer of this.

Most dinnerware and glassware departments and specialty shops have had trouble at one time or another with customers who seek flawless perfection in the tableware merchandise they buy.

Such perfection can be achieved only in assembly-line products, of course. It is not possible or even desirable in quality ware whose manufacture depends so much on the skill and artistry of individual craftsmen.

Slight variations and tiny imperfections in glassware pieces are actually a confirmation of craftsmanship and individual artistry. Most customers who appreciate good glassware understand this. For those who don't, here is a series of questions and answers that a salesperson can use to promote better understanding of the product.

Does a "seed" or bubble glassware constitute a flaw?
No. One of these tiny "seeds" or bubbles the size of a pinpoint may sometimes be observed in a piece of glassware when it is examined closely against a strong light. The bubble is formed by gases when chemicals are united in the fusing or melting of the raw ingredients. It does not affect the quality or the beauty of the glass.

Should all pieces in a set be exactly alike?
No. There are almost always slight variations in diameter, height, and other dimensions in any group of tumblers, goblets, plates or other articles of glass. These variations are usually so slight that they can be detected only with a micrometer, rarely by the naked eye. This is the hallmark of the fine hand craftsmanship.

What is a Cord?
A cord is an almost invisible difference in density in the glass which occurs during the fusing of the molten glass. It is visible only by the fact that it reflects light. When a goblet with a cord in it is filled with water, no light is reflected and the cord becomes invisible.

Is a mold mark a sign of imperfection?
No. A mold mark is merely a ridge on a molded glassware piece that indicates the point at which the mold that formed the item was separated for removal of the finished ware. If it is overly prominent, however, it may be an indication of careless workmanship.

What is a shear mark?
A shear mark is a slight puckering of the glass caused when the artisan snips off excess molten glass when shaping the piece, as for example the end of the handle of a pitcher. It is a normal characteristic of glass and should not be considered a flaw.

Is handmade glassware really made by hand, or merely hand-finished?
The production of handmade glassware is indeed a hand process. The skilled hand and eyes of many men, working in teams, go into the making of every piece. The amazing thing is that such a high degree of excellence can be attained; that piece after piece coming from any individual or group of glass blowers or pressers is so nearly and accurately a duplicate of every piece.

Why can't small irregularities be entirely eliminated from handmade glass?
For the very reason that the glass is handmade. No matter how deft the touch of the sensitive hands of glass craftsmen, it is impossible to eliminate completely small variations. These should not, therefore, be considered flaws. Glass is one of the trickiest materials to work with. Even machine-made glassware cannot be made absolutely perfect. But consider this: Even the finest diamond, examined under a jeweler's loupe, rarely reveals absolute perfection.

How can the salesperson and the customer judge the quality of glassware? There are certain simple tests and guides. Look for clarity and luster by holding the piece against a pure white background. Good glassware is quite clear, while inferior grades show a cloudy bluish or greenish tinge.

Quality glass is also marked by a permanent polish or luster that results from fire-polishing.

Look for smooth edges. Glassware edges should be even, never rough or scratchy. In hand-cut ware, the design should be sharp and accurate. In etched ware, each tiny detail should be distinct and clearly defined.

Fine handblown glass frequently contains lead, which improves its clarity and adds to its weight. If a piece of stemware rings with a clear musical tone when struck lightly, this indicates lead content. Lime glass, on the other hand, does not have the resonance, but this does not make it any less desirable. The lime in such glass adds to its toughness and strength.

- Reprinted from China Glass & Tableware

GUARANTEE

All Tiara gifts are guaranteed to be of fine quality and craftsmanship within the limits of the arts represented. All products are guaranteed for life, and should breakage occur, either accidental or otherwise, or any other damage, replacement will be made at fifty percent [50%] of the current price, provided the receipted guest selection card is sent to Tiara Exclusives as proof of purchase. The receipted guest selection card will be returned to you along with your replacement merchandise.

A fee of three dollars [$3.00] to cover packing, shipping and indemnity must be included with each order for replacement.

There shall be no limitation upon this guarantee, and replacement policy, except in the case of discontinued items, in which event, the Company will no longer be responsible, or liable, for this replacement. Credit 50% toward item of equal or greater than value.

Tiara Glass Leaflets 1997-98

Holiday Scents

5018

5017

5016

868

from

Tiara Exclusives

102

Hostess Special Purchase

Hostesses booking and holding a Giftarama
in November with $150.00 or more in net sales
can select any catalog item valued at
$19.90 or less and pay only $8.00!
OR:
Select #102 Season's Greetings Platter,
crystal/decorated and pay only $6.00!

Limit: One Hostess Special Purchase
Item per qualifying Giftarama.

HOLIDAY CANDLE SETS

Each Votive Set includes a dozen 12-hour scented votives and 3 pc. Stackable Votive Holders in crystal.
Save $4.30 on each set!

5013	**Alabaster Votive Set** fragrant gardenia *Juego Votivo Alabastro* *fragancia gardenia*	$17.50
5014	**Ivy Votive Set** evergreen mist *Juego Votivo Hierba* *bruma siempre verde*	$17.50
5015	**Scarlet Votive Set** spiced apple *Juego Votivo Escarlata* *manzana con especias*	$17.50

Each Reflections Pillar Set includes a 3" x 6" Pillar, a 3" x 9" Pillar and a pair of Reflections Candle Holders, crystal.
Save $5.20 on each set!

5010	**Reflections Pillar Set** fragrant gardenia *Juego Velon Reflexión* *fragancia gardenia*	$20.50
5011	**Reflections Pillar Set** evergreen mist *Juego Velon Reflexión* *siempre verde bruma*	$20.50
5012	**Reflections Pillar Set** spiced apple *Juego Velon Reflexión* *manzana con especias*	$20.50

Tiara's Holiday Ball Set includes three ball candles (red, green, and white) and one Celestial Candle Holder.

682	**Ball Candle Set** *Juego de Vela Forma Bola*	$11.50

On the Cover

868 Holiday Basket, red   **Booking Prize**
Cesta Festiva, rojo
Hostesses, earn this stunning basket with a
November Giftarama of $150.00 or more
and two qualified bookings.

5016 2 pc. Octagon Set   **$19.50**
evergreen mist
2 pzas. Octágono, bruma siempre verde

5017 2 pc. Octagon Set   **$19.50**
fragrant gardenia
2 pzas. Octágono, fragancia gardenia

5018 2 pc. Octagon Set, spiced apple   **$19.50**
2 pzas. Octágono, manzana con especias
Gift giving is made easy with 2 pc. Octagon
Sets by Lancaster Colony Candles. Each 2
pc. set includes one 24 oz. and one 12 oz.
Octagon Jar.

Holiday Starter Sets

Beautiful Starter Sets to show off
your Holiday Table!

115 12 pc. Ponderosa Pine   **$37.50**
Starter Set, crystal
*12 pzas. Juego Inicial Ponderosa Pine
cristal*
Save $18.20!

935 12 pc. Sandwich Starter Set   **$37.50**
peach
*12 pzas. Juego Inicial Sandwich
durazno*
Save $13.20!

527 12 pc. Sandwich Starter Set   **$37.50**
spruce
*12 pzas. Juego Inicial Sandwich
abeto*
Save $13.20!

FESTIVE *A*CCENTS

Decorate for the holidays with these special offers! Prices on this page only are good through December month-end.

017 **Pair Venetian Candle Holders**, crystal
Candeleros Veneciano Par cristal
$19.50

364 **Pair Venetian Candle Holders**, decorated red
Candeleros Veneciano Par decorada/rojo
$19.50

640 **Pair Bayberry Tapers**, red
Par Velas Bayberry, rojo
$2.00

641 **Star Pillar**, red
Velon Forma Estella, rojo
$5.50

670 **Pair Ponderosa Clearfire**, crystal
Par Ponderosa Clearfire, cristal
$14.50

735 **Angelica Candle Lamp** crystal/decorated
Lámpara Angelica, cristal/decorada
$19.50

5008 **Balsam Lites Set**
Juego Lucites Balsam
(Includes 2 bags Balsam Pine Shimmering Lites and a pair of Pineapple Votive Holders in crystal.)
$19.50

Customer Special Purchase

It's so helpful to us when you pay your order
in full! We would like to offer you special savings!

Customers placing a paid-in-full order
of $29.90 or more on the day of the Giftarama
can add on any catalog line item valued
at $19.90 or less and pay only 1/2 price!

Entire Customer order must be paid in full.
Orders placed in the absence of a
Giftarama (outside orders) are not eligible for
this offer. Limit: One 1/2-price selection
per qualifying guest.

Your Tiara Associate:

Effective: November 1996

We Honor:

#20100

March Specials

from

Tiara Exclusives

MARCH ISSUE

362

Hostess Special Purchase

Hostesses booking and holding a Giftarama
in March with $150.00 or more in net sales
can select any catalog item valued at
$19.90 or less and pay only $8.00!
OR:
Select #362 – Sunswept Lamp,
yellow/crystal, and pay only $10.00.
Regularly valued at $34.90.

Limit: One Hostess Special Purchase
Item per qualifying Giftarama.

STARTER *Sets*

Save an unbelievable $13.20 on Sandwich and $18.20 on Ponderosa Pine Starter Sets.

115	**Ponderosa 12 pc. Starter Set,** crystal *Vajilla Inicial 12 pzas. P. Pine, cristal* (Includes 4-Dinner Plates, 4-Mugs, and 4-Salad Plates)	$37.50
527	**Sandwich 12 pc. Starter Set,** spruce *Vajilla Inicial 12 pzas. Sandwich, abeto* (Includes 4-Dinner Plates, 4-Cups, and 4-Saucers)	$37.50
935	**Sandwich 12 pc. Starter Set,** peach *Vajilla Inicial 12 pzas. Sandwich, durazno* (Includes 4-Dinner Plates, 4-Cups, and 4-Saucers)	$37.50

Add-on one of these matching items for an incredible 1/2 of the regular catalog price when you purchase one of the above starter sets.

163	**P. Pine 4 pc. Goblets,** crystal *4 pzas. Copa, cristal* With the purchase of #115	$9.95
488	**4 pc. Salad Plates,** spruce *4 pzas. Plato para Ensalada, abeto* With the purchase of #527	$8.95
934	**4 pc. Salad Plates,** peach *4 pzas. Plato para Ensalada, durazno* With the purchase of #935	$8.95

On the Cover

054 **Daisy Vase Combo** $26.50
crystal
Combo Vase Margarita, crista
This stylish, hand-blown duo
salutes Spring when filled with
your favorite fresh-cut flowers. Set
includes one 7¼" and one 5¼"
Daisy Vase. Regularly valued at
$34.80, you save $8.30!

Captivating Crystal

236 **Lord's Supper Tray** $13.50
crystal/etched
*Santa Cena del Señor
cristal / grabado*

229 **Lord's Supper Tray** $13.50
cranberry
*Santa Cena del Señor
cranberry*

5035 **Ponderosa 4 pc. Clearfire** $19.50
crystal/green
*Ponderosa Pine 4 pzas. Vela
Clearfire, cristal / verde*
Save $20.10!

SCENTED $\mathcal{T}$REASURES

5032	24 oz. and 12 oz. Octagons, lilac *Tarros Llenados, lila blossom* Save $4.30!	$18.50
5033	Sunburst 6 pc. Pillar/Holder Set *6 pzas. Rays de Sol Velon/Sostendor* Includes a 6" Pillar, a 9" Pillar, and a 4 pc. Sandwich Coaster Set/crystal Save $7.20!	$24.50
5034	Lilac Blossoms 6 pc. Pillar/Holder Set *6 pzas. Flor del Lila Velon/Sostendor* Includes a 6" Pillar, a 9" Pillar, and a 4 pc. Sandwich Coaster Set/crystal Save $7.20!	$24.50
5036	24 oz. and 12 oz. Octagons, sunburst *Tarros Llenados, citrus* Save $4.30!	$18.50

Customer Special Purchase

It's so helpful to us when you pay your order
in full! We would like to offer you special savings!

Customers placing a paid-in-full order
of $29.90 or more on the day of the Giftarama
can add on any catalog line item valued
at $19.90 or less and pay only 1/2 price!

Entire Customer order must be paid in full.
Orders placed in the absence of a
Giftarama (outside orders) are not eligible for
this offer. Limit: One 1/2-price selection
per qualifying guest.

Your Tiara Associate:

Effective: March 1997

We Honor:

#20100

November Specials

103

867

5008

from
Tiara Exclusives

Hostess Special Purchase

Hostesses booking and holding a Giftarama
in November with $150.00 or more in net sales
can select any catalog item valued at $19.90 or
less and pay only $8.00!

OR:

Select #304 Twelve Days of Christmas
Drinkware Set, crystal/decorated
for only $10.00!
Each set includes a dozen 12 oz. Tumblers
with one depicted for each of
the Twelve Days of Christmas.

Limit: One Hostess Special Purchase
Item per qualifying Giftarama.

FUNCTIONAL *Table* SETTINGS

These services will make setting a beautiful table simple. Each 12 piece
set includes 4 Tumblers, 4 Dinner Plates, and 4 Soup Bowls.

175   12 pc. Ponderosa Pine Table Set $49.50
crystal
***12 piezas Servicio de Mesa Ponderosa
cristal***
Save $12.20!

969   12 pc. Sandwich Table Set $49.50
peach
***12 piezas Servicio de Mesa Sandwich
durazno***
Save $13.20!

475   12 pc. Sandwich Table Set $49.50
spruce
***12 piezas Servicio de Mesa Sandwich
abeto***
Save $13.20!

Cake Dome Special

011 **Village Guild Cake Plate & Dome $29.50**
crystal/etch
Pastelera Domo Village Guild
cristal/grabado
Any cake will look more delicious in this 13"
Cake Plate and large dome.

On the Cover

103 Peace on Earth 13" Platter $14.50
crystal/etch
Paz en la Tierra Platon 13"
cristal/grabado

867 Sweetheart Lamp $29.50
ruby/crystal
Lámpara, rubi/cristal

5008 4 pc. Shimmering Lites Set $14.50
crystal/balsam pine
4 piezas Juego Luz Tremulantes
cristal/pino balsamina
Includes 2– 8oz. bags of Shimmering Lites,
balsam pine, and a pair of Pineapple Votive
Holders, crystal.
Save $7.30!

Punch Set Special

250 Sandwich 14 pc. Punch Set $45.50
crystal
14 piezas Juego Ponche Sandwich,
cristal
Includes 9 qt. Bowl, 12 Cups and
a clear acrylic Ladle.
Save $14.40!

HOLIDAY *G*IFTS

5065 3 pc. Holiday Basket Set $29.50
3 pzas. Juego de Cesta Festival
Save $5.20 on this 3 pc. set that
includes a 24 oz. Octagon Jar,
evergreen mist, a 12 oz. Octagon
Jar, spiced apple, and an Octagon
Jar Basket, black.

364 Venetian Candle Holders $19.50
1 pair, red decorated
*Candeleros Venenciano, 1 par,
decorado rojo*

680 3 pc. Holiday Ball Candle Set $5.00
red/white/green
*3 piezas Juego Festivo Velas Forma
Bola, rojo, blanco, verde*

640 2 pc. Bayberry Candle $2.00
red
2 piezas Velas Baya del Laurel, rojo

6 pc. Ball Candles, choice $14.90
   3005 Fragrant Gardenia
   3105 French Vanilla
   3205 Sunburst
   3305 Cherry Grove
   3405 Lilac Blossom
   3505 English Rose
   3605 Evergreen Mist
   3705 Wild Berries
6 piezas Velas Forma Bola, escoja

With the purchase of any 6 pc. Ball Candle in
your choice of fragrance add on:

211 Celestial Candle Holder Pair $3.00
crystal
Par Candelero Celestial, cristal
Save $5.90!

Customer Special Purchase

It's so helpful to us when you pay your order
in full! We would like to offer you special savings!

Customers placing a paid-in-full order
of $29.90 or more on the day of the Giftarama
can add on any catalog line item valued
at $19.90 or less and pay only 1/2 price!

Entire Customer order must be paid in full.
Orders placed in the absence of a
Giftarama (outside orders) are not eligible for
this offer. Limit: One 1/2-price selection
per qualifying guest.

Effective: November 1997

We Honor:

#20100

Your Tiara Associate:

Mail to:

Gift Ideas

614

625

from

Tiara Exclusives

Refreshing Spearmint

Capture the freshness of the great outdoors in your own home with invigorating Spearmint Ponderosa Pine.

858 **Ponderosa Pine 74 oz. Pitcher** **$19.90**
spearmint
Jarra, menta verde

862 **Ponderosa Pine Ice Teas** **$22.90**
spearmint
Vaso para Te Helado, menta verde
(18 oz.) 4 pc.

581 **Votive Bridge** **$15.90**
black
Sostendor Votivo forma puente, noir
The 29" long bridge holds four of your favorite votive holders for a stunning display. (Votive holders and candles not included.)

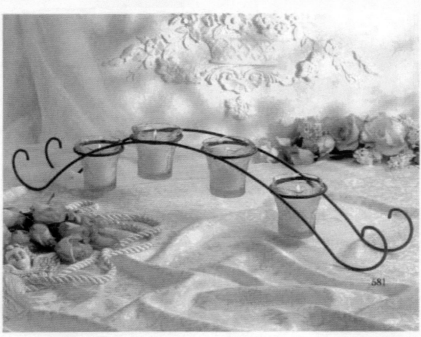

866 Ponderosa Pine $12.90
Three-Part Relish, spearmint
*Bandeja de 3 Compartimientos
menta verde*
(12 ½" dia.)

869 Ponderosa Pine $12.90
Serving Plate, spearmint
Plato de Servicio, menta verde
(12 ½" dia.)

875 Ponderosa Pine $12.90
Egg Tray, spearmint
Bandeja para Huevos, menta verde
(12 ½" dia.)

3312 3 pc. Square Candle $9.90
cherry grove
*3 pzas. Velas Cuadrada
Bosque de Cereza*
(3" x 3")

599 Match Stick Holder $9.90
black
Sostendor de Fosforos, noir
The 14 ½" holder will allow you to
reach hard to light wicks with ease
and control.

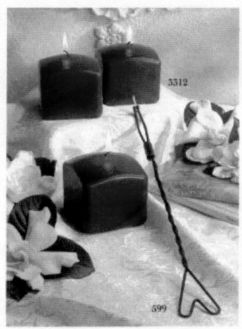

863   **Ponderosa Pine Mugs** $18.90
spearmint
*Vaso con Asa para Refresco
menta verde*
(9 oz.) 4 pc.

877   **Ponderosa Pine** $17.90
2 pc. Vegetable Bowls, spearmint
*Cuencos para Verduras
menta verde*
(7 ¾" dia.)

582   **Screen Taper Holder,** brass $29.90
Malla Sostenedor de Vela, bronce
This attractive holder houses your
favorite taper or formal candle. The
brass 13" screened chimney highlights
the warmth of the candle flame.
(Candle not included.)

583   **Screen Pillar Holder,** brass $29.90
Malla Sostenedor de Velón, bronce
The 9 ½" brass chimney adds a touch
of elegance to any 6" or 9" pillar.
(Candle not included.)

584   **Pillar Pedestal,** brass $18.90
Pedestal de Velón, bronce
(8 ½" high, 3" dia.) Candle not included.

753

731

614　Icy Trillium Serving Bowl　$14.90
crystal/etched
Cuenco de Servico Icy Trillium
cristal/grabado
Detailed pattern with etched highlights combine to form this stylish
10½" classic.

623　Icy Trillium　$19.90
4 pc. Salad Bowls
crystal/etched
4 pz. Juego Ensalad Icy Trillium
cristal/grabado
(6½" dia.)

$500 Level
Hostess Treasures Item

753　Empress 4 pc. Goblets
crystal/green
Vasos Empress, cristal/verde
(14 oz., 8½" high)

$250 Level
Hostess Treasures Item

731　Empress 4 pc. Flutes
crystal/green
Vasos Champán Empress
cristal/verde
(7 oz., 9½" high)

565	**Bowl Tripod** $14.90	577	**Angel Votive Holder** $14.90

565 **Bowl Tripod** $14.90
black
Cuenco Trípode, noir
A perfect holder for Sandwich or
Ponderosa Pine Soup Bowls filled
with potpourri. (8 ¼" high) Bowl
not included.

577 **Angel Votive Holder** $14.90
black/crystal
Votivo Silueta de Angel, noir/cristal
An eye-catching votive holder that
will enhance any wall.
(10" high x 8" wide, includes crystal
votive cup.)

Your Tiara Associate:

Effective January through July 1998.

#21215

September Specials

from

Tiara Exclusives

924

Hostess Special Purchase

Hostesses booking and holding a Giftarama
in September with $150.00 or more in net sales
can select any catalog item valued at $19.90
or less and pay only $8.00!

OR:

Select #924 – 3 pc. Child's Set, peach
and pay only $6.00!

Limit: One Hostess Special Purchase
Item per qualifying Giftarama.

LUNCHEON SETS

131 **7 pc. Ponderosa Pine Luncheon Set,** crystal $29.50
     7 pzas. Juego de Almuerzo Ponderosa Pine, cristal
     (Set includes #164, #166, #176)
     Regularly $51.70 – You save $22.20!

478 **12 pc. Sandwich Luncheon Set,** spruce $29.50
     12 pzas. Juego de Almuerzo Sandwich, abeto
     (Set includes #445, #487, #488)
     Regularly $47.70 – You save $18.20!

986 **12 pc. Sandwich Luncheon Set,** peach $29.50
     12 pzas. Juego de Almuerzo Sandwich, durazno
     (Set includes #934, #945, #946)
     Regularly $47.70 – You save $18.20!

On the Cover

Purchase any **two** 24 oz. Octagon Jars at the regular price ($12.90 each) and get a third 24 oz. Octagon Jar for ***half price!***

Choose from:

618	Spiced Apple	3000	Fragrant Gardenia
3100	French Vanilla	3200	Sunburst
3300	Cherry Grove	3400	Lilac Blossoms
3600	Evergreen Mist	3700	Wild Berries
4100	Green Apple	4300	Tropical Fruit

5125
5126
5008

Specials of the Month

5008   4 pc. Shimmering Lites Set $15.50
crystal/balsam pine/peach
*4 pzas. Juego Laz Tremulantes
cristal/pino balsamina/durazno*
Set includes: One bag of Shimmering Lites, peach, one bag of Shimmering Lites, balsam pine and #704 – Pineapple Candle Holders.
Regularly $21.80 – you save $6.30!

5125   Aromatherapy 3 pack, Peppermint $14.50
Aromaterapia, menta

5126   Aromatherapy 3 pack, Ocean Mist $14.50
Aromaterapia, bruma de mar

5035
905

Close Out Special!

905   4 pc. Tumblers $9.50
cherokee rose
*4 pzas. Vasos Tipo Tumbler
cherokee rose*

5035   4 pc. Ponderosa Pine $19.90
Clearfire, crystal/green
*4 pzas. Ponderosa Pine Vela Clearfire
cristal/verde*

030

879

$\mathscr{G}$IFT $\mathscr{I}$DEAS

030   4 pc. **Hunter Horn Mugs**, crystal $19.50
*Vaso con Asa Forma Trompeta de Caza
cristal*
Regularly $25.90 – You save $6.40!

879   3 pc. **Buffet Set**, spearmint $24.50
*Juego de 3 piezas para Aperitivos
mente verde*
(Set includes: one each – #866, #869, #875)

Customer Special Purchase

It's so helpful to us when you pay your order in full! We would like to offer you special savings! Customers placing a paid-in-full order of $29.90 or more on the day of the Giftarama can add on #900 – Sandwich Puff Box & Cover, peach or #588 – Sandwich Ftd. Compote, spruce for only $6.00!

Entire Customer order must be paid in full. Orders placed in the absence of a Giftarama (outside orders) are not eligible for this offer. Limit: One Customer Special Purchase selection per qualifying guest.

Effective: September 1998

We Honor:

#30100

Your Tiara Associate:

Mail to:

Other Books on Glass by Angela Bowey.

Available from Amazon (search Angela Bowey) or see www.glass-time.com

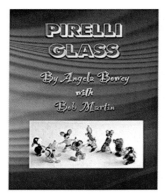

Pirelli Glass offers a definitive guide to identify and learn more about Pirelli Glass including the people who worked there and the history of the company and its products. How did Pirelli came to work so closely with the Scottish paperweight makers Vasart, and the range of Pirelli/Vasart products. Chapters 3 to 6 show all the known Pirelli glass models from company catalogues, the Disney cartoon figures and commissions for the Guinness Company, plus those known from Pirelli advertisements, from Pirelli labels, or confirmed by the glass artists who made them (Bob Martin and Mick Munns). If you are a collector or a trader in this kind of glass, invest in this book – you will enjoy it!
.

New Zealand Glass includes many original catalogue pictures and dozens of photographs. This is the expanded 2nd Edition of this comprehensive guide to understanding and identifying New Zealand Glass. New in the 2nd Edition - an expanded section on the glassware made by Crown Crystal Glass in Australia in the years before New Zealand had its own glass factory. If you are a collector of New Zealand Glass or a Trader in Glass, you need the information offered here. It is a really useful book for identifying New Zealand Glass.

London Lampworkers is the first in a trilogy on Pirelli, Bimini and Komaromy Glass. What figurines and other glass did these London Lampworkers really make; how can you identify a genuine piece; and is yours worth hundreds or is it just a ten dollar copy? This short introductory book will help you identify Pirelli, Bimini and Komaromy glass as well as introduce the people who made it. What is it about Pirelli, Bimini and Komaromy that makes them stand out from other lampworkers of the mid 20th century? What is lampworking, who made it and what is its history?

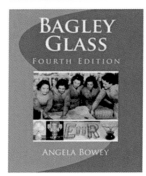

Bagley Glass is the fourth edition of this book about one of the most prolific English makers of art deco pressed glass from the 1920s until 1975. It has hundreds of pictures to help you identify Bagley glass. Who were the Bagleys, where was Bagley's Crystal Glass Company, what did they make and when did they make it? Did Bagley make your piece of glass? Whether its a vase or a bowl, a jug, a plate, or a boudoir set, there's a section that shows the patterns Bagley made with all the patent numbers registered by Bagley. This is a really useful book for identifying Bagley patterns and items.

Made in the USA
Middletown, DE
29 May 2023

31654559R00197